LAND LAW

LAND LAW

Fourth Edition

Denise Artis, LLB, LLM

Principal Lecturer in Law, University of Central Lancashire

John Houghton, LLB, Solicitor

Senior Lecturer in Law, University of Central Lancashire

Series Editor: C.J. Carr, MA, BCL

BLACKSTONE
PRESS LIMITED

This edition published in Great Britain 1995 by Blackstone Press Limited, 9-15 Aldine Street, London W12 8AW. Telephone: 0181-740 1173

© Denise Artis and John Houghton, 1987

First edition, 1987
Second edition, 1989
Third edition, 1992
Fourth edition, 1995

ISBN: 1 85431 383 5

British Library Cataloguing in Publication Data
A CIP cataloguing record for this book is available from the British Library

Typeset by Montage Studios Limited, Tonbridge, Kent
Printed by Bell & Bain Limited, Glasgow

CONTENTS

implied covenants — Specimen examination question — Usual
covenants — Specimen examination question — Revision summary — Suggested additional reading

PREFACE

It is said that Oliver Cromwell once described English land law as a 'tortuous and ungodly jumble'. The same remark could no doubt have been applied by generations of land law examiners to the examination scripts of their students. The aim of this book is to assist law students to unravel some of the jumble and enable them to write exam answers which, if not perfect, will at least reveal to the examiner a grasp of the principles of land law.

This book is not designed as a replacement for a standard textbook but we have endeavoured to set out the main themes of each topic and show how they may be handled under exam conditions. While we have aimed the book mainly at law undergraduates, we have borne in mind the fact that land law is a part of many other courses and tried to cater for the needs of those students as well. In this fourth edition we have endeavoured to make the book as up to date as possible and have spent some time in an effort to explain in detail those cases, which, in our experience, students find so difficult to understand and have tried to emphasise the increasing growth and importance of registration of title. The text is up-to-date to February 1995 and includes several new cases two of the most important being the decision of the House of Lords in *Prudential Assurance Co. Ltd* v *London Residuary Body* [1992] 3 WLR 273 which has clarified the position as to the certainty and duration of leases and *Rhone* v *Stephens* [1994] 2 All ER 65 which gives positive guidance on covenants on freehold land. In relation to statutory changes since the last edition the Access to Neighbouring Land Act 1992 is included.

Guidance to further specific reading is also included for the first time at the end of each chapter. It should be remembered however, that for general in depth discussion covering all aspects of land law the following textbooks are useful: Sir R. Megarry and H. W. Wade, *The Law of Real Property*; K. J. Gray, *Elements of Land Law*; and J. Mackenzie and M. Phillips, *A Practical Approach to Land Law*.

We would like to take this opportunity of expressing our grateful thanks to Shirley Houghton and Joan Jemson for typing what was sometimes an almost illegible manuscript, Simon Taylor, a colleague at the University of Central Lancashire, for allowing us to use his exam question on matrimonial property, and to Heather Saward for her useful and encouraging comments on the text.

Finally, may we wish all those who are setting out on the study of land law the best of luck. We hope you find that, like a trip to the dentist, it will not hurt half as much as you think it will.

Denise Artis
John Houghton
January 1995

TABLE OF CASES

1 EFFECTIVE STUDY TECHNIQUES

INTRODUCTION

Land law, or property law as it is sometimes titled, is an important subject in that as well as forming an integral part of most law degrees, many professional bodies require their students to study and pass examinations in land law. Fortunately, it is also a subject which touches our everyday life as it concerns mutual rights and obligations between people in respect of land, e.g., rights and obligations between a landlord and his tenant, between a mortgagee (perhaps a building society or bank) and the mortgagor (the borrower), or between neighbouring landowners. It is therefore a subject to which students should be able to relate.

From the outset it is advisable to approach the study of this subject positively and enthusiastically. This is particularly important where a course is semesterised as this means it is taught over a period of approximately 14 weeks (or in some cases 12 weeks), which does not allow much time for you to ease your way into the subject. Sometimes land law seems to strike fear into quite intelligent students. Don't let it! Students' comments at the beginning of a course have on occasion been negative, such as: 'I'm not looking forward to studying land law, it's too difficult', or 'I started reading the introductory material and I can't understand a word of it', or even 'Why doesn't the lecturer speak in English. He/she uses incomprehensible language: an incorporeal hereditament — whatever's that? I knew I wasn't going to like it.' At the end of the course, sometimes after the student has completed his/her revision, some of the same students have commented, 'I quite enjoy land law now. It all came together in the end.' For others less fortunate, often those who remained in a negative frame of mind, the material did not come together in the end.

The object of this book is to help you to come to grips with land law but not at the end, right from the beginning. Land law is complex because its roots are based in the feudal system which has been subject to continual change throughout the centuries. This has the effect of making land law a 'building block' subject in that the fundamental principles must be first understood before any real progress can be made. Chapter 3 explains these fundamental principles on which English land law is based. This will, we hope, help you to form that solid foundation so necessary for the study of land law. Subsequent chapters help you to build on that foundation by covering the major topics in land law. In doing so they will show you that even though the principles interlock, land law can be approached logically, building on your understanding and hence increasing your confidence. No one can guarantee that you will get a first-class honours degree by reading this book, but we hope that it will dispel any fear of land law, encourage a positive approach, help you understand and come to grips with land law at the outset, and hence increase your chances of success.

At this point, we should emphasise that students should not just aim 'to pass' land law. 'If only I can just pass I will be happy' is a plea sometimes heard. This is not good enough and is another example of negative thinking. You should aim to pass land law as well as you are able. To do this requires a gradual build-up of knowledge and confidence as you progress through the year, or semester, as the case may be. This book will, we hope, help you to do this, e.g., at the end of every lecture topic, read the topic in this book, discuss it with your friends, pursue points you do not understand in the textbook, read articles and discuss them. *This* is the way towards achieving your goal, *not* 'Oh, I don't understand this — it's boring', filing the lecture notes away apathetically and on to another topic.

PROBLEMS ENCOUNTERED THROUGHOUT THE COURSE

A good attitude is essential. However, that is not to say there are no problems to be overcome. There are. The most common are: terminology, the fact that land is different, and the dual nature of land law.

Terminology

Unfamiliar words and phrases make land law seem complicated, especially during the first few weeks. It may help to give some thought to why land law has its own language. The strange words and phrases are there not merely to make the student's life difficult but are a form of shorthand achieving precision and uniformity. To take a simple example; to describe someone as having a 'fee simple absolute in possession' may seem unnecessarily clumsy, but the form of words tells us so much — namely, that he has the largest estate in land which it is possible to have, that it is inheritable generally and that he has the legal estate and therefore is the legal owner, because the estate is in possession, i.e., it does not arise in the future but he can take possession of the land now. It also tells us that if he dies intestate (without making a will) and he has no one capable of inheriting the property, then his estate will go to the Crown (a relic from feudal times!). Similarly 'remainders' and 'reversions' are ways of describing types of landholding so that if A, holder of the legal title in Blackacre grants 'a life interest to B and in remainder to C for life', A can be described as holding the reversion and C the remainder (both future interests) in that when B dies, Blackacre will pass to C and, on C's death, the land will revert to A or his heirs.

It is important to understand words and phrases used. Ask your lecturer at the end of the lecture or seminar tutor, or even friends during discussion, or better still look them up yourself and make a note of their meaning in the margin alongside the word(s) in your lecture notes so as not to forget it. The glossary in the front of Megarry and Wade, *The Law of Real Property*, is useful in this respect, or use *Stroud's Judicial Dictionary of Words and Phrases*. Do not just ignore words you do not understand. Find out. It will only take a minute or two and it will make studying easier. It will also prevent you from making simple but nevertheless serious mistakes in an examination. For example, if the question asks you to outline and assess the rights available to a mortga*gor*, you must be sure you know that the mortgagor is the borrower and formulate your answer accordingly — one word, yet an all-important one. We have paid special attention in this book to explaining terminology.

Land — A Unique Commodity

Land is treated differently from other types of property such as cars. Land cannot be bought and sold in the same way as a car, and dealings in land are generally required to be in writing (see the Law of Property (Miscellaneous Provisions) Act 1989 which repeals s. 40 of the Law of Property Act 1925). You must get used, at the outset, to the idea that land differs from other types of property and is a unique commodity in that:

(a) it is of a finite quantity, and
(b) several people may have rights and obligations in the same piece of land at the same time.

In respect of one piece of land alone there are endless possibilities. For example, the owner-occupier will probably have a mortgage with either a building society or bank, a room in the house may be occupied at a rent by an acquaintance, there may be a right of way across the garden exercisable by a neighbour, and there may be a restrictive covenant on the land preventing him from keeping pigs. Alternatively, the whole house may be occupied by a tenant, or a person with a life interest in it, a licensee, or even a squatter. As we said, the possibilities are endless. Land law has therefore developed via statute and case law, with the object of regulating the relationship between the various persons holding different interests in the land and placing on them various rights and obligations. For example, we said that the owner-occupier would probably have a mortgage: this relationship gives rise to obligations on the part of the mortgagor to make repayment for the loan plus interest, and gives the right to the mortgagee to seek repossession and sale of the house should the mortgagor fall into arrears over a period of time. Because it is the mortgagor's *home* that is in issue the law developed further to provide safeguards for the mortgagor and mitigate the harshness of the remedies available to the mortgagee.

The point is that if you give some thought to why land is unique then you will gain some useful insight into why land law has developed in the way it has, and why it will go on developing and changing. To quote Megarry and Wade: 'The system is certainly still complex ... partly as a result of its continuous growth through the centuries and partly because of a social need for a highly developed system of private property in land'.

Dual Nature of Land Law

One of the problems students have to understand is that unlike Continental land law which is based on the Roman concept of *dominium* (see Gray, p. 39), English land law recognises the separation of the legal title to land from the 'use and enjoyment' of that land. In other words, it recognises that A can have legal title to land while B can be entitled to the use and enjoyment of that land, for example, where A has legal title to the land but B provided part of the purchase money, *both* A and B would be entitled to the 'use and enjoyment' of the land, B acquiring an equitable interest. This 'dual' nature of land law is the result of the contributions made by 'law' and 'equity', in particular the development of the trust. The position is as follows:

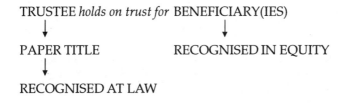

TRUSTEE *holds on trust for* BENEFICIARY(IES)

PAPER TITLE   RECOGNISED IN EQUITY

RECOGNISED AT LAW

For example, the situation in which A and B have both contributed to the purchase price but the legal title is in the name of A alone can be represented as follows:

A: TRUSTEE   *holds on trust for*   A and B
   ↓   ↓
PAPER TITLE   RECOGNISED IN
                                           EQUITY AS ENTITLED
                                           TO USE AND ENJOYMENT

This duality is a difficult concept at first and you should not worry too much at the beginning as the lecturer will probably only introduce the concept and then gradually develop it throughout the course. At the outset, however, you should bear in mind that the terms 'law' and 'equity' are technical terms. If you have not met these terms before, here is a brief explanation. Law and equity correspond to the two systems of justice, 'common law' and 'equity', which were administered in separate courts until the Supreme Court of Judicature Acts 1873 and 1875 which established that the rules of law and equity should be administered by all the courts of the land, so that the remedy obtained should no longer depend on the precise court in which the plaintiff brought his action. Equity mitigated the harshness of the ancient common law in the interests of 'fairness' and 'justice' at the expense of tradition and formality. Its contribution to land law can be seen not only in the development of the trust but in the development of the equitable doctrine of notice (see chapter 3), the equity of redemption in mortgages (chapter 6) and the recognition of equitable leases (chapter 10) (to mention but a few contributions). Nowadays the two systems are administered as one, but interests in land are still *classed* as legal and equitable with important consequences. These are dealt with in chapter 3.

STUDY TECHNIQUES THROUGHOUT THE YEAR

Whether your course is semesterised or continues across the academic year it is important not to miss lectures, otherwise they become disjointed and the 'golden thread' linking the lectures to the course is broken. This is particularly so if the course lasts only for 12 or 14 weeks. Similarly, seminars (tutorials) are important as they are forums where views can be exchanged and problems sorted out. Sometimes your performance at seminars is assessed (this is discussed in chapter 3) but even if that is not the case seminars can still fulfill functions described above and should be attended for that reason as well as for assessment purposes.

Preparation both for lectures and seminars is important if you are to maximise the benefit obtainable from attending those classes. You may feel that this will result in an overload of work, but if you get into the habit of reading and researching a topic before a lecture or seminar then it will become easier. Organisation is the key. Spread your workload across the semester or year, do not leave it until just before the seminar to be assessed or just before the examination. In this way you will minimise any stress and gradually build up your knowledge. Remember that land law is a 'building block' subject and early preparation to understand the basic principles and terminology is essential. Once you have mastered these then the study of the various topics within the land law syllabus becomes easier.

The Value of Lectures

Most universities in their undergraduate law courses have moved away from what might be called 'traditional' lectures, i.e., imparting detailed informa-tion on a particular topic, towards encouraging a 'student-centred' learning approach. This puts the emphasis on the students to discipline themselves into reading and researching the detail guided by their tutors who provide among other things an overview of the area, guidance on relevant reading materials and problematic areas. In this culture the value of lectures is enhanced. Textbooks, no matter how good, are no substitute for being in a lecture theatre, listening, taking notes and asking questions. Textbooks should be read before and after a lecture to gain background to a topic and to add detail to what has been said in the lecture. In that way you can gain the most from lectures, i.e., be prepared — then you can listen and jot down any important/relevant points.

The Value of Seminars (or Tutorials)

'You only get out what you put in!' is the motto here. Seminars and tutorials are for your benefit even when used as part of the assessment process. Use them to your advantage.

Tutors may use them to achieve various objectives:

(a) To explain involved and problematic areas of law already outlined and discussed in the lectures.

(b) To help students to utilise that law and apply it to fact situations.

(c) To add to that law already discussed, whatever the objective (or objectives).

(d) As a vehicle to assess a student's understanding of the area being discussed and his/her ability to contribute orally to that discussion.

Here is the place, amongst a small group of students and the tutor, to sort out any problems you might have. *Ask* if you are confused about something; *enter* into the discussions and put forward your ideas. Of course, to do so confidently, requires preparation. That is why we prefaced our comments with the phrase, 'You only get out what you put in!' Put in the work, prepare the material provided to you by the tutor and you will benefit from a seminar or tutorial. It is no use sitting there expecting the tutor to do all the talking — tutorials are *not* mini-lectures, the tutor is there to guide discussion, provoke thought, and sort out problems. If you do not enter into the spirit of the discussions, then you will learn very little, if anything at all.

To the shy student, a word of advice. Whilst preparing for seminars, jot down the points and cases you feel are most important — not too detailed or too many — then you can refer to them during the seminar. Do make an effort to contribute to the discussion. Don't let a seminar pass without making at least one point, only in that way will your confidence grow.

Statutes and Relationship with Case Law

Get used to dealing with statutes and the construction of statutes. Your previous experience of law may well have dealt with essentially case-law-based subjects such as contract and tort so that you have become familiar with reading law reports and citing authority. Land law is still to a large extent based on statute, namely, the 1925 legislation, so that you may be faced with learning a new set of skills. The emphasis put on statute and the depth of knowledge of particular sections required varies from course to course, but there are certain sections of the Law of Property Act (LPA) 1925 in particular which are basic to the study of land law and which must be understood (LPA 1925, s. 1(1), (2) and (3), outlining legal estates and legal interests, for example).

Neither can you study the law of easements without an understanding of LPA 1925, s. 62. It is therefore useful to sort out the key sections in each particular area and ensure that you understand their major requirements even if you are unable to remember the precise wording. For example, an addition to your lecture notes on easements alongside s. 62 could be:

> In LPA 1925, s. 62, a conveyance of land will pass to the purchaser 'all ... privileges, easements, rights, and advantages whatsoever, appertaining or reputed to appertain to the land ... or, at the time of conveyance, ... enjoyed with ... the land' subject to a contrary intention.

In noting this section you will need to add the definition of 'conveyance' in LPA 1925, s. 205(1)(ii); consider relevant case law on what the courts understand by 'privileges ... rights ... at the time ... enjoyed' etc. For example, in *Wright* v *Macadam* [1949] 2 KB 744 it was held that storage of coal in a coal shed provided by the landlord amounted to a right enjoyed by the tenant at the time of the conveyance (namely, the grant of a further tenancy). The right therefore passed under s. 62 as a full easement. (Remember that a right will not pass if there is evidence of the parties' intention that it should not pass.)

In construing the Law of Property Act 1925 generally, you should always bear in mind that it is a *consolidating* statute and is not therefore intended to change the old law except in so far as it is inconsistent with it. This leads to a conservative interpretation of the statute by the judges. This is illustrated by *Beswick* v *Beswick* [1968] AC 58, in which the House of Lords took a very narrow approach to LPA 1925, s. 56 (which concerns a third party being treated as a covenantee: see chapter 8). Reference was made to the predecessors of the section. (See particularly the speech of Lord Upjohn when he states: 'Section 56 of the Law of Property Act 1925 has a long history behind it. . . . No one has ever suggested that that section [i.e., the Real Property Act 1845, s. 5, which was replaced by LPA 1925, s. 56] was intended to do more than supplant the old common law rule relating to indentures *inter partes* in relation to realty.') Whilst this approach to LPA 1925 must always be borne in mind you must also remain aware that in some situations social or commercial practice necessitates a wider construction, e.g., the approach taken by Brightman LJ in *Federated Homes Ltd* v *Mill Lodge Properties Ltd* [1980] 1 WLR 594 by the use of LPA 1925, s. 78, as a means of automatic annexation of a covenant to land, and not merely as a word-saving provision.

USE OF TEXTBOOKS AND ACADEMIC ARTICLES

Use of Textbooks

A textbook is the student's friend and is invaluable. Choose one good textbook, one that you can understand and feel comfortable with. This is better than buying or borrowing several (assuming you have the money to use so extravagantly). Quality and not quantity is important. You can pass land law with one good book provided you supplement it with articles etc. Your choice will depend to a large extent on titles recommended for your course. If there is a choice given, go and look at the relevant books in the bookshop or library, particularly before purchasing, and ascertain as far as you can which you find the easiest to read and understand. A good friend it will be but, as stated earlier, it should not replace the lecturer as your main guide to the complexities of land law. Its value lies in being able to read the relevant chapter *in advance* of the lecture and so enable you to glean some idea of the intricacies of the topic to be discussed.

If that is not possible — the chapter may be too long or too detailed, for example, in parts — then read it *after* the lecture and add comments in the margin beside your lecture notes, adding to them and clarifying them. In this way you may be able to sort out any minor problems as they arise. For example, in your lecture notes dealing with LPA 1925, s. 1, you may have written:

LPA 1925, s. 1(1), limits the number of legal estates capable of existing to two:

fee simple absolute in possession
term of years absolute.

This can be added to after reading your textbook as follows:

LPA 1925, s. 1(1), limits the number of legal estates capable of existing to two:

fee simple *absolute* in possession	'Absolute' used to distinguish from a determinable or conditional fee simple.
term of years *absolute*	'Absolute' has no special significance, merely denotes relationship between landlord and tenant (Gray, p. 79).

In order to be able to add comments to your notes, you must space them out and not cram them together.

We do not intend to discuss the various textbooks on the market, except to say that some may be more academic and less practical than others, which may reflect the nature of your course. Often it is helpful for undergraduates to refer initially to a book covering the basic principles such as Riddall, Dalton or Megarry's *Manual*. Once you feel confident with the material then progress to a more thorough academic and detailed text such as Megarry and Wade, Gray, or Cheshire and Burn. In this way you do not feel out of your depth and gradually build up your knowledge of a particular topic. One thing we can say about land law books is that they are now making greater efforts to show how the law relates to the real world, such as the problems of cohabitees. Students studying for professional examinations may prefer a more compact text. Books by Curzon or Mackenzie and Phillips will probably be helpful in this respect.

Case books, such as *Maudsley and Burn's Land Law: Cases and Materials*, are useful as a guide to leading cases and course material where there is little time or opportunity to read cases in full. Remember that they are never a substitute for reading cases in the law reports, a lesson which hopefully law students will have learnt from the first term of the first year. An advantage of case books is that they may provide extracts from articles or papers which may not be available to the student, e.g., Commonwealth journals.

Use of Articles and Reports

Articles vary greatly in their approach and depth. Those which appear in legal journals like the *Conveyancer and Property Lawyer*, the *Law Quarterly Review* or *Modern Law Review* are usually very academic and of a high standard. They can be complex, however, for the undergraduate. Those which appear in the *Law Society Gazette* or *New Law Journal* are orientated toward practitioners and adopt a practical approach to explaining the law. Both these types of articles are very helpful especially to undergraduates as they are written by leading academics or practitioners who provide an insight into the law. It is always useful to read Law Commission reports which not only indicate possible future developments but also give a general review of the existing law. Reports on mortgages, matrimonial property and covenants in freehold land are examples.

Students studying for professional external examinations will be more familiar with articles in journals published by their own professional body, in particular the *Estates Gazette*, the *Chartered Surveyor* or the *Journal of Planning and Environmental Law*. Again, in such journals articles take a practical approach and can be very helpful. Every attempt should be made to keep abreast of recent case law and developments.

Preparation for your seminar or tutorial may involve reading various articles referred to by your tutor or lecturer. He or she does not intend that every article must be photocopied, coloured in with fluorescent pen and filed away, or long copious notes of detail made. What the tutor is in effect asking you to do is to read the suggested article, and note any salient points made by the author. After all, reproduction of and comment on these points is all you will have time for in the tutorial or indeed, if relevant, in the examination. As an example, you could read the article by S. Moriarty, 'Licences and land law: legal principles and public policies' (1984) 100 LQR 376.

Your final notes should look something like this:

The article is concerned with which remedy will attach to an estoppel licence and the extent to which contractual licences can bind third parties.

Looks at remedies available by comparison of the cases of *Dillwyn* v *Llewellyn*, *Inwards* v *Baker*, *Pascoe* v *Turner*. Argument is that the remedy given is governed by the nature of the representation to which it gives effect, e.g., in *Pascoe* v *Turner*, T was led to believe by P that the house was hers. Therefore the court ordered transfer of fee simple. Attempt at explaining court's approach can be made by paying closer attention to precise content of representations.

Situation where monetary remedy is awarded is based upon creation of a co-ownership interest, e.g., *Dodsworth* v *Dodsworth*, *Re Sharpe*. Even though occupation may be intended, the nature of co-ownership is that a co-owner may end up with a share of capital, e.g., as a result of an application under LPA 1925, s. 30.

Conclusion: estoppel intended to give effect to informal arrangements, remedy will be selected which best gives effect to what the person was told he could have.

In relation to contractual licences and third parties, the author begins with the orthodox view that contract cannot bind third parties.

Considers the extent to which contractual and estoppel licences differ.

Concludes may be fundamentally different but may arise from the same set of facts, e.g., *Errington* v *Errington*.

Compares *Williams* v *Staite*, *Tanner* v *Tanner*, *Chandler* v *Kerley*. In all three cases one party led to believe by the other party that he had a right to occupy and has acted to his detriment: only in *Williams* v *Staite* is there found to be estoppel.

Concludes distinctions in cases based on general difference between contract and estoppel, i.e., consideration rather than reliance — for consideration must be reciprocity based on request. Argues that contractual licences should bind third parties since would lead to an odd result that person who had incurred a detriment as a result of another's request would get no proprietary right, but would if suffered detriment as a result of his own act.

Distinguishes *King* v *David Allen & Sons Ltd* and *Clore* v *Theatrical Properties Ltd* on the basis they are commercial, not domestic, arrangements made between businessmen; in both cases no legal right was created because of a defect in form.

Discusses objections to informality, mainly on evidentiary basis, i.e., what is the content of the agreement concerning land? Considers that lack of writing may prevent knowledge of full extent of intention but does not prevent assessment of minimum protection envisaged.

Final conclusion: if courts recognise estoppel as a proprietary interest this will prevent diversity of remedies and lead to reforms necessary to accommodate it more harmoniously within the structure of English land law.

CONCLUSION

Now having acquired a positive confident approach to land law and hopefully in possession of a suitably comprehensive set of lecture notes you are in a healthy position to go forward to prepare for the ultimate challenge — the examination. The following chapter will offer guidance and suggestions on how to undertake this preparation in order to make the best use of the knowledge you have acquired during the year.

2 ASSESSMENT

Methods of assessment vary across courses. Professional courses and some undergraduate courses may continue to use the more traditional three hour unseen examination paper but more frequently additional or alternative forms of assessment are being used to assess different skills. Your course may include one or more of the following, all of which are discussed below:

(a) examination (which may be seen or unseen);
(b) coursework;
(c) seminar performance.

THE EXAMINATION

General

Many hurdles have to be jumped in life, and examinations are but one of them. To perform in a race as well as you are able, you need to *train* regularly and consistently. Build up your strength slowly but surely to peak on the day of the race. Preparation for an examination in land law is exactly the same:

(a) *Train* by following the advice in chapter 1 and work consistently throughout the year getting your notes into a manageable size and suitable for revision use.

(b) *Build up your expertise* as the examination gets closer, by drawing up a realistic revision timetable.

(c) *Commence* this build-up in good time — not too early or too late, but giving yourself enough time to build up confidence for the great day.

(d)   *On the day* of the examination meet the challenge with confidence. You are at your peak and so show the examiner your talents.

As examinations approach, draw up a realistic revision timetable. Make sure you leave enough time for revision and remember it is better to take your time over revision. Spread it over several weeks, in order to build up slowly, rather than cram everything in at the last minute. How much time you will need depends on you. It will vary with each individual student.

In order to use your time to best effect, however, we have found from personal experience that spreading your revision *across* the subjects you are studying, rather than totally revising each subject in turn, is more beneficial. Rather than spending, say, one or two weeks revising the whole of land law, then another week or two revising the whole of a different subject, say crime, etc., spend two days revising *one topic* within land law, e.g., easements, then two days revising *one topic* of another subject, say, theft in crime etc. Continue alternating across the subjects revising different topics each time. This will enable you to build up your confidence in all the subjects slowly and surely, prevent you becoming bored, and give you an incentive to continue. It will also prevent you from falling into the trap of having revised one or two subjects very well, but others hardly at all, perhaps because time ran out and some subjects were left to the last.

Once you have drawn up your timetable, you have to decide when to start revising. This again is a personal decision and will depend on whether you are studying full time, part time, day release or evening. Those studying part time will need to begin sooner, as their revision time is probably limited to evenings only. Full-time undergraduate students, we suggest, will need about six weeks to undertake their revision if they are attempting four or more examinations. It will, of course, depend on the number of examinations to be sat and the revision timetable should reflect this.

Always leave at least a day immediately prior to the examination free to refresh your memory on the topics you have revised earlier and clear your mind of everything else. Do not spend the evening before the examination or the morning of the examination trying to cram in last-minute details. You will find that the dubious benefit obtained in terms of acquiring titbits of information is outweighed by the fatigue that will result and probable panic that will ensue. If you have kept to your timetable and paced yourself, you will not feel the need to cram, only to refresh your memory ready for the challenge of the day.

Is there a Difference in Approach to Preparing for a Seen or Unseen Paper?

The answer is 'yes'. The *seen* paper will usually involve a problem type question involving interrelating areas of law which you will have some time (not necessarily a long time) to research before answering the question. It will require not only in depth knowledge of those interrelating areas but an ability to apply that knowledge to factual situations, thus preventing mere regurgitation of legal principles. Your research and analytical skills will be tested to the full.

The *unseen* paper on the other hand, normally offers a wider choice of questions and is more dependent on memory than the seen paper. Although application of legal principle to factual situations is also important, the questions are less likely to have complicated interrelated problems but test your knowledge over a wider area.

Is there a Difference in Approach to Preparing for a Three Hour and a One and a Half or Two Hour Examination Paper?

The answer is 'no'. Whilst you will not have as many questions to answer and hence not as many topics to revise for a shorter one and a half hour or two hour examination, nevertheless the topics you choose to revise will have to be researched, and answered, in the same depth as for a three hour paper. Your answers, however, must be directed to the specific question given and timed so that, if possible, an equal amount of time is given to answering each question. A word of warning if the exam is a 'seen' exam. The temptation to utilise all your research material may result in you losing track of time and your answer becoming unbalanced.

Preparation should involve not only substantive research but time management. Ask yourself 'How will I set out my answer to a question on [a certain topic]?' Prepare a plan and try it out.

Selecting Topics for Unseen Examinations

The number of topics covered in a land law examination will vary depending on the type and length of the examination. Professional courses may adhere to the traditional unseen three hour examination in which case you will normally be required to answer four or five questions out of nine or ten set. If the examination is timed for a shorter period, say one and a half hours, the number of topics tested is restricted and you will probably be required to answer two out of four questions. Sometimes one question is compulsory. Where that is the case you will no doubt be informed by your tutors. The only guidance we can provide is to warn against restricting your revision so that you only revise an equal number of topics to questions. For example, if four or five questions are required to be answered, then revision of five topics is unlikely to be adequate revision. Topics may not appear, or if they do, may appear in an unusual or difficult form, or mixed with a topic not revised. This is particularly the case where a compulsory question is set, as the object of such questions is often to test whether a student can apply their knowledge to a factual situation which may require consideration of more than one topic. For example, a question may require an understanding of the formalities to create a lease, it may then bring in the terms of the lease, both express and implied and remedies for breach. It is not inconceivable that the question may also raise the problem of a landlord mortgaging the lease and then falling into arrears of payments, requiring an appraisal of the probable effects of this on the tenant.

If an attempt is made, however, to revise every topic, it is likely that they may have been treated too superficially so that a good, in-depth answer is unlikely to be forthcoming. It cannot be stressed too strongly that questions must be answered in as much depth as possible. A happy balance which will enable a choice of questions is needed.

How to achieve this balance? The following guidelines may help:

(a)   For undergraduates, the overall content of the examination paper will reflect the course which has been taught. The sum of the tutorial and lecture programme delimiting the boundaries of the subject for examination purposes. Those studying for a professional examination, however, will need to turn to the relevant syllabus provided by the professional body.

(b)   Again in respect of undergraduates, it is highly likely that those areas on which a lot of time has been spent during the year will get an adequate airing on the examination paper.

For those benefiting from a correspondence course the short weekend (or other) lecture programmes available will usually give some indication of the emphasis, or lack of it, placed on certain topics.

(c)   Any new developments are likely to be incorporated into the paper; for instance the problems for an occupier establishing an overriding interest protected by s. 70(1)(g) of the Land Registration Act 1925 (see, for example, the recent cases of *Lloyds Bank plc* v *Rossett* [1991] 1 AC 107 and *Abbey National Building Society* v *Cann* [1991] 1 AC 56 discussed in chapter 3). It must be remembered, however, that examination papers (for both undergraduates and students taking professional examinations) are set quite some time before the actual examination date and whilst students must always keep up to date with new developments and be able to incorporate them into all their answers, it is the 'burning issues' alive *at the time of setting the paper* which are likely to arise.

It is stressed that the above are only suggestions and students must be guided wholly by the content and bias of their particular course.

Most land law courses will cover a range of more or less standard issues. A typical land law programme inevitably covers some or all of the following topics:

(a)   The 1925 legislation.
(b)   Future interests and the rule against perpetuities.
(c)   Settlements.
(d)   Co-ownership and matrimonial property.
(e)   Licences.
(f)   Easements and profits à prendre.
(g)   Covenants.
(h)   Mortgages.
(i)   Leases.

Leases is a vast topic in itself and the amount of this topic covered in any one course will vary. Some will deal only with creation and express and implied covenants in the lease. Others will include the protection afforded to residential tenants by the Rent Act 1977, the Housing Act 1988 and the Protection from Eviction Act 1977 (as amended), and to business tenants by the Landlord and Tenant Act 1954. Students must be guided by their own course content.

Tentative advice about selecting topics to revise is:

(a)   Learn the topics you find most interesting.
(b)   Remember there are certain fundamental principles in land law which are inherent in every topic. For example, it will always be necessary to consider whether the land in question is subject to the unregistered or registered system of conveyancing, whether the interest in the land is a legal or equitable one, and, if it is equitable, is it overreachable or does it require protection by registration?

Revision of any particular topic must therefore be based on an understanding of the fundamental principles of the 1925 legislation.

Question Spotting

In preparing for the exam, a useful exercise is to look at several past exam papers and try to answer some of the questions under exam conditions, i.e., give yourself 30 minutes to answer the question including planning the approach you will take. Looking at past questions will give you some idea of the layout of previous exams and the standard expected. This will lead to the exam game of 'question spotting'. In addition, where the exam is internally set, you will be able to get some guidance as to likely examinable topics by the time devoted to particular areas in lectures and tutorials. If your lecturer's pet topic is conditional and determinable fees simple then you can probably assume that a question on that topic will appear on the exam paper. Where you are doing a professional course with externally set exams, then question spotting is more difficult, but again past papers will be of some assistance.

For example, past exam papers may show the law of mortgages is regularly examined but that the rule against perpetuities is never examined, even though it appears on the syllabus. Equally, consulting past papers may give some clue to the particular aspect of a topic that interests the examiner, e.g., not only may mortgages be regularly examined, but the examiner may invariably examine one aspect of that area of law such as the equity of redemption or mortgagees' rights. On professional courses, gauging the depth of knowledge required may be difficult so that you should look at examiners' comments on previous exam scripts if these are generally available. One final thing to remember, if question spotting, is that exams are set some considerable time before you sit the paper, so that what appears to be especially topical just before the date of the examination, may not have been particularly important where the exam was set. For example, *Williams & Glyn's Bank Ltd* v *Boland* would not have aroused much comment when decided at first instance, but became extremely important in the light of the later Court of Appeal and House of Lords decisions. Having said that, you should keep as up to date as possible with current law and, in fact, some professional courses specifically state that a knowledge of recent legislation and case law will be expected. One final point, if you are on a professional course, keep an eye on your professional journal for recent changes in the law and also for any announcement about recent developments stating whether knowledge will or will not be expected of them for exam purposes.

IN THE EXAMINATION ROOM

Once in the exam room, keep the following advice in mind.

Read the Entire Paper Carefully

The instructions, which are not always the same from year to year, should be read thoroughly. Note how many questions are on the paper, how many you need to answer, whether there are any compulsory questions and, if the paper is split into sections, how many questions from each section you need to answer. Read the entire paper first rather than begin by looking for particular topics. Don't panic if the areas you had hoped for don't immediately appear, take some time to assess the whole paper.

Select the Questions you Intend to Answer Carefully

Allocate the time allowed for answering the question(s) with care. If you have to answer several questions do not spend too long on one question with the result that you do not answer all the questions, or only spend a few minutes on the last one, then valuable marks will be lost. To avoid this, some students prefer to leave their best question until last, so that if they do run short of time they will be able to write an answer to it quickly, almost without thinking. Whilst this may appeal to some, others prefer the alternative approach of starting with their best question. This has the advantage of helping you get over any nerves and build your confidence: you are not rushing and therefore should produce a really good answer which will get you a good mark. If you do find yourself in the unenviable position of running out of time, however, answering your last question in note form is better than no answer at all.

Professional examinations often have a different structure from those of degree examinations. In the former the maximum marks which can be obtained for each question are often indicated. Take careful note should this be the case and avoid spending too much time answering questions where few marks are available.

Plan Every Answer

Make sure before you begin the answer that you are clear what the question requires and spend a few minutes planning your answer carefully or if it is a seen paper spend time planning and timing your answer before entering the exam room. For example, the following is a fairly specific question which requires you to understand the basic intention of the Settled Land Act 1925 and the life tenant's obligations with regard to the remaindermen.

'The Settled Land Act enables settled land to be dealt with freely and at the same time affords full protection for the rights of persons beneficially interested in the land.' Discuss.

You do *not* need, therefore, a long introduction on the definition of settled land and requirements for creation of a settlement under the Act. Your plan should look something like this:

1 Introduction: intention of SLA — free alienability of land.
2 Land can be dealt with freely:

   (a) Because tenant for life (T for L) etc. has legal estate, ss. 19 and 20.
   (b) Can be disposed of (notice to trustees required).

      (i)   Can be sold (*Wheelwright* v *Walker*, best consideration.)
      (ii)   Can be exchanged (s. 38(3)).
      (iii) Can be leased (best rent) (s. 42).
      (iv)   Options can be granted etc.

(c)   Other powers of T for L: consent of trustees needed, e.g., cutting and sale of timber etc.

(d)   Other powers of T for L: improvement etc.

3   Protection of beneficiaries:

(a)   Trustees receive and hold purchase money (ss. 18 and 75).
(b)   Beneficiaries' interests overreached on sale.
(c)   Supervisory powers of trustees.

Comment. How effective is this protection?
N.B. Cannot curtail T for L's powers: *Re Paget's Settled Estates* (1885); *Re Acklom* (1929).
Conclusion: Act balances two conflicting interests — public and private.
Has it achieved what question says it does?
Comment briefly on reform: Scammell 1957, Potter 1944.

Note that the question says 'Discuss', you do not therefore get credit for writing a long list of everything you know about settled land. On the contrary, this will indicate to the examiner you do not understand the material. Show the examiner you have understood the basic principles and then display your point of view drawn from the cases or articles you have read. (See later chapters for other plans.)

Problem questions can be easier than discussion questions because it will normally be clear what you have to do. The question itself is in effect guiding you, preventing you from going off at tangents into irrelevancies. When faced with a problem question, identify the area of law involved and then plan out the basic requirements before applying the principles to the given facts. You may find it helpful to follow these suggested guidelines:

(a)   *Read the problem question very carefully* and identify the area or areas of law involved. Is it concerned, for example, with easements or licences or leases etc?

(b)   *Check for the possibility of overlap.* Always remember the possibility of a mixed question, e.g., a question on cohabitees' property may be argued as a licence, if you decide there is no possibility on the facts given of co-ownership.

(c)   *Identify clearly the main facts.* Are you required to advise any particular party? Who will be the likely plaintiff(s) and likely defendant(s)?

(d)   *Identify clearly the main issues* involved bearing in mind (b) above. For example, if the question is concerned with easements, is it seeking to test your ability to differentiate between rights capable of being easements and others such as vague general rights which are not? Or is the question testing whether you can decide whether an easement has been acquired by one party and if so how?

(e) *Recall the basic principles, any statutory provisions and leading cases* on the topic, such as LPA 1925, s. 62, if easements are concerned, and cases such as *Re Ellenborough Park* [1956] Ch 131, *Wheeldon* v *Burrows* (1879) 12 ChD 31, *Sovmots Investments Ltd* v *Secretary of State for the Environment* [1979] AC 144 (see chapter 7 for full list).

(f) *Apply the basic principles* etc. to the question and present a clearly argued case based on appreciation of the facts given.

(g) *Check every answer.* Try to leave sufficient time at the end of the examination to read your answers over quickly and rectify any serious errors, or insert any last-minute points you have remembered.

It is also worth remembering that because land law is heavily dependent on formality, words that are *not* in the question may be as important as those that are, e.g., if a question says 'A grants a right of way to B' do not assume this creates a legal easement. The missing words there are 'by deed'; you need therefore to discuss not only acquisition by way of an express grant, but also the possibility of an easement being acquired by implication or in equity.

Writing the Answer

Following the above guidelines on how to approach problem questions, and the advice on discussion questions, should enable you to organise your material ready to commence writing the answer. In doing so, always write legibly, show a good command of grammar and, most important of all, ensure that you get the basic information across to the examiner. If you can show this grasp of the basics then you can build upon it in order to improve the overall marks per question. Cut out irrelevance and keep to the requirements of the question. This can especially be a problem when citing cases. You must support your answer with relevant authority, but you do not need to recite the facts in great detail. What is important is the *principle(s) of law* enunciated in the case and the status of the court.

For example, if the question requires you to discuss the protection of equitable interests you could begin by noting whether the question indicates if the Land Registration Act 1925 applies, explaining briefly that the mechanics of protecting equitable interests differ depending on whether the title to land is registered or not. You may then wish to use the case of *Midland Bank Trust Co. Ltd* v *Green* [1981] AC 513. You can do this by commenting that in this case (which involved land with unregistered title) the House of Lords, reversing the Court of Appeal, held that if an equitable interest, which is capable of registration as a land charge under the Land Charges Act 1925 (now 1972) is *not* registered, then it will be void as against a purchaser of the legal estate — a purchaser being someone who gives valuable consideration in money or money's worth, valuable consideration having the same meaning as in the law of contract. In that case, an option to purchase, capable of being registered as a Class C(iv) land charge, was not in fact registered. It was therefore held to be void and unenforceable. Interestingly, it was also decided that as the Land Charges Act remains silent on the need for bona fides, this must have been deliberate and no such requirement will be read into the Act. To quote Lord Wilberforce: 'The case is plain: the Act is clear and definite. Intended as it was to provide a simple and understandable system for the protection of title to land, it should not be read down or glossed: to do so would destroy the usefulness of the Act.' The same principle applies to land with registered title although the equitable interest will be entered on the relevant charges register.

It is not an irrelevance to discuss possible alternative points of view. The examiner may sometimes set a question requiring such discussion to ascertain whether a student has really thought about a paritcular area of law and not just learned it parrot fashion. For example, a question such as:

'The law relating to restrictive and positive covenants over land is unduly complex and in need of reform.' Discuss.

Here the examiner is searching to see how deeply you have studied this area of law. He is looking for wide reading and an ability to summarise various academic views on the topic *and* some original comment from the candidate to show that you have a view and how you have formulated that view.

It is unlikely that you will be provided with statutory material in a land law exam, simply because there is so much of it. If it is provided, however, remember that it can be a double-edged sword. It may be comforting to have statutes available, but it is no substitute for knowledge of the provisions of the Act. If you don't know the main provisions then you will waste precious time in searching through the many provisions of, say, the LPA 1925 to find the section you need. If you do know the outlines of the sections then the statute will be of benefit to you in that you will be precise in your answer and be able to interpret the statute for the examiner's benefit.

A final point. While writing your answer, keep referring back to your plan *and* to the question to make sure you are answering the question given and not what you would like the question to be. You would be surprised how often this happens! It is especially important to refer back to the question when formulating your conclusion. Every answer should end with a conclusion. It can be short if you wish, but in some way should tie together all the arguments in your answer and show the examiner you really have understood that area of law.

If the question, for example, asked you to compare and contrast legal and equitable interests in land, you could conclude by saying something along the lines:

Legal interests, being proprietary interests and 'rights *in rem*', are clearly superior to equitable interests, the status of which has been shown to be debatable, being regarded in the main as 'rights *in personam*'. Whilst equitable interests are not therefore binding on the whole world, protection is provided for holders of equitable interests as outlined in this essay, namely by the doctrine of overreaching, the registration of the equitable interest and where necessary the equitable doctrine of notice.

COURSEWORK ASSESSMENT

An increasing factor in degree courses is that of coursework to supplement the exam. You may find that on your course, success does not depend solely on passing the exam. It may be that one or more pieces of coursework done during the year will count towards the final mark given. In law degrees, this is likely to be no more than 20 to 25 per cent of the total exam mark, because of the requirements of the legal profession regarding exemption from the first part of the professional training.

If coursework forms part of your assessment then it can benefit you in two ways. First and obviously, the better your coursework mark, the less pressure there is in reaching the overall pass mark in the exam. Your coursework mark will probably not affect your overall mark dramatically because in most courses the coursework has a fairly low weighting. However, coursework can make the difference between passing and failing or put you into a higher class. Second, it is likely that any coursework topic you do is likely to be an important part of the course with the possibility of a question in the exam (unless it is the policy on your course to preclude you from answering a question related to your coursework). You could therefore benefit in that you will have had the opportunity of revising thoroughly a topic which is likely to be examined. Use coursework not merely as a means of answering the question you are set, but also as an opportunity to research thoroughly a particular topic. This will also be of benefit if the coursework requires you to present your answer before fellow students in a tutorial. A well researched answer will give you the confidence to deal with the issues in the question and deal with any questions you may receive during the tutorial and thereby improve your overall mark.

A word of warning. If you do get a good grade in your coursework, do not rest on your laurels. You must continue to aim for as good a mark as possible in the examination in order to do yourself justice. The temptation is there to then relax a little. Do not fall into the trap of thinking you can take it easy after completing your coursework assessment — you need to work consistently. On this point of consistency — it is also unwise to expend too much time on coursework at the expense of other subjects. Try to spread your work as evenly as possible.

Even if there is no coursework assessment, you will probably be given pieces of written work to do throughout the academic year. You should do the pieces of work set, partly as revision and partly as practice in dealing with the sort of questions you are likely to meet in the exam. Hopefully, when marking the answer, your lecturer will make comments on errors or misunderstandings and give you some indication of the way your answer should be framed. This may particularly be the case if you are on a part-time course. It is obviously a chore to have to write answers to questions, especially if you are at work during the day, but the benefit is in getting guidance which may otherwise be hard to come by.

In land law, as we said at the outset, the ultimate key to success is *hard work* and *organisation*. Don't be afraid of land law, its principles are no more difficult than any other area of law, but you must get to grips with terminology and the different approaches of law and equity as early in your course as possible. If you are clear on these, then what may appear incomprehensible at first will then become understandable. We hope in the remaining chapters of this book to show how this can be achieved.

The following chapter, chapter 3, deals with the basic foundations on which land law is built — principles which are essential to the understanding of land law, which we said at the outset is a 'building block' subject. These principles flow through all the specific topics which follow and for that reason are dealt with in some detail in chapter 3.

SEMINAR PERFORMANCE

A novel approach, but one being used increasingly, is to assess a student's performance in seminar. There is no uniform pattern of how this is done. Some courses assess a student's performance at *every* seminar calculating an average mark at the end of the course which will contribute to the overall mark. The overall mark may be made up of a mark for coursework and/or examination. Other courses assess the performance of a student at one or two seminars where they may be required to present a paper and/or lead discussion. If this affects you, it is important to check any guidelines issued for your course which may lay down the criteria on which marks may be awarded. Some of the following general points may be helpful:

(a) Tutors are looking for you to *contribute orally* to the seminar discussion. Reading prepared notes is not the best way to gain marks, rather you need to show that you have carried out independent study or research into the topic under discussion by either asking questions or *listening* to what other students say and *responding* appropriately.

(b) Try *not to dominate* a seminar, this is not contributing, rather it shows an inability to listen and think clearly before speaking. On the other hand, sitting in a corner and not responding to questions will not gain marks no matter how well you have prepared the material or done your research.

Your tutor will try to ensure that everyone has the opportunity to contribute but if you are shy you should help yourself by getting into the habit of making a comment, or pointing out a useful case report you have found, at each seminar.

(c) If your course requires you to present a seminar paper or lead discussion, it would enhance your performance if you prepared a handout or OHP transparency summarising the main issues you have identified. This would be of benefit both to yourself and to the rest of the seminar group. Remember, you should be able to respond to questions from the rest of the group.

CONCLUSION

As assessment in undergraduate courses varies, you should shine in at least one of the skills being assessed. It is a matter of taking a positive attitude to improve your performance. If you are weak in one method of assessment, for example oral skills, then seek advice and work at improving that particular skill.

3   THE 1925 LEGISLATION

INTRODUCTION

Although given the title 'the 1925 legislation', this chapter is much wider. It looks at three interlocking areas. These are:

(a)   Land holding before 1926.
(b)   The intervention of equity.
(c)   The changes wrought by the 1925 legislation including registration of title.

The reason for doing this is that in any study of English land law it is fundamentally important to grasp as soon as possible the main foundations upon which the law is based *and* in doing so the student can then see why the 1925 legislation effected the changes it did and whether or not they are effective.

The majority of courses approach land law in this way but not all set detailed examination questions on the historical development of that law. The depth in which you as a student study the pre-1926 law will depend on the lecturers at your particular institution. Professional courses, however, are unlikely to set examination questions on the historical aspects. *All* students, however, will find it invaluable to have an appreciation of how the law has developed. The *changes* wrought by the 1925 legislation and subsequent developments *are* often a source of examination questions and these can be quite varied.

LANDHOLDING BEFORE 1926

Tenures and Estates in Real Property

As we said above, in any study of English land law it is fundamentally important to grasp as soon as possible to the main foundations upon which that law is based. A useful historical outline can be found in *The Law of Real Property*, 5th ed. by Sir Robert Megarry and H. W. R. Wade. The first foundation to note is the system of subinfeudation developed by the Normans as follows.

All land was taken by the Crown in 1066 and was (and still is) owned entirely by the Crown. The Crown then granted interests in that land amounting to less than full ownership.

Tenants holding directly from the Crown became known as tenants *in capite* (tenants in chief). It was usual for them to grant lesser interests to persons of lower rank than themselves. The tenants *in capite* becoming known as mesne lords and their tenants as tenants in demesne. Hence the feudal system, of which you are probably aware developed along the lines shown in figure 3.1.

This system of subinfeudation continued expanding until the statute *Quia Emptores* 1290 which prohibited further alienation of land by subinfeudation. (The effect of this prohibition was that the Crown was still the only owner of land but the feudal tree was gradually eliminated at each and every transfer of the land till at the present time nearly all 'landowners' are tenants *in capite* of the Crown.) Hence the position today regarding a person dying intestate (i.e., without making a will) and without heirs is that his or her estate will devolve to the Crown.

As has been indicated above land was granted to tenants on certain conditions, these being the consideration that the tenant in demesne had to provide for the mesne lord. This consideration was normally in the form of some service to be provided by the tenant for his lord. Very soon the forms of service required of a tenant could be seen to fall into certain well defined categories or classes and the set of conditions of service imposed on the tenant denoted the tenure of his interests, i.e., tenure varied according to the service required of the tenant.

The forms of tenure and service are explained in more detail in the textbooks and therefore will not be discussed here except to remind students that unfree tenure differed from free tenure. A free tenant knew in advance what services he was to provide whereas an unfree tenant could be required to perform any service at the will of the lord.

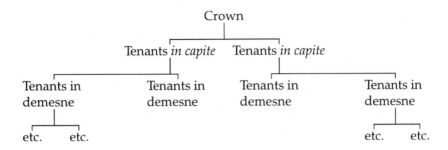

Figure 3.1

The Decline of Tenure

Together with the prohibition of alienation by subinfeudation the statute *Quia Emptores* had the effect of preventing any further forms of tenure from developing.

The system started to fall into decline from this point and many services required of tenants became commuted to monetary payments to the lord to be made either periodically, or once and for all, on the transfer of the interest.

The Tenures Abolition Act 1660 accelerated the decline but the final nail in the coffin of tenure was the reform of the law of real property in 1925.

Estates

It is frequently said that the tenure of a landholding represents the 'quality' of a person's interest since the type of holding each person enjoyed depended on the form of services he had to provide for his mesne lord; there is an obvious difference in quality between a free tenant knowing the services he had to provide and an unfree tenant or villein whose services were unknown. If this then was the quality of the holding it was also necessary to quantify the holding in the sense that a grant of land was always made for a specified period of time, e.g., a grant of 'Blackacre to X in fee simple' meaning that X could enjoy Blackacre indefinitely. As we mentioned before with tenure, X could not own the land itself he could merely enjoy a right to use it for a certain period of time specified in the grant to him. It is that extent of time that is known as the *estate*.

There were two main classes of estate: estates of *freehold* and estates *less than freehold*, the difference being that a freehold estate when granted was of uncertain duration whereas an estate less than freehold was clearly for a finite period when granted.

If we look first at the freehold estates we can see that this classification could be broken down further to show the various different indefinite periods for which an interest could be granted as follows:

(a)   *Estate in fee simple.* This was the largest estate known to the law and was the estate granted to a man and his heirs without any restrictions whatsoever. The estate continued for so long as the original grantee and any of his heirs survived. In effect this was and is the nearest thing to full ownership of land.

The word 'fee' in the phrase fee simple estate indicates that the estate is inheritable, i.e., if the grantee does not dispose of it during his lifetime (*inter vivos*) or by will it passes automatically to his heir. The word 'simple' denotes that it is inheritable generally, i.e., by the general heir of the holder being either ascendants, descendants or collaterals. This is to distinguish this fee estate from the following.

(b)   *Fee tail.* This was an estate given to the grantee 'and the heirs of his body' — one that devolves upon the lawful issue of the grantee in order of descent but not upon ascendant or collateral heirs. The word 'tail' derives from the French '*taillé*' meaning cut down: it is an estate cut down from being 'simple'. The estate may be further limited by a stipulation that it may only descend through male or alternatively female heirs. It is then known as an estate in tail male (or female), e.g., 'Greenacre to X and the heirs male of his body'.

(c)   *Life estate.* As is implied by the name, this estate lasts for as long as the life in question. This can cover the straightforward situation of the grant of 'Greenacre to X for his life' and also a grant such as 'Whiteacre to Y for so long as Q lives' which is known as the *estate pur autre vie* ('for another life').

(d)   *The base fee.* This estate is being mentioned here in order to cover fully the various freehold estates. It is a variation on the fee tail brought about in the following manner.

Suppose a grant was made of 'Blueacre to A for life, remainder to B and the heirs of his body', i.e., a life estate followed by a fee tail estate. It became possible, through a series of legal manoeuvres, to 'bar the entail', turn it from an entailed interest into something resembling a fee simple. These actions were originally known as fines or recoveries, depending on the method used, and then later it was possible to take action under the Fines and Recoveries Act 1833. The basic point was that some of the actions enabled the entail to be barred without the permission of the person who is B in our example. If this was done then the estate became in effect a fee simple, i.e., alienable by the present holder *inter vivos* or by will or if he failed to alienate it then it passed to his general heirs but only for so long as B's tail lasted, i.e., the 'fee simple' ended if and when B's line of descending heirs died out; this was the base fee. Incidentally, under these various actions, if B consented to the barring of the entail the interest became a proper fee simple and was treated accordingly.

Estates Less than Freehold

These are the estates, alternatively known as leaseholds, which originally played no part in the system of real property. They were the personal estates of certain duration. Originally they were not recognised by real actions, which dealt only with freeholds of uncertain duration, but they came to resemble interests in real property because of their connections with the same subject-matter, land.

This distinction between freehold estates and estates less than freehold was of great importance. Consider the following examples. Suppose a grant was made of 'Mauveacre to Z, aged 90 years, for 50 years if he lives so long'. Here Z is 90 years old and is unlikely to live to be 140 years old to enjoy his whole interest. Nevertheless since the *maximum duration of his interest is certain* it was an estate less than freehold. A grant of 'Mauveacre to Z, aged 90 years, for his life' which would have had exactly the same practical effect, would however have been a freehold estate since the duration of his interest is *uncertain*.

Nature of the Fee Simple Estate

In practice the fee simple amounts to absolute ownership of the land concerned, the most ample estate known to the law. It ensures:

(a)   A right of alienation, i.e., free disposition by will or deed, the original restrictions on disposition by will had disappeared by the 15th century.

(b)   The right to everything in, on or over the land. '*Cuius est solum eius est usque ad coelum et ad inferos*' (he who owns the soil owns all to the heavens and to the centre of the earth), and with that ownership he may do everything he wishes with the land. However:

(i)   There may be self-imposed restrictions, e.g., restrictive covenants.

(ii)   Use of land may incur a liability in tort for nuisance, e.g., *Ryland* v *Yates* (1914) 58 SJ 612 (swarms of flies); *Rylands* v *Fletcher* (1868) LR 3 HL 330.

(iii)   Statutes have removed some property rights: petroleum vests in the Crown (Petroleum (Production Act 1934), coal vests in the National Coal Board (Coal Act 1938; Coal Industry Nationalisation Act 1946); uranium etc. vest in the United Kingdom Atomic Energy Authority (Atomic Energy Authority Act 1954).

(iv)   Ownership of airspace is not exclusive: aircraft may fly over at reasonable heights by virtue of the Civil Aviation Act 1982 (*Bernstein* v

Skyviews & General Ltd [1978] QB 479) though other interferences with airspace may be actionable (*Clifton* v *Viscount Bury* (1887) 4 TLR 8).

(v)   There are restrictions on the use of water.

(vi)   Restrictions are imposed by 'modern social legislation' — Town and Country Planning Acts, Rent Act 1977 etc.

(vii)   Wild animals have no owners unless tamed.

(viii)   Treasure trove belongs to the Crown by prerogative right (*Attorney-General* v *Trustees of the British Museum* [1903] 2 Ch 598).

See Curzon, *Land Law*, for a full list of limitations.

When can Estates Exist in Time?

Any estate in land may exist at any time in one of three ways:

(a)   *In possession*, giving an immediate right to possession and enjoyment of the estate.

(b)   *In remainder* and (c) *in reversion*, both of which exist in the future, i.e., give a future rather than present right to possession. The distinction here is that a remainder gives an interest to some person not previously entitled to the land, a reversion is the residue of a grantor's interest after he has given away some lesser estate in possession to another person.

Examples:

(a)   A owns Blackacre in fee simple and makes a grant to 'B for life, remainder to C in fee simple'. B has a present life estate, therefore, *in possession*. C has a future fee simple estate, therefore, *in remainder*.

(b)   A owns Blackacre in fee simple and makes a grant to 'B for life', remainder to C in fee tail', B has a present life estate *in possession*. C has a future fee tail, therefore, an estate *in remainder*. A has retained the outstanding fee simple, therefore, *has a reversionary interest*.

The Intervention of Equity

The most fundamental distinction in the law of real property is that between legal and equitable interests in land. The distinction is historical in that certain rights could be enforced in the common law courts (i.e., the King's ordinary courts) and these were known as legal rights. Other rights were not protected by the common law courts but came to be protected by the Chancellor in his Court of Chancery if he deemed this equitable. Although the Judicature Acts 1873 to 1875 amalgamated the two jurisdictions, the dual system produced is what makes land law in England and Wales so unique. It is a concept which must be grasped early in your course.

Equitable rights were (and still are) inferior to legal rights in that a legal right would be enforced against everyone, whereas an equitable right would be enforced only against a person whom the Chancellor considered was unable in good conscience to deny liability.

The Distinction between Legal and Equitable Rights

Legal rights are 'rights *in rem*', i.e., real rights which were historically protected by real actions through which the claimant could recover his land from any person who had seized it wrongfully.

Equitable rights are 'rights *in personam*', i.e., personal rights protected historically by personal actions. This meant that the owner of a personal right in property could sue someone who had wrongfully dispossessed him but he could not ask the court to compel the return of the land itself. He had to make do with monetary compensation if the person wrongfully dispossessing him chose to stay put.

Furthermore, a *legal interest* in land is a right in the land itself, so that whoever acquires the land subsequently is bound by the legal right and takes the land subject to it whether he had notice of it or not.

Equitable interests, however, give rise to personal actions against individuals and do not bind successors in title of a legal estate unless such successor in title purchases the property *with notice* of the prior equitable interest.

An example of the difference between legal rights and equitable rights is the trust. If land is conveyed 'to a trustee in fee simple on trust for B (the beneficiary) in fee simple', then the common law would treat the land as belonging absolutely to the trustee and allow him to do what he liked with it regardless of B. Equity would compel the trustee to manage the land for B's benefit and convey it to him according to the terms of the trust, i.e., equity would recognise B's personal rights and enforce them against the trustee. But this was an equitable right *in personam*, enforceable against a trustee alone so that if he died or conveyed the land elsewhere B had no redress. However, later, this doctrine was extended to cover:

(a) Anyone who took a conveyance of the land *with notice* of the trust.
(b) The trustee's heir.
(c) Anyone to whom the land was given.
(d) Executors or creditors of the trustee.
(e) Anyone *except* a bona fide purchaser of the legal estate for value without notice of the prior right.

The Purchaser Without Notice

The plea of a bona fide purchaser of the legal estate without notice is an 'absolute, unqualified, unanswerable defence'. The onus of proof lies on the person setting it up:

(a) *Bona fide.* The purchaser must act in good faith.
(b) *Purchaser for value:*

(i) Value includes money, money's worth (stocks, shares) other land (i.e., part exchange), marriage.
(ii) The value need not be full value but it must have been actually paid or given before the purchaser receives notice of the equitable right.
(iii) A purchaser includes mortgagees.

(c) *Of a legal estate.* In order to gain absolute priority the purchase must be of a legal estate. Where a mere equitable interest is acquired then priority runs in accordance with time and as between competing equities the first in time normally prevails.
(d) *Without notice.* There are three kinds of notice:

(i) *Actual notice.* A person has actual notice of all facts of which he has actual knowledge, however that knowledge is acquired, except that vague rumours will not suffice. By statute a number of rights are registrable in the Land Charges Register and registration constitutes *actual notice* whether the purchaser searches or not. Good faith is irrelevant (*Midland Bank Trust Co. Ltd v Green* [1981] AC 513).
(ii) *Constructive notice.* A person has constructive notice of all those facts of which he would have acquired actual notice had he made those enquiries and inspections which he ought reasonably to have made. The standard of prudence is that of men of business under similar circumstances. Thus a purchaser has constructive notice of a fact if:

(1) He actually had notice that there was *some* incumbrance and a proper enquiry would have revealed what it was.
(2) He has, whether deliberately or carelessly, abstained from making those enquiries that a prudent purchaser would have made.

(iii) *Imputed notice.* If a purchaser employs an agent, e.g., a solicitor, any actual or constructive notice which the agent receives may be imputed to the purchaser.

Remedies Granted

(a)   Specific performance — an order ordering someone to carry out his obligations.

(b)   Injunction — an order preventing someone doing something or making someone put right something already done.

(c)   Damages i.e., monetary compensation.

Example of Equitable Rights

(a)   *A trust.* This arises where a donor grants his legal estate to trustees to hold for the benefit of a named beneficiary or beneficiaries. The beneficiary will have an equitable interest and the courts will compel the trustees to administer the property for the benefit of the beneficiary.

(b)   *A mortgage.* This arises where a mortgagor charges his land to a mortgagee as security for a loan. Equity will allow the mortgagor *at any time* after repayment of the loan falls due, and despite any contrary provisions in the mortgage, to recover his land by paying the mortgagee whatever is due to him under the loan together with costs. (Mortgages can be legal or equitable — see chapter 6.)

(c)   *Restrictive covenants.* Normally a contract is binding upon and enforceable by the parties alone. But during the 19th century it was held that if a landowner covenants (promises by deed) not to use his land in a certain way for the benefit of neighbouring land, the covenant could be enforced in equity against successors in title of the covenantor thus imposing an equitable burden on the land.

(d)   *Estate contracts.* When a person contracts to purchase an interest in land, he is at once considered to have an equitable interest in that land even before he has paid the price and has had the legal estate of the vendor conveyed to him (see *Midland Bank Trust Co. Ltd v Green* [1981] AC 513 where failure to register an estate contract as a land charge rendered it unenforceable).

Creation of Equitable Rights

Equitable rights can be created or arise in three diffrerent ways:

(a)   *Informality*, where the proper formalities for the creation or conveyance of a legal estate are not observed, e.g., noncompliance with Law of Property Act 1925, s. 52, which requires, amongst other things, that leases of more than three years be created by way of a deed. If such a lease is not in a deed it may, if in writing, be recognised in equity.

(b) *Inability,* where the grantor only has power to create or convey an equitable interest, i.e., he who has merely an equitable interest can only convey an equitable interest.

(c) *Intention,* where the grantor intended and provided that an equitable interest should arise. See, for example, *Lloyds Bank plc* v *Rosset* [1991] 1 AC 107 where it was held that no intention to grant an equitable interest in the matrimonial home arose. This important case is discussed later in this chapter under 'Registration of title' and in chapter 5.

THE 1925 LEGISLATION

Fundamental changes were made to English land law in legislation commonly called 'the 1925 legislation' comprising the following Acts:

1922 Law of Property Act.
1924 Law of Property (Amendment) Act.
1925 Trustee Act.
1925 Settled Land Act.
1925 Law of Property Act.
1925 Land Registration Act.
1925 Land Charges Act, now 1972.
1926 Law of Property (Amendment) Act.

The first two made the most substantial alterations to the law but were then consolidated into the Law of Property Act 1925 (LPA 1925) before they all came into force on 1 January 1926.

The aims of the legislation were twofold:

(a) Amendment and modernisation of existing law, e.g., abolition of outdated tenure (as mentioned before).

(b) Simplification of conveyancing procedure. As you will be aware 'conveyancing' denotes the method of transferring estates and interests in land. As there were numerous legal estates prior to 1926 the problem was as follows. Suppose A wished to acquire the legal title to Blackacre and Blackacre was owned by various people under the following disposition: 'Blackacre to W for life, remainder to X for life, remainder to Y in fee tail, remainder to Z and his heirs'. There are four legal estates in Blackacre here:

W has a life estate in possession.
X has a life estate in remainder.
Y has fee tail estate in remainder.
Z has fee simple estate in remainder.

Before 1926, in order to acquire legal title to Blackacre, A, in our example, would have had to acquire *all those four* legal estates from their owners. It would be no use acquiring some of them, e.g., if he acquired the estates of W, X and Y, Z *could still enforce his legal fee simple remainder against A* since it is a fundamental principle that *a legal estate is enforceable against any person with any interest in the land whether he knows of that legal estate or not.*

Hence conveyancing was a complicated, messy, expensive problem in need of some simplification which was then achieved by the following steps:

Step One: Reduction of the Number of Legal Estates to Two

By LPA 1925, s. 1(1) the only two estates capable of subsisting, or being created, or conveyed at law are:

(a)   The *fee simple absolute in possession* (freehold estate).
(b)   The *term of years absolute* (leasehold estate).

Section 1 then went on to restrict the number of legal interests that could exist in land to five (i.e., the number of interests in other people's land rather than estates in your own land that would henceforth be recognised by the common law).

By LPA 1925, s. 1(2) the only interests or charges in or over land capable of subsisting or being created or conveyed at law are:

(a)   An easement, right or privilege in or over land for an interest equivalent to a fee simple absolute in possession or term of years absolute.

(b)   A rentcharge in possession issuing out of or charged on land, being either perpetual or for a term of years absolute.

(c)   A charge by way of legal mortgage.

(d)   Any other similar charge on land which is not created by an instrument.

(e)   Rights of entry exercisable over or in respect of a legal term of years absolute or annexed to a legal rentcharge.

Note the effect of LPA 1925, s. 1(1) and (2): only one freehold and one leasehold estate can exist at law after 1925 and the only interests that can exist at law after 1925 (with the exception of (c), a mortgage, which is a topic in itself for later) are those that would exist for a similar period of time to the legal estates. If you note the wording of the provisions of LPA 1925, s. 1(2), all the legal interests must exist either perpetually, as does a fee simple absolute in possession, or for a period equivalent to a term of years absolute.

The effect of *step one* then made conveyancing simpler in that so far as freehold conveyancing was concerned there could *only be one legal estate of freehold.*

If you return to our quoted example above, 'Blackacre to W for life, remainder to X for life, remainder to Y in fee tail, remainder to Z and his heirs', no estate satisfies the test of LPA 1925, s. 1(1) (even Z's fee simple is in remainder, note, not in possession).

Before moving to the next step the following points should be noted:

(a)   Section 1(1) and (2) refers only to the interests mentioned being *capable* of existing etc. at law. It *does not say* that they *must* be legal. There are certain other conditions to be satisfied before an estate can be legal, especially LPA 1925, s. 52(1), which requires a legal estate or interest to be created or conveyed by deed. If you combine s. 52(1) with s. 1(1) or s. 1(2) it therefore follows that the creation of an easement over Blackacre by a grant 'to A in fee simple' or of an estate in Blackacre 'to A in fee simple' without the use of a deed will prevent them being a legal interest or estate respectively despite s. 1(1) and (2).

(b)   The meaning of 'fee simple absolute' has already been explained but note 'absolute' denotes a fee simple which is not determinable or conditional.

Step Two

The obvious question to ask after step one is what happens to all the other estates and interests that were legal before 1926 but do not now fall within the provisions of LPA 1925, s. 1(1) and (2)? The answer is provided by LPA 1925, s. 1(3) — all other estates, interests and charges in or over land take effect as equitable interests. So if we return to our example: 'Blackacre to W for life, remainder to X for life, remainder to Y in fee tail, remainder to Z and his heirs', all these former legal estates before 1926 are now converted to equitable estates or, as they are more properly called under the 1925 legislation, *equitable interests*.

What has happened to the legal estate or estates? The answer is that a legal fee simple absolute in possession is held on trust to give effect to the equitable interests of the beneficiaries to the trust, W, X, Y, Z. The exact method of creating and controlling this trust will be studied later but essentially it can be represented in the following manner: 'Blackacre to W for life, remainder to X for life, remainder to Y in fee tail, remainder to Z and his heirs' effectively becomes: 'Blackacre *to trustees* in fee simple absolute in possession (the legal estate) *on trust for* W for life, remainder to X for life, remainder to Y in fee tail, remainder to Z and his heirs'.

The trustees in effect hold the present legal freehold to give effect first to W's interest, then to X's, then to Y's entail, until the time when Y's entail dies out, whereupon the fee simple of Z ceases to be in remainder and becomes an estate in possession. The trust then comes to an end since Z's interest now fulfills the requirements necessary to be legal itself.

During the time this is happening, which may be many years, the conveyancing is made simpler by the fact that there is only one legal estate for a purchaser to concern himself with, not four as was the case before 1926.

Those of you with inquiring minds may now be asking yourselves the following question: 'So a lot of what were legal estates before 1926 are now only equitable interests. I know that by and large this does not affect the protection those interests are given but what about the problem of the bona fide purchaser for value of the legal estate in the land without notice of the equitable interest? Surely a person who prior to 1926 had a legal estate could enforce it against any person irrespective of whether that person knew of the interest? Now, unless he has the fee simple absolute in possession, his estate is merely an equitable interest and not enforceable against the bona fide purchaser for value without notice. Isn't his interest therefore less valuable and less well protected because of this?

This is where step three comes in.

Step Three

Let us suppose we have the following situation *after* 1926. Blackacre is conveyed on trust for W for life, remainder to X for life, remainder to Y in fee tail, remainder to Z and his heirs. We know from what has just been said above that it is the legal estate, the fee simple absolute in possession, that is held in trust to give effect in equity to the equitable interests of W, X, Y and Z.

Suppose that A, acting in good faith, wishes to purchase the legal estate. Can he simply, by paying his purchase money to the trustees, get that fee simple absolute in possession from them and hold that fee simple absolute in possession free from the equitable interests of W, X, Y and Z?

The answer to that question lies in a closer examination of the *equitable doctrine of notice*, i.e., if someone *purchases a legal estate* whilst acting in *good faith* with *no notice* of the *equitable interests* existing in the same property he or she takes free of those equitable interests.

The forms of notice, discussed earlier, were, however, based upon investigation of both the property itself and the title deeds. Clearly this system of investigation was open to defects ranging from negligence to sheer oversight in the complexity of deeds involved and the Commission investigating real property law in the 19th century suggested alterations that reached maturity in the concept of overreaching in the 1925 legislation.

The Concept of 'Overreaching'

Let us suppose again that we have our trust of land, 'Blackacre on trust for W for life, remainder to X for life, remainder to Y in fee tail, remainder to Z and his heirs', and again let us suppose A wishes to purchase it. The effect of the new concept of overreaching is quite startlingly simple. If A pays his money to at least *two* trustees, or a trust corporation, of the trust he may take the legal estate free from the equitable interests of W, X, Y and Z which are transferred to the purchase money. This can be illustrated as follows:

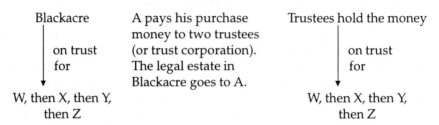

Blackacre
on trust
for
W, then X, then Y,
then Z

A pays his purchase
money to two trustees
(or trust corporation).
The legal estate in
Blackacre goes to A.

Trustees hold the money
on trust
for
W, then X, then Y,
then Z

A now holds Blackacre legally free from any equitable interests. This is often expressed in the following manner: 'A is legally and beneficially entitled to Blackacre'. That is to say, he has not only the legal, paper title but also, since it is free of equitable interests, all the benefit of his entitlement as well. He can enjoy it for himself without having to have regard to the other person's interests. W, X, Y and Z on the other hand now no longer have interests in the land but in the money. W for his life, then X, then Y and the heirs of his body, then Z and his heirs get the monetary equivalent of the fee simple. Notice here is irrelevant: the operation takes place automatically in this sort of situation.

This concept of overreaching is quite jurisprudentially acceptable to equity, for equity acts not against the thing itself, like the common law, but against any person seeking to interfere with the equitable owner's enjoyment of his interest. Equity does not, therefore, insist that W, X, Y and Z enjoy interests in the land but that they have a claim against the trustees for interference with what they are entitled to.

It is important to emphasise that there must be at least *two* trustees (or a trust corporation) before overreaching can occur. One will not suffice. Useful cases to illustrate this are *Williams & Glyn's Bank Ltd* v *Boland* [1981] AC 487 and *City of London Building Society* v *Flegg* [1988] AC 54. In the first of these cases there was only *one* trustee, the husband who had the matrimonial home conveyed into his name alone. Hence the wife's beneficial interest (established as she had contributed to the purchase of the home) was *not* overreached: it remained an interest in the property itself and was not converted into the monetary equivalent. The practical result of this was that the bank, to which the husband had mortgaged the property without informing his wife, could not obtain possession of the property.

By contrast in the second of these cases there were *two* trustees. A married couple had purchased a house to accommodate themselves and the wife's parents. The parents' names were not on the title deeds but they had contributed to the purchase price and so had a beneficial interest in the house.

Unfortunately for them, their interest *was* overreached as there were two trustees. When there was default in making mortgage repayments in relation to extra borrowing of which they knew nothing, the building society was entitled to obtain possession.

These cases are discussed again on pages 44 and 91.

The system of overreaching works simply and effectively where the equitable interest is capable of having a monetary value, but consider the situation shown in figure 3.2.

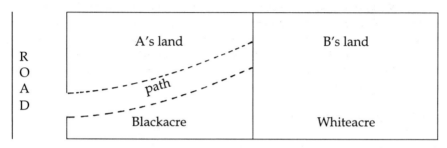

Figure 3.2

B owns Whiteacre; A owns Blackacre. In order to enable B to gain access to the road, A grants to B a right of way over Blackacre by way of the path for B's life. If you refer back to LPA 1925, s. 1(2), you will see this cannot be a legal easement since it is not equivalent to a fee simple or a term of years absolute. It is therefore an equitable easement. If overreaching were to be applied here it would mean that if a purchaser P came forward to buy Blackacre from A, then P could pay his purchase money to two trustees and B could claim his share of that purchase money representing his former easement over Blackacre. That is not a lot of use to B, particularly if it was his only access to the road; so the system of overreaching breaks down. Something else is needed here.

That something was provided by the retention and improvement of the system of notice.

Extension of System of Registration of Charges

The 1925 legislation abolished to a great extent the old pre-1926 system of actual, constructive and imputed notice as being unsafe and unsound and produced a system of registration in a Land Charges Register under the Land Charges Act 1925 (now the Land Charges Act 1972). This introduced a system whereby *registration of certain interests constituted actual notice* to a purchaser and *if not registered* even actual, constructive or imputed notice by any other means was irrelevant and of *no effect on the purchaser* (see *Midland Bank Trust Co. Ltd* v *Green* [1981] AC 513 discussed in chapter 2).

The Land Charges Act 1925 established a number of registers and a complete outline of the system may be gleaned from the textbooks.

At the same time the Land Registration Act 1925 provided for the extension of registered title. This was a wholly new system of conveyancing which now covers the majority of the country. This new system provides for registration of titles on transfer and of third-party rights. This is discussed in more detail later.

Throughout land law you will see that by and large equitable interests are protected by one or other of these two methods, 'overreaching' or 'registration'. However, there are occasions where there are defects in these schemes requiring a retreat to actual or constructive or imputed notice under the old doctrine of notice (for example see specimen examination question 1 at the end of this chapter).

ANALYSIS OF INTERESTS

You ought now to be able to analyse any interest in land and identify the proprietary interests involved in it. However basic or uninteresting this is, all problems of land law are to be solved by adopting this first basic approach.

You should now be able to decide:

(a) Who owns an interest.
(b) The exact nature of the estate or interest in question.
(c) Whether it is in possession, remainder or reversion.
(d) Whether that interest is legal or equitable.

For example a grant of Blackacre 'to A during B's life, then to C for life, then to D in fee tail, then to E in fee simple absolute'.

Who owns interest?	A	Not B, he is merely used to describe the length of A's interest.	C	D	E
What sort of interest is it?	Life estate pur autre vie.		Life estate.	Entailed interest.	Fee simple absolute.
Possession, remainder or reversion?	Takes it immediately, therefore in possession.		Must wait until A's interest ends, therefore in remainder.	Must wait for A and C's interests to end, therefore in remainder.	Must wait for A, C and D's interests to end, therefore in remainder.

Legal or equitable?	Equitable, not within LPA 1925, s. 1(1).	Not within s. 1(1), so equitable.	Not within s. 1(1), so equitable.	Prima facie within s. 1(1) but not in possession, so it is equitable.

REGISTRATION OF TITLE

The revised system of registration of title contained in the Land Registration Acts 1925 to 1988 and the Land Registration Rules, *must* be kept separate from the system of registration of *charges* under the Land Charges Act 1925, now 1972. Students must get it clear in their minds that the two systems are quite distinct: the Land Charges Act will *only* apply where the old system of conveyancing is used (involving investigation of title deeds for at least the previous 15 years), i.e., where *title* to the land is unregistered. Although perhaps more properly a topic covered in a conveyancing syllabus most land law syllabuses do include the basic principles relating to registration of title (but not the detailed procedure), not least because the system has gradually been extended to all areas of England and Wales. Both systems of conveyancing will, however, be relevant for some considerable time as the legislation only provides for registration of title to the legal estate on its *transfer*. For the same reason most examination papers will contain a question seeking to ascertain whether or not you understand the system. In addition, most papers will state in the rubric whether the facts in any given question relate to registered or unregistered land. It is important to note this and direct your answer accordingly. All major textbooks contain chapters on registration of title. The main work is Ruoff and Roper, *The Law and Practice of Registered Conveyancing*. It is, however, too detailed for land law students (other than students of conveyancing). The most helpful and up-to-date appraisal is to be found in *Maudsley and Burn's Land Law: Cases and Materials*.

The questions below are ones you should ask yourself when revising this area:

(a)   What is the system of registration of title all about?

(b)   What is the effect on the legal estate if title is not registered in an area of compulsory registration?

(c)   Do I know the three features of the system, namely, the mirror, curtain and insurance principles?

(d)   Am I aware of any recent developments?

Depending on your notes, you may think of more questions. It helps to list them and then work through them.

What is the System of Registration of Title all about?

The system provides for the registration of *legal titles* to land and the *protection* of other interests in and over land. Only interests capable of existing at law under LPA 1925, s. 1 are registrable. Other interests, called 'minor interests', are protected, not by registration as separate titles but by entry on the register by means of a notice, restriction, caution or inhibition. In addition there are overriding interests that are binding on a purchaser even though they are not entered on the register. Such interests, defined in LRA 1925, s. 70, are a source of contention. Details of equitable beneficial interests, i.e., those existing behind a trust, are not disclosed on the title deeds as they are 'overreachable' on sale.

What Title may be Registered?

Only the two estates capable of being legal by virtue of LPA 1925, s. 1, may be registered, i.e., the fee simple absolute in possession and the term of years absolute. With respect to leases the Land Registration Act 1986 amended the 1925 Act. It lays down the test for determining whether an unregistered lease of property in a compulsory registration area should be registered. This is whether there is a sale and whether its term exceeds 21 years (or there is 21 years or more to run). See D.C.S. Phillips (1986) 130 SJ 579. Remember that short leases, although not registrable, may amount to overriding interests within LRA 1925, s. 70(1)(k), i.e., leases for any term of interest not exceeding 21 years whether granted at a rent or gratuitously (see LRA 1986, s. 4(1)), and therefore anyone dealing with the registered title will take subject to such a lease whether or not he could have discovered its existence. Most leases of this sort are already covered by s. 70(1)(g) (i.e., rights of persons in actual occupation or in receipt of rents and profits), but not all.

What is the Effect on the Legal Estate if Title is not Registered?

In areas of compulsory registration (designated as such by order), dealing in land after a given date must be carried out under the new system of conveyancing. Furthermore, the Housing Act 1985, s. 154, requires that tenants in the public sector exercising their right to buy given to them under that Act should receive registered titles. If the title is not registered where necessary, LRA 1925, s. 123, provides that 'every conveyance on sale of freehold land ... shall ... become void' if not registered after *two months* (or authorised extended period) from the date of the conveyance. In practice this is mitigated as the registrar (or a court) may allow a later date provided there is a reasonable excuse.

Do I know the Features of Registration of Title?

The mirror principle   The register is intended to operate as a mirror, accurately reflecting the totality of estates and interests affecting the registered land. Ask yourself, 'What of overriding interests within LRA 1925, s. 70(1)? These are very important as they bind the proprietor of registered land even though he has no knowledge of them and no reference is made to them in the register. They are defined in s. 70 of the Land Registration Act 1925. Of particular interest to students is the category of overriding interest in s. 70(1)(g), namely:

> The rights of every person in actual occupation of the land or in receipt of the rents and profits thereof, save where enquiry is made of such person and the rights are not disclosed.

The recent decisions of *Abbey National Building Society* v *Cann* [1991] 1 AC 56 and *Lloyds Bank plc* v *Rosset* [1991] 1 AC 107, following on the heels of the two already important cases of *Williams & Glyn's Bank Ltd* v *Boland* [1981] AC 487 and *City of London Building Society* v *Flegg* [1988] AC 54, embody the criteria needed to establish an overriding interest protected by s. 70(1)(g). These decisions are likely to provide a fertile ground for examiners' questions both as part of the 1925 legislation and overlapping into matrimonial property and will therefore be dealt with below in detail.

Criteria necessary to establish an overriding interest
It is important to realise that not all occupiers can successfully claim an overriding interest as illustrated in the cases of *Flegg*, *Cann* and *Rosset* where the claims failed, for differing reasons. One method of approach is to list the criteria necessary to establish an overriding interest and relate those criteria to the facts given in the question. Such a list may look like this:

The claimant of an overriding interest must:

(a)   be able to establish an equitable interest in the property,
(b)   prove this equitable interest has not been overreached,
(c)   have been in actual occupation at the time of the creation or transfer of the legal estate.

Taking each criterion in turn the student should then explain them in more detail and apply them to the given fact situation.

Establishing an equitable interest
There are various ways in which an occupier can establish an equitable interest, for example, by making a financial contribution, direct or indirect, to the purchase price of the property.

Examples which could be quoted are the *Boland* and *Flegg* cases where direct contributions were made and, by comparison, the *Rosset* case where helping with renovations to a derelict property was insufficient to be regarded as establishing such an interest.

The *Rosset* case involved the acquisition of a semi-derelict property as a matrimonial home with the husband as sole registered proprietor. The exchange of contracts took place on 23 November 1982 but renovation work had started on 7 November with the vendor's assent. Between 7 November and the completion date renovations were effected by builders and Mrs Rosset devoted almost every day to aiding them. Unknown to his wife, Mr Rosset took out a mortgage to secure an overdraft for the renovation work and subsequently defaulted on his repayments. Consequently the bank sought to repossess. Mrs Rosset claimed she had an equitable interest in the property combined with her vicarious actual occupation via the builders and hence an overriding interest binding on the bank.

The House of Lords held that the labour done by Mrs Rosset was not sufficient to create an inference of common intention that she should have an equitable interest in the property. Hence the question of whether Mrs Rosset was in actual occupation was not pursued. There are several articles discussing this case and it is always helpful to supplement your notes with any criticisms or comments from them. See, for example, M.P. Thompson, 'Establishing an interest in the home: *Lloyd's Bank plc* v *Rosset*' [1990] Conv 314; C. Bell, 'Overriding interests and actual occupation' (1990) 134 SJ 709.

The equitable interest must not be overreached
As figure 3.3 illustrates, overreaching of an equitable interest prevents an overriding interest from arising as LRA 1925, s. 70(1), refers to 'interests ... for the time being subsisting in reference [to registered land]'. Interests which are overreached, i.e., converted into the proceeds of sale, are of course no longer interests in land. It should be emphasised that payment of the purchase money to two trustees or a trust corporation is required for overreaching to take place.

The cases of *Boland* and *Flegg* (discussed earlier in relation to overreaching) are so important that at the risk of becoming boring, the facts are detailed here:

In *Williams & Glyn's Bank Ltd* v *Boland* [1981] AC 487, a husband was registered as sole proprietor of the matrimonial home where he and his wife lived. The wife had made a substantial contribution to the purchase, which entitled her to a share in the house. She had not protected her interest by entering a notice, caution or restriction on the register. The husband, without the wife's consent, charged the house to the plaintiff bank to secure his business indebtedness. The bank never enquired whether the wife had any interest in the house. It now claimed repayment of the loan and possession of the house. The House of Lords (Lord Wilberforce, Viscount Dilhorne, Lords Salmon, Scarman and Roskill) held that the wife had an overriding interest within LRA 1925, s. 70(1)(g), being a 'person in actual occupation'.

In *City of London Building Society* v *Flegg* [1988] AC 54, the House of Lords, reversing the Court of Appeal, distinguished *Boland's* case on the ground that in that case there was only *one* registered proprietor whereas in *Flegg's* case there were *two* (husband and wife). As there were two, the equitable interest of the wife's parents (which arose from their contribution to the purchase price of the house) was capable of being overreached. Hence the parents' equitable interest was not an interest 'subsisting in reference' to land and could not be protected as an overriding interest even though the parents occupied the house.

Several articles have been written on these two cases which students may refer to, including W.J. Swaddling [1987] Conv 451 and P. Hargrove [1988] Fam Law 17.

Williams & Glyn's Bank Ltd v *Boland*

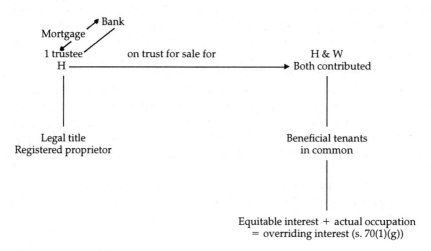

City of London Building Society v *Flegg*

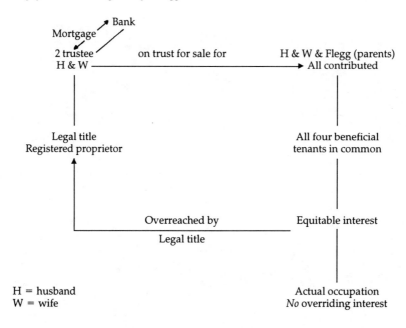

H = husband
W = wife

Abbey National Building Society v Cann

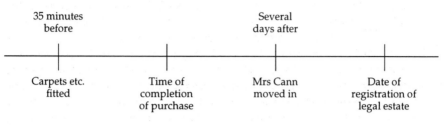

Figure 3.3

The date for determining an overriding interest
The House of Lords in the recent cases of *Abbey National Building Society v Cann* [1991] 1 AC 56 and *Lloyds Bank plc v Rosset* [1991] 1 AC 107 ruled that the dates for determining the existence of an overriding interest and 'actual occupation' were different. A claimant must have been in actual occupation at the time of creation or transfer of the legal estate whereas the relevant date for determining the existence of an overriding interest protected by LRA 1925, s. 70(1)(g), affecting the estate transferred or created is the date of registration.

The reason for the different dates was said to prevent a conveyancing absurdity. On this point a useful judgment is that of Lord Oliver of Aylmerton in the *Cann* case who states that it would be absurd if:

> a mortgagee after completion and after having made inquiries and parted with money be bound by the interest asserted by a newly arrived occupant coming between completion and registration of his charge.

To illustrate this point the *Boland* and *Cann* cases are useful. In *Boland*, the wife was clearly in actual occupation of the matrimonial home at the date of the creation of the mortgage of the matrimonial home taken out by her husband. Even if it was not registered until later (and it can usually take some weeks) she had an overriding interest. Compare the position of Mrs Cann (see below), who was not held to be in 'actual occupation' at the relevant time.

In *Cann* (see figure 3.3) Mrs Cann bought, in the joint names of herself and her son George, a house of which she had been sitting tenant. George assured his mother she would always have a roof over her head. Two years later this property was sold and another purchased in George's sole name and was bought by means of a £15,000 mortgage of which Mrs Cann was fully aware. The house was subsequently sold for £45,000 and a maisonette purchased for £34,000 again in George's sole name. £4,000 was needed to achieve the purchase and contemporaneously with the purchase of the maisonette

George mortgaged it to a building society for £25,000 without the knowledge of Mrs Cann. The vendor vacated the maisonette 35 minutes antecedent to the completion of the purchase at which time carpets had been laid and furniture placed in the premises. Mrs Cann moved in several days later. George subsequently fell into arrears and the Abbey National sought repossession. The House of Lords held that Mrs Cann was not in actual occupation at the date of transfer (i.e., completion of the purchase in this case). The acts done 35 minutes prior to completion were of a 'preparatory character'. Some degree of permanence and continuity is required, ruling out a 'mere fleeting presence'.

Interesting articles abound on this case, including, J.A. Greed, 'A Cann of worms?' (1990) NLJ 815, 867; M. Beaumont, 'A home in old age - a conveyancing absurdity' (1990) LS Gaz, No. 19 (23 May 1990), 24, and No. 28 (25 July 1990), 27.

The curtain principle   Only the legal title is shown on the register. All trusts are kept off the title as the beneficial interests behind the trust will be overreached on sale, i.e.:

Legal title
———————————————————CURTAIN
Trust details

The insurance principle   The State guarantees the accuracy of the registered title in the sense that an indemnity is payable from public funds if a registered proprietor is deprived of his title or is otherwise prejudiced by the operation of the scheme (LRA 1925, s. 84). The indemnity is payable by the Chief Land Registrar out of moneys provided by Parliament. The register will, of course, be rectified under the terms of LRA 1925, s. 82, wherever possible. For an interesting discussion of the circumstances under which rectification or indemnity should be used, see *Clark* v *Chief Land Registrar* [1993] All ER 936, ChD. Whether or not rectification is a *right*, as Judge Mervyn Davies in *Blacklocks* v *J.B. Developments (Godalming) Ltd* [1982] Ch 183 seemed to think, or obtainable at the *discretion* of the court in the cases listed in s. 82(1) as Templeman J remarked in *Epps* v *Esso Petroleum Ltd* [1973] 2 All ER 465 at 472 is one of several interesting points discussed in an article by D.G. Barnsley, entitled 'Rectification, trusts and overriding interests' [1984] Conv 361.

The Opening of the Register

The Land Registration Act 1988 was brought into force on 3 December 1990 opening the register to inspection by the public. Copies may be made provided the appropriate fee is paid and any conditions laid down in the rules complied with. The advantage of the Act is that registered titles will no longer be secret and dependent upon the registered proprietor's consent for disclosure, e.g., a potential developer of land will be able to discover whether any covenants affect the land before making a bid to purchase and applying for planning permission.

A useful discussion of the reasoning behind opening the register is to be found in the Law Commission's Report No. 148.

CONCLUSION

English land law, although based on fundamental principles, is dynamic, slowly building on these principles and so responding to change. Those principles (principles which make it unique), and in particular the changes brought about by the 1925 legislation, have been outlined in this chapter. Grasping an understanding of them is important, not only to be able to answer questions set specifically on them but because they form a spring-board to understanding the topics dealt with in the subsequent chapters.

SPECIMEN EXAMINATION QUESTIONS

Question 1

The plea of a purchaser of a legal estate for value without notice is 'an absolute, unqualified, unanswerable defence' (per James LJ in *Pilcher* v *Rawlins*, 1872).

What does equity understand by the doctrine of notice? Has the importance of this doctrine been diminished by the 1925 property legislation?

Suggested Approach

Read the question carefully and ascertain what the examiner is looking for, then answer it without going off at tangents. This question is straightforward. It is concerned with the equitable doctrine of notice and the effect on it of the system of registration of charges extended by the 1925 legislation. It does not require an answer based on 'everything I know about the 1925 legislation'. Unfortunately, this happens sometimes — a student will see the words '1925 property legislation' and will promptly exclude all other aspects of the question. Needless to say, such an answer will probably not even gain a pass mark no matter how accurate the material produced is, for it is not answering the question given. A further point is that although in essence the question is divided into two parts, there is no indication that equal marks will be available for each part. Consequently, the question should be treated as a whole. Do not spend an undue amount of time on either part.

One way of embarking on a question of this nature is to indicate to the examiner in your introduction that you are aware of what is required and indicate briefly the direction in which your answer will progress. For example:

> The doctrine of notice was developed by equity to mitigate the harshness of the common law which only recognised legal rights (legal rights are good against the whole world). Eventually this doctrine established that equitable rights would also be good against the whole world, that is, all *except* 'a bona fide purchaser of the legal estate for value without notice of the equitable interest' (or a person claiming through such a purchaser).
>
> This is what James LJ is referring to in the quotation given, when he states that the plea of the purchaser of a legal estate for value without notice 'is an absolute, unqualified, unanswerable defence'. The date was 1872 and to a large extent the doctrine of notice has been replaced by the extension of the system of registration of charges brought about by the 1925 legislation (namely the Land Charges Act 1925 now 1972). Not all equitable rights are registrable, for example, those arising through acquiescence. In those situations the doctrine will still apply. In areas of compulsory registration of title the Land Registration Act 1925 also caused the importance of the doctrine to diminish.

A different approach would be simply to give the examiner what he wants by defining what is meant by the doctrine of notice in a brief introduction:

> The equitable doctrine of notice, referred to by James LJ in the quotation given, established that equitable rights would be good against everyone *except* a bona fide purchaser of the legal estate for value without notice of the equitable interest (or a person claiming through such a purchaser).

Whichever approach is adopted the essay should then develop by dissecting the wording of the doctrine itself, for the question asks you to 'explain'. For example:

> Equity, by referring to a bona fide purchaser of the legal estate for value, requires that there is in fact a purchaser and the legal title to the land has not been received by way of a gift, whether by will or *inter vivos* grant or obtained by way of adverse possession (after 12 years) as it was in *Re Nisbet and Potts' Contract* [1906] 1 Ch 386 (a squatter). Such a purchaser must act in good faith and give value, i.e., provide some form of consideration, and must take without notice of the equitable interest.
>
> Notice is of three types, actual, constructive and imputed, i.e., a person is deemed to have actual notice of all facts of which he has acquired

knowledge, no matter how, and constructive notice of that which he would have discovered had he made the sort of investigation that a prudent purchaser would have made, e.g., undertaking inspection of the land and making enquiries of any person in occupation, plus an examination of the vendor's title — this can be done either by the purchaser himself or more usually by his solicitor. Any actual or constructive notice received by the agent employed by the purchaser (e.g., solicitor) is imputed to the purchaser (*Jared* v *Clements*) provided the agent acquires it when acting as such and in the course of the particular transaction (LPA 1925, s. 199).

Moving to the second part of the question — the effect of the 1925 legislation on the doctrine of notice — there is a lot of ground to cover and little time to do it, so be direct: (a) explain the extension of the system of registration of charges, then (b) identify those equitable rights (with examples) which are not registrable and to which the doctrine will still apply. For example, on point (a):

> The 1925 legislation abolished to a great extent the old pre-1926 system of actual, constructive and imputed notice as being unsafe, preferring to extend the system of registration of charges. Under the Land Charges Act 1925 (now 1972) many important interests, mainly equitable (such as equitable easements and restrictive covenants) and some legal (e.g., puisne mortgages), are registrable. At the same time the Land Registration Act 1925 provided for registration of title and third-party rights. The effect of both these Acts is that in respect of registrable interests, the old doctrine of notice has no application. Registration itself constitutes actual notice to all persons for all purposes connected with the land. Notice by any other means is irrelevant. If *not* registered then the interest is *void* as against certain classes of purchaser (LPA 1925, s. 198). As Megarry J states: 'The test is now the state of the register not the purchaser's mind'. For example, in *Hollington Bros Ltd* v *Rhodes* [1951] 2 TLR 691 an unregistered estate contract was declared void, and in the leading case of *Midland Bank Trust Co. Ltd* v *Green* [1981] AC 513 the House of Lords (reversing the Court of Appeal) similarly held that an unregistered estate contract, namely an option to purchase land, was void for non-registration. Whilst these cases involve land with unregistered title the same principle applies to registered title.

Depending on the length of time still available, a good student may wish to comment on the *Midland Bank* case and the approaches taken by the Court of Appeal and the House of Lords. For example:

> The House of Lords made it clear that bona fides is a concept of equity. Lord Wilberforce stating that when notice came to be regulated by statute the

requirement of good faith became obsolete. Neither does statute require a purchaser to pay more than a nominal amount. This contrasts with the Court of Appeal, particularly the judgments of Lord Denning MR and Everleigh LJ (Sir Stanley Rees dissenting), who considered that a purchaser should pay an 'adequate' sum by way of consideration, 'adequacy' going further than the meaning given to it in the ordinary law of contract — otherwise the door would be open to fraud.

On point (b) it should be explained that not all interests are registrable, e.g., equitable rights of re-entry for breach of a leasehold covenant (*Shiloh Spinners Ltd* v *Harding* [1973] AC 691), equitable rights arising by acquiescence (*E.R. Ives Investment Ltd* v *High* [1967] 2 QB 379) and, of course, restrictive covenants entered into before 1925. In such situations the doctrine of notice still applies.

Finally, a conclusion to complete the question. Always re-read the question before concluding. A few lines directly aimed at answering the question are better than a long meandering conclusion which only confirms to the examiner that you don't really understand anything about the equitable doctrine of the notice but have merely regurgitated what you have read. For example:

> The importance of the equitable doctrine of notice has indeed been diminished in importance by the 1925 legislation, in particular due to the expansion of the system of registration of charges by the Land Charges Act 1925 (now 1972). It has *not* been replaced completely, however, because certain equitable interests are not registrable. In addition in areas of compulsory registration of title, the Land Registration Act 1925 clearly adds to its decline.

The question does not specifically ask for a detailed discussion of the effects of the Land Registration Act 1925 on the doctrine and it can therefore be assumed that this is not required as it would be impossible to cover the material in the time available. You may, however, wish to comment briefly that should the title to the property be registered under the Land Registration Act 1925 then a person who can establish a beneficial interest and who is also in actual occupation of the property may have an overriding interest within s. 70(1)(g) of that Act and such interests bind third parties without registration.

Apart from pure essay-type questions like question 1, it is quite common for examiners to set questions similar to question 2 in order to ascertain whether or not you can apply your knowledge to given situations.

Question 2

State with reasons, whether the following grants are today capable of creating legal estates or interests in land:

(a)   a grant by deed, of Blackacre to Y in fee tail;

(b)   a grant, in writing, of a yearly tenancy of Whiteacre to Z at a rent of £200 per annum;

(c)   a grant of a restrictive covenant over Greenacre to a neighbouring landowner;

(d)   a grant, by deed, of a right of way over the grantor's land, for the life of the grantee;

(e)   a grant, by deed, of realty to X for life, at an annual rent of £200.

Comments

Read the question carefully, as always, and note that *reasons* are asked for your answers and it is the *position post 1926* which the examiner is interested in — an answer which spends time explaining the position pre 1926 will not therefore be relevant: valuable time will have been wasted without gaining any extra marks. You might think the above comment is superfluous — 'Who would even consider doing that?' you might ask. Yet some students *do* just that. They tend to write an answer which represents what they have learned rather than what the question is asking and if they know the position pre 1926 will tend to tell the examiner all about it. Don't let this be you, for the examiner will not be at all impressed! Answer the question given.

Suggested Approach

Such a question as this does not require a yes or no answer. It is quite searching and unless you are confident that you know why the grants described in the question can amount to legal estates or interests or not, it should be avoided. There is no room for guesswork or 'waffle'. The question requires specific answers to specific situations.

A suggested framework would be:

(a)   Such a grant, albeit by deed, cannot be legal. Since 1926, by virtue of LPA 1925, s. 1(1), only two estates are capable of being legal, the fee simple absolute in possession and the term of years absolute. The grant given to Y is neither. It is 'in tail' and is necessarily equitable by virtue of LPA 1925, s. 1(3).

(b)   The grant, in writing to Z, of a yearly tenancy is capable of creating a legal estate (being a term of years absolute within LPA 1925, s. 1) provided it satisfies all the three conditions set out below. These conditions must be met before there can be an exception to the general rule, contained in LPA 1925, s. 52, that a lease cannot create a legal estate unless it is made by deed. The lease must:

(i)   take effect in possession (possession not being confined to physical possession but including receipt of rents and profits, e.g., from subtenants in actual physical possession), and

(ii)   be for a term not exceeding three years, whether or not the lessee is given power to extend the term, and

(iii) be at the best rent reasonably obtainable without taking a fine (a 'fine' in this sense being a lump payment made in consideration of a reduced rent).

Having stated the position the student must progress the answer by applying the above conditions to the lease given. It should be pointed out, for example, that it will depend on whether the £200 per annum is indeed 'the best rent reasonably obtainable'. It should be explained that the yearly tenancy (a periodic tenancy) is treated at law as a grant for one year, which, if not determined at the end of that year, will automatically and without any fresh letting run for another year and so on from year to year. It is not certain, however, that it will endure for more than three years. It therefore meets the requirement described in (ii) above (see, e.g., *Hammond* v *Farrow* [1904] 2 KB 332).

(c)   A grant of a restrictive covenant is necessarily equitable, for LPA 1925, s. 1(2), identifies five interests capable of being legal. A restrictive covenant is not one of those five and therefore cannot be legal.

(d)   A right of way is classed as an easement, i.e., a right exercisable over the land of another. LPA 1925, s. 1(2)(a) mentions 'an easement, right or privilege in or over land for an interest equivalent to an estate in fee simple absolute in possession or a term of years absolute' as being one of the only five legal interests 'which are capable of subsisting or being conveyed or created at law'.

The grant in the question being for the *life* of the grantee (even though it is by deed) does not satisfy the necessary requirement of s. 1(2) and consequently is *not* capable of being a legal interest and must be equitable.

Whether or not the grant by deed by X in part (e) of the question is classed as a legal or an equitable estate is complicated by the fact that an annual rent of £200 is payable. In your answer you must distinguish between commercial and family arrangements. For example:

It will depend on whether the transaction is commercial in nature or whether it is in the nature of a family settlement. If it is commercial then the grant will be considered to be a lease for 90 years, for LPA 1925, s. 149(6), converts leases let at a rent, for life, into such a term. It is therefore capable of being a legal estate and as it has been created by deed this will meet the criteria of LPA 1925, s. 52. If, however, it is by way of a family settlement then, despite the fact that a rent is payable, X will have a life interest which is not capable of existing as a legal estate and is necessarily equitable (LPA 1925, s. 1(3)).

As Megarry and Wade state in *The Law of Real Property*, 'The distinction is not always clear-cut'. Consequently, marks may be gained by a comment to that effect together with the example of a case illustrating the point. One such case is *Re Catling* [1931] 2 Ch 359. In that case a testator devised a house to trustees on trust to grant a lease thereof to his widow at the rent of £1 a year, the tenancy not to be determined while the widow made the house her principal home. The widow claimed that the will made her a tenant for life under the Settled Land Act 1925. Bennett J disagreed and it was held that as a matter of construction the widow was 'a tenant under a lease at a rent'.

SUGGESTED ADDITIONAL READING

Although the history of land law is unlikely to be part of a modern course, an understanding of the history is a useful building block. You could consult:

A. W. Simpson, *An Introduction to the History of Land Law*, 2nd ed., 1986 (Clarendon Press).
J. G. Riddall, *Introduction to Land Law*, 5th ed., 1993 (Butterworths), which gives a clear and concise account of tenures and estates.
L. B. Curzon, *Land Law*, 6th ed., 1993 (Pitman), which gives a useful overview of the areas discussed in this chapter.
D. Hayton, *Registered Land*, 3rd ed., 1981 (Sweet & Maxwell) which provides a more detailed discussion of the system of registration of title.

4 SETTLEMENTS AND FUTURE INTERESTS

INTRODUCTION

As we have seen in chapter 3 one of the fundamental effects of the 1925 legislation is to reduce the number of legal estates in land to two and convert those other estates, capable of being legal prior to 1926, into equitable interests existing behind a trust of the legal estate in the land. In land law the word 'settlement' is synonymous with 'trust'. Rather than speaking of 'trusts over land' it is more common to speak of 'settlements of land'. Land law students therefore need to have a clear grasp of the principles involved in the creation and administration of settlements. The first part of this chapter will help you to understand these principles and guide you on tackling your revision. The second part deals similarly with 'future interests', namely, those equitable interests behind the trust which merely give an entitlement to future possession, e.g., a disposition such as: 'Blackacre to A for life, *remainder to B* in fee tail, *remainder to C* and his heirs'. The whole disposition can be generally referred to as a 'settlement'. After 1925 it should be read as follows: 'Blackacre to trustees in fee simple absolute in possession on trust for A for life etc.' In addition, B and C's equitable interests only entitle them to possession of Blackacre at some time in the future.

MAIN ISSUES

As explained 'settlement' is synonymous with trust. In its general sense it is used for *all* kinds of arrangements whereby property is given to particular persons in succession. In fact the essential element of a settlement is a series of interests created by a single gift, whether will or deed. Settlements of land fall into two categories: the *strict settlement* governed by the Settled Land Act 1925 (SLA 1925), originally used as a means of keeping land in the family, and the *trust for sale*, governed by the Law of Property Act 1925, used as a means of providing income and capital from the sale of the land for members of the family.

An approach which can be useful when revising both settlements and future interests is to leave the detailed provisions until later. Rather begin by bearing in mind at the outset:

(a)   the original objectives of the settlor, and

(b)   the overall philosophy behind the legislation, i.e., that whilst recognising that each person should be able to dispose of his land as he pleases, it is not in the interests of public policy for land to be tied up for long periods of time. The legislation attempts to balance these two conflicting aims.

A brief comment on this delicate balance could form a useful introductory or conclusive paragraph to an examination question. It would show the examiner that you have done more than learn the legal provisions but have thought about why the law has developed in the way it has. For example, if confronted with a question on settlements, you could, after stating the two conflicting interests, comment as follows:

The legislation attempts to balance these aims by extending the use of the trust for sale and by allowing land held on a strict settlement to be disposed of (sold, leased etc.) by the person entitled under the settlement to possession of the settled land for his life. So successful has the legislation been in promoting the former in fact that E.H. Burn in *Cheshire and Burn's Modern Law of Real Property* suggested that if it were now enacted that *all* settlements of land must be created by way of trust for sale nothing would be lost. In fact, paradoxically, today it is easier to keep land from being sold by way of a trust for sale (as in *Re Inns* [1947] Ch 576) than by way of a strict settlement.

A great deal of academic debate has centred around the issue and you should consider the views of Professor M. M. Lewis (1938) 54 LQR 576 and Professor G. Grove (1961) 24 MLR 123 both recommending an amendment to the Settled Land Act 1925 to vest the legal estate in the settled land in the settlement trustees. Prefessor Potter (1944) 8 Conv (NS) 147 favoured a scheme whereby a strict settlement could only be created where there was intention to do so and Professor Scamell in (1957) 10 CLP 152 favours the conversion of all settlements into trusts for sale (as does E. H. Burn as commented earlier).

Once you have grasped what the law is attempting to achieve and why, it helps in understanding the detailed statutory provisions, which would otherwise seem purely regulatory. Some degree courses may study in some detail the historical development of settlements prior to 1926. It is not our intention to concern ourselves with this. Should this be part of your course we refer you to standard texts, especially *The Law of Real Property* by Megarry and Wade.

In order to ascertain whether students understand this area of law, examination questions tend to be quite searching and require:

(a)   a detailed knowledge of the machinery and administration of both types of settlements,

(b)   an awareness of the purpose and effectiveness of the legislation, and

(c)   the ability to make a comparison between both types of settlement.

Remember also that whilst this part of the chapter is concerned with 'settlements' as a separate area of law, often examinable as such, an understanding of the trust for sale is also important to be able to come to grips with other topics, especially co-ownership and matrimonial property dealt with in later chapters, so you ignore the trust for sale at your peril.

STRICT SETTLEMENTS

What is a Strict Settlement?

Inherent in all examination questions is the problem whether the settlement in question can be classified as a strict settlement or a trust for sale, for this is a prerequisite to deciding who is entitled to the legal estate. It is useful therefore to consider SLA 1925, s. 1, in some detail with examples, because faced with such a problem it is useful to be able to state that the settlement given is, for example, a strict settlement (and not a trust for sale) because it falls within a certain subsection of SLA 1925, s. 1.

Settled Land Act 1925, section 1

A strict settlement arises whenever land is limited in trust by deed, will, or document in order to create any of the interests laid down in SLA 1925, s. 1, provided no immediate and binding trust for sale is imposed.

The interests listed in SLA 1925, s. 1, are referred to by technical terms but are, by and large, the estates, with which we have already become acquainted in chapter 3, which cannot exist at law after 1926, i.e., all estates *other than* fee simple estates, for example, life estates and all fee simple estates *other than* fees simple absolute in possession.

The text of the list of interests in s. 1(1) follows in the left-hand column with our commentary in the right-hand column.

Interests in SLA, s. 1(1)	*Examples*
(i) limited in trust for any persons by way of succession; or	For example, 'to A for life, remainder to B absolutely' — what were formerly a life estate and a future fee simple absolute in remainder now exist as equitable interests behind a trust.
(ii) limited in trust for any person in possession — (a) for an entailed interest whether or not capable of being barred or defeated;	For example, 'to A in fee tail, remainder to B absolute' — the old fee tail estate which cannot be legal after 1926.
(b) for an estate in fee simple or for a term of years absolute subject to an executory limitation, gift, or disposition over on failure of his issue or in any other event;	Although this may not look like it, this provision refers to a conditional fee simple. The last words, 'or in any other event', give that away. For example, 'to A on condition he does not marry Miss B, remainder to C absolutely' — a condition subsequent.
(c) for a base or determinable fee or any corresponding interest in leasehold land;	For example, 'to A until Preston North End Football Club are promoted to Division 1, then to B in fee simple' — the old determinable fee simple.
(d) being an infant, for an estate in fee simple or for a term of years absolute; or	A slight variation from the above principle here. Prior to 1925 an infant could hold any legal estate in land, but after 1926, LPA 1925, s. 1(6), provides that an infant cannot hold even a fee simple absolute in possession or a term of years absolute. His interest therefore exists in equity only behind a trust of the legal estate.
(iii) limited in trust for any person for an estate in fee simple or for a term of years absolute contingently on the happening of any event; or	This is the other conditional fee simple, subject to a condition precedent, e.g., 'to A on condition he marries Miss B, remainder to C absolutely'.
(iv) charged, whether voluntarily or in considera- tion of marriage or by way of family arrangement, and whether immediately or after an interval, with the payment of any rentcharge for the life of any person, or any less period, or of any capital, annual, or periodical sums for the por- tions, advancement, mainten- ance, or otherwise for the benefit of any persons, with or without any term of years for securing or raising the same.	This is a non-commercial arrangement for protecting a financial provision for someone by charging it on land given otherwise to someone else. For example, 'Blackacre to A in fee simple subject to a payment of £500 per annum charged on Blackacre to my widow during her widowhood'.

Machinery of the Strict Settlement

As explained before this involves holding the legal estate, usually the fee simple absolute in possession, on trust to give effect to all the equitable interests outlined in the settlement. If you return to the introduction at the beginning of this chapter you can see again that we referred to a conveyance of Blackacre, namely, 'to A for life, remainder to B in fee tail, remainder to C and his heirs'. This, we said, after 1926 became: 'Blackacre to trustees in fee simple absolute in possession on trust for A for life, remainder to B in fee tail, remainder to C and his heirs'. This can now be seen to be settled land falling within the provisions of SLA 1925, s. 1(1)(i) and (ii).

Once you can recognise a strict settlement and identify it as such then your revision should progress to the machinery of the strict settlement, the way in which SLA 1925 deals with all the equitable interests involved and attempts to protect them, whilst at the same time allowing the overreaching provisions of the 1925 legislation to apply in order to allow free conveyance of, and dealing in, the legal estate.

It is important always to know exactly who holds the legal estate and in what capacity, as an examination question usually seeks this information. Remember that although the legal estate is held on a trust and there are trustees of it, their main functions (outlined in revision summary 2) can be described merely as 'managerial'. The legal estate is not held by them — except in special circumstances such as where the tenant for life wishes to purchase the settled land for himself — but by one of the following:

(a) The tenant for life — a person of full age whose interest is in possession (SLA 1925, s. 19) — this will be the person with the life interest, A in our example above.

(b) Where there is no tenant for life, SLA 1925, s. 20, endows certain persons with the powers of tenant for life. So, for example, in the case of a settlement arising under s. 1(1)(ii)(a), where land is limited in trust 'for A in fee tail remainder...', A in this example would be a person with the powers of the tenant for life.

(c) The statutory owner — where there are no persons within (a) or (b). This is of particular importance where land is limited in trust for an infant (a settlement under s. 1(1)(ii)(d)). Statutory owners may be expressly named in the settlement deed or, if the deed is silent, the trustees are the statutory owners.

What is often forgotten by students is the balancing of the public and private interest mentioned earlier. The tenant for life, the person with powers of tenant for life or statutory owner is not given the legal estate in order for him to benefit personally from the powers which are given to him in that capacity (summarised in revision summary 1) but in order to achieve the object of the legislation, namely to allow the free disposition of land. The wishes of the settlor however must not be ignored. Consequently the tenant for life (etc.) holds the legal estate on trust. He is therefore a trustee, in the true sense of the word, both of his own beneficial life interest and the equitable interests of the other beneficiaries. He may therefore be held liable in damages for any breach of trust in dealing with the settled land. To illustrate consider the following settlement: 'Blackacre to A for life, remainder to B for life, remainder to C in fee tail, remainder to X, a charity'. This can be represented as follows:

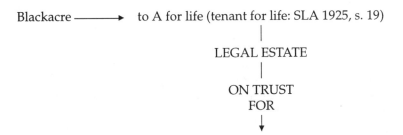

Blackacre ⟶ to A for life (tenant for life: SLA 1925, s. 19)

LEGAL ESTATE

ON TRUST
FOR

A for life, B for life, C in tail, remainder to X, charity

Further safeguards are provided by the SLA to ensure that the private wishes of the settlor are not forgotten, and to offer a measure of protection to the beneficiaries. These include:

(a)   in respect of the most important statutory powers, e.g., sale, the tenant for life must give notice to the trustees (see revision summary 1); and
(b)   in a few cases he cannot exercise those powers without consent of the trustees (see revision summary 1); and last but not least
(c)   the purchase money must be paid to two trustees or a trust corporation. In the absence of trustees, therefore, it follows that a tenant for life (or statutory owner) cannot exercise any powers.

Should it be necessary to discuss these safeguards, examiners will also be looking to see whether students have considered their effectiveness in light of the fact that the trustees of the settlement are under no obligation to interfere in an improper transaction (SLA 1925, s. 97), although they may if they wish bring the matter before the courts as they did in *Wheelwright* v *Walker* (1883) 233 Ch D 752 per Pearson J. They may waive notice altogether or accept less than the required one month's notice (SLA 1925, s. 104(4)), and they may accept a general notice from the tenant for life that he intends to exercise his powers under SLA 1925 'from time to time'.

Not very effective safeguards you might think, and yet remember that delicate balance between private and public policy. The legislators did not wish to prevent the tenant for life from exercising his powers altogether and yet they felt the need to protect the beneficiaries. To illustrate this balance consider the position if the tenant for life exercises his power of sale without giving the required notice to the trustees. A purchaser dealing with the tenant for life in good faith is not required to enquire whether notice has in fact been given to the trustees (SLA 1925, s. 101(5)). Why? Because the land is no longer 'tied up' by the settlement, the transaction is therefore in line with public policy and the beneficiaries still acquire their interest which the settlor wished them to have, except that these are 'overreached' on sale and thereby converted into money.

Powers and Duties

The revision summaries at the end of this chapter provide a checklist of the main powers and duties of the tenant for life and trustees of the strict settlement provided by SLA 1925. Not only should you know these, but you should be able to comment on them, e.g., the powers of the tenant for life are wide-reaching and most importantly *cannot be curtailed* in any way, for SLA 1925 prevails over any attempt by the settlor to do so — otherwise the purpose of the Act would be frustrated! — any such attempt will be void (SLA 1925, s. 106(1)).

Students must take care, however, when dealing with attempts to curtail the power(s) of the tenant for life (such as a residence qualification) because such attempts will only be rendered void if they fetter the *statutory powers* of the tenant for life. A residence qualification, therefore, that provides for the tenant for life forfeiting his interest on ceasing to reside on the settled land will be void in the event that the tenant for life ceases to reside as a result of exercising his statutory powers, such as sale or leasing. In this event the tenant for life will still be entitled to his life interest, represented by the income from the purchase money, or rent from the lease. If, however, the tenant for life ceases to reside on the settled land *merely because he wishes to live somewhere else* then the forfeiture will be operative and the life interest will be lost. Examiners often test a student's knowledge of the powers of the tenant for life by including residence qualifications in settlements. In answering such a question the case of *Re Acklom* [1929] 1 Ch 195 is invaluable. In that case one testator, in his will, bequeathed his house (held on lease) and furniture etc. to trustees upon trust to permit his sister to reside there after his death and have use and enjoyment of everything for her life. He directed the trustees to sell after his death, or during her life if she did not wish to reside there, but gave them a power to postpone sale as they might think proper and divide the proceeds between charities. On the testator's death his sister went into immediate possession. Seven years later she went abroad temporarily leaving servants to look after the house. About a year later she was prevented from returning to England due to ill health and so let the house on a periodic tenancy. Later she sold it, having the powers of tenant for life.

A summons was taken out by the trustees of the settlement asking the court to decide what, if any, interest she had in the proceeds of sale. The court held that she had *not* forfeited the power of sale by her temporary absence and therefore she had a proper interest in the proceeds of sale. Maugham J said that SLA 1925, s. 106, clearly applied. This rendered any provision, limiting or preventing a tenant for life from exercising his power of sale, *void*. Therefore if the sister was in the position to exercise the powers of a tenant for life, a provision whereby the proceeds of sale should, under the terms of the will, pass to the charities was void (following *Re Paget's Settled Estates* (1885) 30 ChD 161). Despite the charities' argument that she had forfeited her interest in the property, not having lived in it for two years prior to the sale, the court decided that there was no evidence that prior to the sale she had finally and irrevocably decided not to live in the property. It was emphasised that she was entitled to give up possession if it was for the purpose of exercising her powers under the Settled Land Act.

TRUSTS FOR SALE GOVERNED BY THE LAW OF PROPERTY ACT 1925

Revision

As explained earlier the legislators encouraged and extended the use of the trust for sale. In addition to *expressly* created trusts for sale — which are easy to recognise having these words or similar: 'to trustees *on a trust to sell and hold the proceeds* for A for life, remainder to B in tail' — *statutory* trusts for sale were imposed in certain circumstances. Most controversial and wide-reaching of those being wherever two or more persons hold land on either a joint tenancy or a tenancy in common (LPA 1925, ss. 34 and 36), i.e., co-owned land. Consequently whenever a couple purchase the matrimonial home and have it conveyed into joint names a trust for sale will arise by statute.

You should keep this uppermost in your mind and Lord Denning might even advise you to draw red hands pointing towards those sections of LPA 1925. This will be developed in the chapter on co-ownership.

It should be remembered that the whole nature of the trust for sale is to ensure a regular income for the beneficiaries and not to keep land tied up for the family.

The freeing of the land is achieved by LPA 1925 which governs trusts for sale. It gives the *trustees for sale* the *legal estate* and imposes on them a *duty* to sell. This does not mean that the property must be sold immediately, however, for coupled with that duty is a *power* to *postpone sale indefinitely*, provided the trustees decide to do so unanimously.

It is worth remembering that it is this power to postpone which gives rise to the paradox, mentioned earlier, that it is, after 1926, easier to keep land in the family by way of a trust for sale than by way of a strict settlement. Unlike the powers of tenant for life under a strict settlement, which we have seen cannot be curtailed, the powers of the trustees for sale can be restricted. In an express trust for sale, for example, the trustees may be required to seek the consent of certain persons, perhaps even the beneficiaries, before sale (see *Re Herklot's Will Trusts* [1964] 1 WLR 583). In a statutory trust for sale LPA 1925, s. 26(3), requires the trustees, in so far as practicable, to give effect to the wishes of the beneficiaries.

STRICT SETTLEMENTS AND TRUSTS FOR SALE COMPARED

You should by now, after reading the above coupled with the detail from your lecture notes and/or standard texts, be able to offer a comparison of the two types of settlement. As guidance see table 4.1. If an examination question is framed to require such a comparison the examiner will want you to develop that comparison — one way would be along the lines taken by Burn to the effect that nothing would be lost if all settlements were to be made by trust for sale.

FUTURE INTERESTS

You should have now safely negotiated the law relating to strict settlements and trusts for sale. It will have been noticed that some of the interests referred to there are not in possession but entitle the owners of them to future possession.

The law makes special provision for these interests by providing rules restricting the sorts of interests that can be held in the future and the length of time they can exist before falling into possession. Put very simply if an interest falls outside the period allowed by the law it is void.

Table 4.1   Strict settlements and trusts for sale compared

Strict settlements	Trusts for sale
1. Object: to keep land in the family.	Object: to provide an income for beneficiaries.
2. Governed by SLA 1925.	Governed by LPA 1925.

3. Legal estate held by either:
    (a) tenant for life (s. 19), or
    (b) person with powers of tenant for life (s. 20), or
    (c) statutory owners (ss. 23 and 26).
	Legal estate held by trustees for sale.

4. Powers of tenant for life etc. are indefeasible, (s. 106) (they cannot be limited or curtailed).	Powers of trustees for sale can be limited, e.g., s. 26, consent of certain persons may be required to the sale (easier to keep land from being sold).
5. Creation: express words	Creation: (a) expressly using words 'on trust to sell' (or similar), or (b) by statute.
6. Doctrine of overreaching applies.	Doctrine of conversion applies.
7. Inflexible: apply to land only.	Flexible: may include *all* kinds of property, including land.
8. Devolution on death of T for L, complicated and expensive.	Less so.
9. Inconvenient	Convenient.

Main Issues

These are more difficult to identify and will vary from course to course. Professional courses will not be concerned with them in as much depth as undergraduate courses. What can be said, however, is that you should:

(a) know the types of future interest that can exist and remember that these are equitable after 1926 and must be held behind a trust,

(b) understand the difference between *vested* and *contingent* interests, and

(c) be able to decide whether a future interest is void or not. To do so you must be able to apply the rules against remoteness with special emphasis on the rule against perpetuities around which most examination questions in this area tend to revolve.

Types of Future Interest

There are *three* main types of future interests:

(a) reversions;
(b) remainders; and
(c) executory interests.

The first two, i.e., reversions and remainders, were the only types known to the common law; the third, executory interests, was a creation of equity and will not be discussed.

A reversion is the undisposed of portion of an estate which, by operation of law, is preserved to a grantor who has parted with a portion of his original estate. In other words it is a future estate in land which returns ('reverts') to the person who originally had the fee simple or to his successors in title. For example:

(a) If, before 1926, A, who was a tenant in fee simple of Greenacre, granted it to B for life; on B's death, the land would revert to A or to A's heirs or assigns.

(b) If, after 1926, A, the owner in fee simple of Whiteacre, grants it to T for a 90-year term, A has a freehold reversion — at the end of T's term, the land reverts to A.

Since 1926 the only *legal* reversions are:

(a) The estate of a tenant in fee simple where the land has been granted to another for a term of years.

(b) the estate of a tenant for a term of years who has granted a smaller term of years to a subtenant.

This follows from LPA 1925, s. 1 (and see also s. 149(5)).

When, at common law, a tenant in fee simple created a particular estate and, by the same instrument, gave the residue of the fee simple to another person, that person's interest was a *remainder*, e.g., if A, the fee simple owner of Greenacre granted Greenacre 'to B for life' (this is the particular estate), with remainder to C in fee simple, C has a remainder. A remainder is therefore a future estate 'which awaits and depends upon the termination of some particular estate'. A remainder differs from a reversion in that:

(a) a remainder originates in a grant or assurance and does not arise by operation of law (as does a reversion); and

(b) the interest limited to follow the preceding or 'particular estate' remains over to some third party and not to the original grantor.

Remember, a remainder after a fee simple is void!

Vested or Contingent Interests

Future interests can be either vested or contingent. It is particularly important to know when a future interest will be classed as contingent because the rule against perpetuities mentioned earlier is only concerned with such interests. It is therefore a prerequisite to answering most questions on future interests to know whether they are vested or contingent.

To summarise:

(a)   A *vested interest* is an interest which is either in possesion at the present time or is ready to take possession immediately on the ending of the prior estate or estates, for example: 'Blackacre to A for life, remainder to B for life, remainder to C absolutely'. All these interests are vested. A has an immediate present right to possession (and his interest is therefore said to be vest in possession). B and C can take immediate possession as soon as the interest preceding theirs ends. This estate is often technically referred to as the 'particular' estate or interest. B can take his life interest immediately A's particular interest ends and C can take his fee simple as soon as B's particular estate has ended. Although they have not got interests in possession they are said to have interests which are 'vested in interest'.

(b)   A *contingent interest* is one which is neither 'vested in possession' nor 'vested in interest'. That is to say, some *further event must occur apart from the mere dropping of the particular estate* before the holder of the interest in question may claim possession. Three examples should show the three conditions necessary before an interest is vested for the purposes of the rule against perpetuities. If these are not met the interest will be contingent.

(i)   The interest must be ready to take effect immediately on the dropping of the particular estate. 'Blackacre to A for life, remainder to B (aged 20) when he attains 25 years of age'. Can B take possession forthwith if necessary? No. He must satisfy the further condition of reaching 25.

(ii)   The identity of the beneficiary must be known. Consider the following: 'Blackacre to A for life, remainder to the eldest child of B (a bachelor), but if he has no such child then to C'. Do we have anyone to take that interest now if necessary? No. We cannot identify the person to take the interest. If B has a child he will take a fee simple; if he does not then C will take it. We cannot tell which it will be.

(iii)   The size of the interest to be taken must be known, e.g., 'Blackacre to A for life, remainder to *all* his children who attain 21 years'. If one supposes A to have two children, X and Y, who are both already 21 years of age, then in general terms they both have vested interests. They can take their interests immediately if A dies. But, for the purposes of the rule against perpetuities, if that interest is likely to vary because of subsequent uncertain events, i.e., other children being born and attaining 21 years of age and therefore varying the interests of X and Y from half to one-third, to one-quarter and so on then it is *not* to be treated as vested for the purposes of that rule.

There are, therefore, *three tests to apply to ensure an interest is vested* and *not* subject to the rule against perpetuities.

(a)   The person to take the interest must be identified.
(b)   The size of that identified person's interest must be certain. This is not a general test for vesting but is so for the purposes of the rule.

(c)   That interest must not be subject to any other condition apart from the dropping of the particular estate.

Rules Against Remoteness

Here again you can see the balancing of the public and private interest, the law regarding it important that the owner of property should not be permitted to use his power of disposition to tie the land up for long periods of time. Hence even before the 1925 legislation the common law discouraged dispositions of property which imposed restrictions on either future alienation or the future enjoyment of that property. The law regulating such dispositions falls under the following heads:

(a)   The rule against perpetuities.
(b)   The rule against inalienability or perpetual trusts.
(c)   The rule against accumulations.

Being the rule most common in examination questions and frequently misunderstood by students it is intended to deal with the rule against perpetuities in detail.

The Rule Against Perpetuities

Stated fully, the rule is this:

> Every attempted disposition of land or goods is void, unless, *at* the *time* when the instrument creating it takes effect, one can say that it MUST take effect (if it takes effect at all) within the *life* or *lives* then in being and 21 years after the termination of such life or lives, with the possible addition of the period of gestation.

Until 1964 a gift was void if it was capable of vesting only after the perpetuity period had expired. There was no 'wait and see' — the slightest possibility that the perpetuity period might be exceeded avoided the gift, and this even if it was highly improbable that the period might in fact be exceeded. For example, by his will made in 1900, A, who died in 1908, gave Greenacre to trustees upon trusts for his daughter D for her life, and after her death for the first child of D who should reach 21. The gift to D's child *is good if D is 'a life in being' at the date of A's death*. And in any event, any child of D can reach the age of 21 only within the perpetuity period, i.e., 21 years after D's death.

But if, on the other hand, the gift had been given to the first child of D to attain the age of 25, the gift would have been void; for D might have died when her eldest child was under four in which case that child might attain 25 outside the perpetuity period. See *Ward* v *Van der Loeff* [1924] AC 653, showing that for the purposes of this rule no person was deemed too old to have children, and W.B. Leach (1952) 68 LQR 35, 46, for an entertaining attack on the developments of the perpetuity rule.

The rule against perpetuities, remember, only applies to contingent interests.

Statutory Changes

Section 163 of LPA 1925 provided that where, in an instrument taking effect *after 1925*, a limitation would be void because *it is limited to vest at an age beyond 21*, it shall be *construed as if '21' had been inserted instead of the greater age*.

Thus if land is limited 'to A (a bachelor) for life, remainder to the first son of A to attain 45 years', this shall be construed as 'to the first son of A to attain 21 years', thereby saving the gift.

Section 163 applies only where the gift would otherwise be void. Thus, for example, if property was given to B contingently on his attaining 30 and, at the time the instrument comes into operation B is 25, there can be no question of substituting 21 so that B can take the gift forthwith; for the gift, as it stands, is good: B is living when the gift comes into operation and he is bound to attain 30, if at all, during his own lifetime and therefore well within the perpetuity period.

The Perpetuities and Accumulations Act 1964

Several important changes in the rule against perpetuities have been made by the Perpetuities and Accumulations Act 1964. Its main provisions are designed to save from invalidity gifts which would otherwise be void by reason of infringing the perpetuity rule (as it stood before the Act).

Section 1 provides that a settlor or testator may specify a period not exceeding 80 years as the perpetuity period instead of the old period of lives in being plus 21 years.

Section 2 abolishes the presumption that a person is never deemed to be incapable of having children, and provides that for the purposes of the rule males under 14 and females under 12 and over the age of 55 shall be presumed (for the purpose of the perpetuity rule) to be incapable of having children. Evidence is admissible to show that a person will or will not be able to have a child.

Section 3 abolishes the principle that there is no 'wait and see' with regard to the perpetuity rule. The view was taken that the validity of a limitation should not depend on facts which *may* occur but on facts which *do* occur, a 'wait and see' principle. Hence it is provided by the section that no interest is to be treated as void for remoteness until it becomes established that it must vest, if at all, after the end of the perpetuity period. This perpetuity period is to be calculated in accordance with s. 1 or by reference to statutory lives, listed in s. 3, and not by reference to common law lives in being, referred to earlier.

Section 4 provides for the reduction of age in a grant to avoid remoteness. Settlors and testators generally provided for the postponement of vesting until the age of 25, and, as this defeated so many settlements, s. 163 of LPA 1925 provided that where the ascertainment of a beneficiary or class of beneficiaries depended on the attainment of an age over 21 or the gift would be void under the rule, the age of 21 was to be substituted for the age in the instrument. Section 163 is repealed in respect of dispositions made after 16 July 1964 and the age contingency is reduced not to 21 but to the age nearest the specified age consistent with the gift being valid.

This section also provides that where in a class gift it was possible for the interest taken by a member of the class to vest outside the period and so render the gift void, that person is to be excluded from the class.

Section 9 exempts from the perpetuity rule options given to a lessee to purchase the freehold or reversion and provides that, as regrads options to acquire for valuable consideration *any interests* in the land, the perpetuity period (when applicable) shall be 21 years.

Section 15 provides that the Act does not apply to trusts for non-charitable purposes.

What most students find difficult is understanding the meaning of a 'life in being'. The easiest way and simplest advice is to ask 'Who is alive (or *en ventre sa mère*) when the instrument creating the interest comes into operation?' (A will, remember, comes into operation on the death of the testator, an *inter vivos* deed when it is executed.) If you follow the specimen examination question below, this should help you to understand the application of the rule.

SPECIMEN EXAMINATION QUESTIONS

Question 1: Future Interests

A testator who died in 1963 left a will by which he gave property on trust for Sarah for life and thereafter for all Sarah's grandchildren whenever born, who should attain 21, in equal shares. At the testator's death Sarah was 75 years old and all her children were dead, but she had one grandchild, Jenny, aged 20. Consider whether Jenny is entitled to the trust property. Would your answer have been the same if the testator had died in 1965?

Suggested Approach

As the rule against perpetuities only applies to contingent interests, the first thing to ask yourself is:

(a)   Is the interest (of Jenny here) contingent? An interest is not contingent unless three requirements are satisfied:

(i)   The identity of the beneficiary must be ascertained.
(ii)   The size of the interest which he or she is to take must be finally settled.
(iii)   Any conditions precedent imposed upon the grant of the interest must have been satisfied.

Therefore, clearly Jenny's interest is contingent, as it will not vest until (i) Jenny reaches the age of 21, and (ii) the size of her interest (which depends on how many grandchildren Sarah ultimately has) is known.

(b)   Will the common law rule or the Perpetuities and Accumulations Act 1964 apply? As the testator died in 1963, clearly the common law rule applies as the Act only affects instruments coming into effect on or after 16 July 1964. The common law rule is that a grant of a contingent interest is void *ab initio* unless it is certain that the interest will vest, if it vests at all, within a life or lives in being when the grant comes into operation plus a further period of 21 years from the expiry of the last life in being plus any relevant gestation periods.

(c)   Who are the common lives in being? All persons who are alive or *en ventre sa mère* when the instrument comes into operation. A will comes into operation on the death of the testator. Therefore, ask yourself:

(i)   Was Sarah alive at the testator's death?
(ii)   Was Jenny alive at the testator's death?

We are told Sarah was 75 at the testator's death, therefore she is a life in being, and she had one grandchild, Jenny, aged 20, therefore she also is a life in being.

(d)   Apply the common law rule to ascertain if Jenny's interest is void *ab initio*, i.e., is there any possibility, no matter how remote, that the gift could vest outside the perpetuity period (i.e., later than 21 years after Sarah or Jenny's death)? Yes, because it is possible that Sarah could have a child after 1963 who would therefore not be a life in being who in turn could have a child. This child would be the grandchild of Sarah and might not attain 21 until more than 21 years after the death of Sarah or Jenny. Therefore the gift is void at common law.

Even though the common law ignores physical impossibilities it takes account of legal ones, for example, in *Re Dawson* (1888) 39 ChD 155 it was argued that though alive at the date of the gift, the person in question could not have another child because she was in her sixties. The argument was rejected. However, in *Re Gaite's Will Trusts* [1949] 1 All ER 459 it was held that a person under 16 is considered incapable of having legitimate children since it is not lawful to marry under that age.

(e)   Would your answer have been the same if the testator had died in 1965? Clearly not because the 1964 Act would apply. As Sarah is 75, it may be presumed that she cannot have a child, thus making the gift valid (for the purposes of the rule against perpetuities). Section 2 of the 1964 Act presumes that a female can only have a child between the ages of 12 and 55, and that a male can only do so over the age of 14. Evidence may be brought, however, to rebut the presumption. There is no need to use the 'wait and see' rule under s. 3(1) of the Act.

(f)   Conclusion. The gift to Jenny would be void *ab initio* if the testator died in 1963 under the common law rule against perpetuities. If the testator died in 1965, it would be valid as the Perpetuities and Accumulations Act 1964 would apply, but Jenny would have to wait until Sarah, who was given a life interest, died before she could take possession of the trust property.

Question 2: Settlements

> In his will, Alan, who died recently, devised No. 3 High Street to his wife, Beryl, for life or for so long as she continued to reside there, remainder to his son, Carl, in fee simple.
>
> Beryl presently lives in No. 3 and, apart from this inheritance under Alan's will, is in poor financial circumstances. She is considering selling No. 3 and buying a smaller property in a cheaper area of town, although she is not convinced that she can settle down at any distance from her family and friends. However, she does require in some way to generate income from her inheritance. Advise Beryl:
>
> (a)   on the effect of the will;
> (b)   whether No. 3, High Street, may be sold;
> (c)   what course of action, other than sale, Beryl might take to produce a source of income.

The best approach to a question such as this is first to identify the disposition generally as a settlement commenting that there is a succession of interests. Develop this by identifying the specific type of settlement. In this case it could be argued on the basis of *Re Acklom* that A has created a strict settlement within SLA 1925, s. 1(1)(i) (but compare *Re Herklot's Will Trusts*).

Moving on to parts (a), (b) and (c) of the question you will note that the question covers virtually the whole of the detailed law of strict settlements. Turning to (a), you will be expected to explain that B has a life interest and C a fee simple in remainder. Both can only exist in equity (LPA 1925, s. 1(3)) behind a trust of the legal estate. B, being of full age and with her life interest in possession, is the tenant for life (SLA 1925, s. 19) and is the holder of the legal estate. There must be trustees of the settlement but as this is a strict settlement they have limited powers and duties.

Part (b) involves a discussion of the main power of the tenant for life, namely, the power to sell the settled land. Note here there is a residence qualification, consequently B, the tenant for life, can sell provided she does so for the purpose of exercising her power under the Settled Land Act (*Re Acklom* and *Re Paget's Settled Estates*). This is because SLA 1925, s. 106, prevents curtailment of the powers of the tenant for life.

Some mention of the fact that the interests of the beneficiary, C, are protected is necessary, e.g., by commenting that A has a duty to obtain the best consideration in money reasonably obtainable and the trustees may apply to court for an injunction to restrain the tenant for life from selling in breach of that duty, as in *Wheelwright* v *Walker*.

On sale the purchaser will take free of any equitable interests, namely C's, which are overreached, provided the purchase money is paid to two trustees or a trust corporation. You may wish to expand further on the duty of C to give notice to the trustees of sale and the effectiveness of that requirement, and the problems which could face a purchaser. For example, if B sold No. 3 High Street merely because she wanted to live elsewhere and not for the purpose of exercising her powers under the Settled Land Act then the settlement would have terminated (assuming C is of full age) and C would be entitled absolutely. Here the innocent purchaser, not knowing that the settlement has terminated could be in difficulty. Two fairly recent articles discuss this point. Warrington, 'The tenant for life and the unlikely purchaser — some further thoughts' [1985] Conv 377 uses the example of a disposition to the widow for life or until remarriage, then to a child absolutely. He points out that were the widow to remarry and then (wrongfully) purport to exercise the statutory powers under SLA 1925, there is a good chance that the innocent purchaser will be in difficulty, and asks 'Does such a purchaser get a good title?' Stone in an earlier article, 'A Settled Land Act problem revisited: sale by a former tenant for life after termination of the settlement' [1984] Conv 354, presents a most coherent argument to say he does, but Warrington, whilst feeling that the solution provided by Stone might well appeal to the courts, does not accept it as necessarily correct and would rather see a more definite solution to the problem, namely, statutory amendment by adding to SLA 1925, s. 5(1), a further paragraph (f) requiring the vesting deed to contain the event(s) that would cause termination of the interest of the person for the time being entitled.

Whilst the example provided differs from the one given in the question there is a clear analogy.

A detailed knowledge of the tenant for life's powers is needed for part (c) — see revision summary 1 — but it is essential that your answer is directed to the question. Do not discuss all the powers, for the question specifically states that B requires a source of income. Remember also that B can do as she likes with her own *life* interest — it is her power to deal with the settled land which is limited, because C's interest must be protected.

Finally a conclusion completes the question well and may impress the examiner. One suggestion is to comment on the purpose behind SLA 1925 and the way in which the legislation has balanced the two conflicting interests, the public and the private, such that A can dispose of his property as he chooses and yet may not tie it up indefinitely. This can be seen in the question given, for B, being the tenant for life, has wide powers of disposition.

REVISION SUMMARIES

1   Powers of the Tenant for Life etc. (including Statutory Owner)

(a)   Powers exercisable upon given notice to SLA trustees:

(i)   Sale for best consideration in money (ss. 38 and 39) (*Wheelwright* v *Walker*).
(ii)   Exchange, for other land (difference can be made up by capital (s. 38(iii)).
(iii) Lease, for best rent obtainable in the circumstances (s. 42(1)(ii)).
(iv)   Granting of an option (in writing).

(b)   Powers exercisable with consent of SLA trustees:

(i)   Disposal of principal mansion house.
(ii)   Cutting and sale of timber.
(iii) Compromising claims (i.e., settlement of disputes relating to the settled land).
(iv)   Sale of settled land chattels (with permission of court).

(c)   Other powers:

(i)   To effect improvement (as distinguished from repairs) of settled land.
(ii)   To select the investments of the capital money within the methods specified by the Act (s. 73).
(iii) To take the lease of other land.
(iv)   To enter into contracts.
(v)   To dedicate highways and open spaces.
(vi)   Any additional powers given by the deed of settlement.

Remember the tenant for life may deal with his own life interest as he wishes.

2   The Main Functions of Settled Land Act Trustees

(a)   To receive and hold capital money (ss. 18(1)(b) and 75(1)).

(b)   To receive notice from the tenant for life of his intention to enter into certain transactions.

(c)   To give consent to certain transactions.

(d)   To act as special personal representatives on death of the tenant for life, for example, land is settled on A for life or until he succeeds to Blackacre, remainder to B for life, remainder to C in fee simple; if B is living at A's death, the land vests in the trustees of the settlement, in their capacity as special personal representatives.

(e)   To act as statutory owner if the tenant for life is an infant or there is no tenant for life.

(f)   To extend the principal vesting deed in cases where one has not been provided in the ordinary course.

(g)   To execute a deed of discharge, where one is necessary, on the determination of the settlement.

(h)   To exercise the powers of the tenant for life if the tenant for life wishes to acquire the settled land for his own benefit (s. 68).

(i)   To exercise the power of the tenant for life where the tenant for life no longer has any substantial interest and either consents to such exercise or unreasonably refuses to exercise his powers.

(j)   To supervise generally the well being of the settled land.

SUGGESTED ADDITIONAL READING

The general textbooks such as Sir R. Megarry and J. W. Wade, *The Law of Real Property*, 6th ed., 1994 (Sweet & Maxwell) and Cheshire and Burn, *Modern Law of Real Property*, 14th ed., 1988 (Butterworths) deal with this area generally. Useful information can be obtained by reading the Law Commission's Consultation Paper No. 133, HMSO on the 'Law of Trusts: The Rule Against Perpetuities' (1993). More specialised texts include the following but are currently awaiting updating and may be out of print, although your library may have them:

B. Harvey, *Settlements of Land*, 1973 (Sweet & Maxwell).
Maudsley, *Modern Law of Perpetuities*, 1979 (Butterworths).

5 CO-OWNERSHIP AND MATRIMONIAL PROPERTY

INTRODUCTION

In this chapter we will be dealing with the situation where a piece of land is owned by concurrent owners as opposed to the situation outlined in chapter 4 where the interests are held successively. We will see that since 1926 the device of the trust for sale has been used to simplify the conveyancing procedure but this has itself created difficulties which can be readily explored by the examiner. The allied topic of matrimonial property, i.e., the respective rights of spouses or cohabitees during the subsistence of their relationship will also be dealt with.

Both these areas are important for examination purposes for either problem or essay questions, not least because there are difficulties in applying the statutory trust for sale to meet changing social needs as between both husband and wife and cohabitees, see, e.g., *Williams & Glyn's Bank Ltd* v *Boland* [1981] AC 487 and *Burns* v *Burns* [1984] Ch 317. This chapter will deal first with the essentials of co-ownership and then look at problems created in matrimonial property.

CO-OWNERSHIP

Main Issues

When undertaking revision of this area of law, your initial objective is to grasp the nature of joint ownership of land after 1926. Once again our advice is that you should leave out the detailed provisions until later and concentrate on mastering basic principles. For example, it is essential to understand the nature of the statutory trust for sale in order to appreciate the difficulties that have arisen from it. This chapter therefore will try to explain the trust for sale in this context and then look at some of the likely problematic areas for exam purposes.

The essential point initially is that before 1926 all forms of co-ownership could exist at law or in equity. By virtue of LPA 1925, s. 34, a trust for sale arises whenever land is conveyed to two or more persons jointly. Consequently after 1926 the legal estate is vested in a trustee or trustees upon trust for the co-owners in equity. The intended effect was to simplify conveyancing so that a purchaser need only concern himself with the holder of the legal estate. The equitable co-owner's interests are not in the land itself but are overreached on sale and converted into interests in the proceeds of sale. For example, if Blackacre is conveyed to A and B jointly and is later sold to C, the effect is shown in figure 5.1.

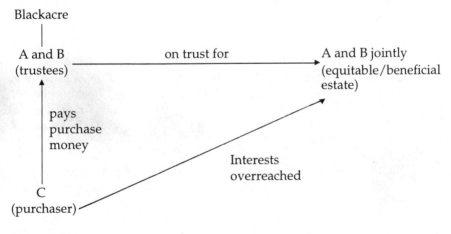

Figure 5.1

It is worth noting at this point that land will also be regarded as co-owned land where there is more than one person with a beneficial interest in the land but only one name is on the title deeds. As *Williams & Glyn's Bank Ltd* v *Boland* [1981] AC 487 illustrates, the court will still impose a trust for sale in these circumstances, i.e.:

on trust for sale for

Legal title   Beneficial co-owners

In order to explain the reasons why the changes made in 1926 were necessary and the complexities that can arise, we must look next at the types of co-ownership.

Types of Co-ownership

Prior to LPA 1925 there were four types of co-ownership: joint tenancy, tenancy in common, coparcenary and tenancy by entireties. For all practical purposes only joint tenancy and tenancy in common now exist and we will deal only with them.

The distinction between joint tenancy and tenancy in common must be understood. It is based upon two concepts; the four unities and the right of survivorship (*ius accrescendi*). The four unities (time, title, interest and possession) must all be present in joint tenancy; in tenancy in common only unity of possession is essential. It must not be forgotten therefore that unity of possession is essential to both forms of co-ownership, i.e., if one person can exclude another from part of the land, they are not co-owners but absolute owners of parts of a plot of land.

The other fundamental concept of joint tenancy is the right of survivorship, i.e., on the death of one joint tenant his share automatically passes to the survivor(s). Ultimately the sole surviving joint tenant will become sole owner but predeceasing joint tenants pass nothing to their estates. In a tenancy in common there is no right of survivorship so that a tenant in common is free to deal with *his* interest as he thinks fit, i.e., he can dispose of it either during his lifetime or by will or it will devolve upon his estate in the event of intestacy. It was because of this that changes were maancy in common could only exist in equity and any dealings with it were taken off the legal title, thus making the conveyancing procedure simpler. Consider the following example.

Whiteacre is conveyed 'to A and B equally', i.e., as tenants in common, and the events and transactions shown in figure 5.2 occur.

Prior to 1926 all these dealings could have taken place *in law*, so that a potential purchaser of Whiteacre would have to investigate *all* the titles in order to discover what he was acquiring. *After 1926* the legal estate would be vested in A and B as joint tenants on trust for themselves as tenants in common. Consequently, the tenancy in common would be equitable and all dealings in it overreached on completion; the purchaser would only need to pay the purchase money to the holder of the legal estate (in our example, A as survivor) and would be discharged from any other interests in the tenancy in common.

Bearing in mind the basic distinctions between joint tenancy and tenancy in common we will now examine a potential source of examination questions, namely, whether a joint tenancy may be converted into a tenancy in common.

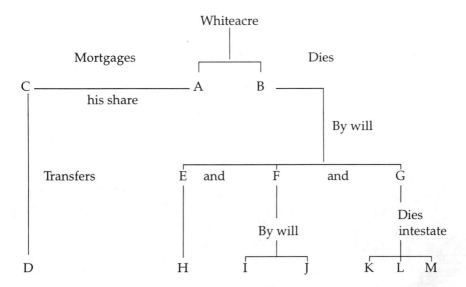

Figure 5.2

It has already been mentioned that if one of the four unities is absent, there can be no joint tenancy, but a tenancy in common may still arise even where all four unities are present. This will arise where the words used indicate that each co-owner will have a specific share in the property, since this is contrary to the joint tenancy concept of all or nothing (*Re North* [1952] Ch 397, in which a gift made to A and B on condition they paid an annuity 'in equal shares' was held to create a tenancy in common). In an exam question it may therefore be necessary to consider whether the donees are intended to take specific shares, in which case there will be tenancy in common. In addition, in some situations equity will presume a tenancy in common although on the face of the deed there is joint tenancy, e.g., where purchase money is provided in *unequal* shares or where property is conveyed as partnership property (see *Lake* v *Craddock* (1723) 3 P Wms 158).

Once you have established that there is a joint tenancy it may next be necessary to consider whether this has been brought to an end. This is done by *severance*, which has the effect of converting the joint tenancy into a tenancy in common. Prior to 1926 this could be done by alienation or acquisition of another interest and after 1926 can be effected by written notice (LPA 1925, s. 36(2)). Before discussing this further, one thing that *must* be remembered is that after 1925 there can be no severance of the *legal* joint tenancy, so that whatever happens to the beneficial interests, the legal estate remains vested in the original trustees, i.e., if land is conveyed to A and B as joint tenants, they hold the legal estate on trust for themselves and will continue to hold the legal estate even if the beneficial joint tenancy is severed.

Alienation arises where one joint tenant, during his lifetime, sells his interest to a third party, since this results in destruction of the four unities. For example, land is conveyed to A and B as joint tenants. B transfers his *beneficial* interest to C. The result is that A and B hold the legal estate as joint tenants on trust for A and C as equitable tenants in common.

Similarly, if one joint tenant acquires the interest of another there is destruction of the unity of interest and tenancy in common results. For example, land is conveyed to A, B and C as joint tenants. A acquires the interest of B. The result is that A, B and C hold the legal estate as joint tenants on trust for A and C as tenants in common (A having two thirds and C one third).

The area of most difficulty as regards severance is the notice in writing provision introduced by LPA 1925. Written notice can be, and in practice frequently is, given by endorsing a notice of severance on the deed of conveyance to the joint tenants. It is, however, unlikely that a devious examiner would have such a straightforward point in his questions and we will therefore look at two of the cases to discover what amounts to notice in writing. In *Re Draper's Conveyance* [1969] 1 Ch 486 it was held that the issue of a summons amounted to notice in writing, but in *Harris* v *Goddard* [1983] 1 WLR 1203 a prayer in a divorce petition for a property adjustment order was insufficient. An examiner will be looking to see whether you understand the distinction between the two cases. To impress the examiner therefore you should stress that the difference is one of intention: the court will ask itself the question, 'Can it be said that the notice is such as to give a clear indication that one co-owner no longer wishes his interest to be joint?' This could be expanded as follows:

In *Re Draper's Conveyance* the parties were divorced and proceedings commenced to have the property vested in the sole name of the wife, thus indicating separation of the joint interest. In *Harris* v *Goddard* there could have been, for example, a reconciliation and no divorce so that petitioning for divorce was not an irrevocable step.

One final point on severance is that under LPA 1925, s. 36, severance can be effected by one joint tenant doing such other acts or things as may have been effective to sever a joint tenancy in personalty in equity. This could be done as regards personalty by a common course of conduct indicating that all joint tenants intended to treat the property as held in common (*Williams* v *Hensman* (1861) 1 John & H 546). This approach was applied by Lord Denning MR to land in *Burgess* v *Rawnsley* [1975] Ch 429 where the parties had orally negotiated the transfer of the interest of one joint tenant to the other without agreeing on the consideration prior to one joint tenant's death. The issue of severance by a course of dealings was further considered in *McDowell* v *Hirschfield, Lipson and Rumney* [1992] 2 FLR 126 where the court took the view that to establish a course of dealing both parties must show a clear intention that their interest should be common not joint. In this case no course of dealing could be established from correspondence in connection with the parties' divorce which had not yet been concluded because of the death of the husband. See also *Gore and Snell* v *Carpenter* (1990) 60 P & CR 456 where it was made clear that in the absence of an express agreement to sever or a sufficient course of dealings negotiations alone would not suffice for severance. Interesting and useful discussions of severance and notice in writing can be found in (1968) 84 LQR 462 (Baker) and [1976] CLJ 20 (Hayton).

It should also be remembered that an equitable joint tenancy cannot be severed by will. A will is only effective from the date of death and is deemed to have been preceded by the right of survivorship vesting the interest in the surviving joint tenant(s).

Before considering an exam question one further point must be borne in mind. It has already been said that the legal joint tenancy cannot be severed and that on the death of one trustee the joint tenancy passes to the others by survivorship. This raises a potential difficulty where only one trustee remains since a sole trustee for sale cannot convey the legal estate without appointing a second trustee. This is now covered by the Law of Property (Joint Tenants) Act 1964 which provides that a sole survivor may convey the legal estate provided that he conveys as beneficial owner or the conveyance contains a statement that he is beneficially interested. After 1 July 1995 the effect of the Law of Property (Miscellaneous Provisions) Act 1994 is that the survivor of joint tenants can no longer sell as beneficial owner. The conveyance will have to contain a statement that the survivor is solely and beneficially entitled. An exam question may require you to point this out and you must remember that the Act does *not* apply if a memorandum of severance has been endorsed on the conveyance nor does it apply to registered titles. In such cases it is safest to appoint a second trustee to convey the legal estate.

We will now consider a typical exam problem in this area before looking at co-ownership as between spouses and cohabitees.

SPECIMEN EXAMINATION QUESTION

In 1980, A, the owner in fee simple of Blackacre, granted the property to his five children, P, Q, R, S and T jointly. Over the last five years the following events have occurred:

(a)   In 1981, P sent a letter, by registered post, to his four brothers stating that he wished to be able to sell his interest in Blackacre to any purchaser he wished. The letter was never received by Q, R, S and T.
(b)   In 1981, T sold his interest in Blackacre to V for £5,000.
(c)   In 1982, Q sold his interest to his younger brother, T, for £5,000.
(d)   In 1983, S and his elder brother, R, died in an aeroplane crash whilst travelling on holiday to Spain.

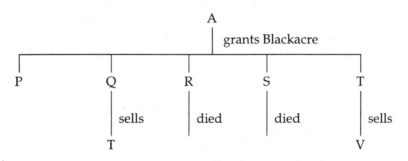

Figure 5.3

The executors are winding up the estates of S and R and seek your advice as to the persons in whom the legal estate and equitable interests in Blackacre are vested.

Suggested Approach

Since the question asks you to consider both the legal estate and equitable interests, it is sensible to deal with them separately and make it clear to the examiner which interest you are considering. It is always helpful therefore to draw a diagram to represent the dealings in Blackacre (figure 5.3) and then consider (a) the legal estate and (b) the equitable interests.

Legal Estate

Begin by explaining that here there is clearly a situation of co-ownership and since the grant was made after 1926 a statutory trust for sale arises (LPA 1925, s. 35). Therefore the legal estate is initially held by the brothers upon trust for sale for themselves as equitable co-owners. However LPA 1925, s. 34(2), provides that the legal estate can be vested in no more than four trustees and that where there are more than four grantees, the trustees are the first four of full age named. As a result the legal estate is initially vested in P, Q, R and S upon trust for sale for P, Q, R, S and T. There can be no severance of the legal joint tenancy (LPA 1925, s. 36(2)) so that none of the dealings in Blackacre has any effect on the legal joint tenancy. However, R and S have died so that their interest in the legal estatass to P and Q by survivorship, and P and Q would now hold the legal estate since there is nothing on the facts to suggest they have surrendered their interest in the legal estate.

Equitable Interest

The first thing to consider is whether the brothers, at the time of the grant, are equitable joint tenants or tenants in common. A useful commentary would be along the following lines:

> A granted the brothers their interest by the same deed (so far as we are aware) and all were given the same interest. Consequently, it can, probably, be said that the four unities necessary for joint tenancy existed. The question tells us the grant was made to the brothers *'jointly'*, which would seem to indicate there were no words of severance and since none of the equitable exceptions applies, it can be said that they were equitable joint tenants.

Next consider the effect of the various dispositions in the joint tenancy:

(a)   P's letter. The issue is whether there is sufficient notice in writing under LPA 1925, s. 36 to amount to severance of the joint tenancy. This requires an application of the relevant case law. For example:

> Since P's letter was sent by registered post his notice would be effective notwithstanding its non-arrival (*Re 88 Berkeley Road NW9* [1971] Ch 648, applying LPA 1925, s. 196). The question is whether P's words showed a sufficient intention to sever. It could be argued that the statement that P wished to be free to sell his interest to any purchaser he wished shows a clear desire to treat his interest as his own and not as joint property. If this is the case then P would become tenant in common with his brothers of Blackacre (P having a one-fifth share) and the brothers would remain joint tenants as between themselves.

Parts (b) and (c) are straightforward exercises no doubt designed by the examiners to see if the student really understands the basic principles behind a joint tenancy and tenancy in common. A long answer is not required: that would waste valuable time. Something along the following lines would suffice:

> T's sale of his interest to V would destroy unity of title with the result that V would become tenant in common with a one-fifth share. Similarly Q's sale to T would again destroy unity of title and T would become tenant in common in respect of Q's share.

In part (d) there is a twist in the question with two of the brothers dying. It is best approached by considering the position before the death of S and R. At that time P, Q, S and R held the legal estate on trust for:

> P (tenant in common with a one-fifth share).
> V (tenant in common with a one-fifth share).
> T (tenant in common with a one-fifth share).
> S and R (joint tenants with a two-fifths share).

Consequently the beneficial interest in S and R's two-fifths share vests by survivorship in the survivor or S and R, but the question says that they died in an aeroplane crash, raising the issue of *commorientes*. An answer could deal with this as follows:

> If two people die together and it is uncertain which died first, the issue is resolved by LPA 1925, s. 184, which provides that in circumstances of uncertainty, the younger is deemed to have survived the elder (see *Hickman v Peacey* [1945] AC 304 in which a number of people in the same house were killed in an air raid). The question only tells us that S and R were killed in an air crash, so it may be that there was clear evidence of who died first, e.g., one being pulled alive from the wreckage and subsequently dying in hospital. In the absence of such evidence S would be presumed to have survived R and the two-fifths beneficial interest would pass to his estate.

Finally, no answer is complete without a conclusion. The question asks you to advise the executors of R and S. An examiner will not be impressed if you omit to do so. Something quite brief will suffice but it must not be omitted. For example:

> The resultant advice to the executors is that the legal estate is held by P and Q upon trust for P, V and T (one-fifth share each) and S's estate (two-fifths share).

One last point. Some students may find it easier to set out the answer as in figure 5.4 and follow the events through. If this approach suits you then provided the legal points are dealt with, there is no reason why it should not be taken.

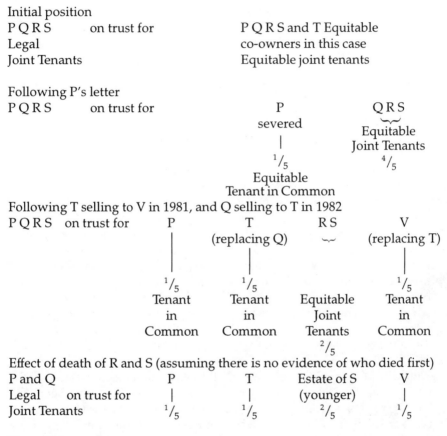

Initial position
P Q R S   on trust for   P Q R S and T Equitable
Legal   co-owners in this case
Joint Tenants   Equitable joint tenants

Following P's letter
P Q R S   on trust for   P   Q R S
                                            severed   Equitable
                                               | Joint Tenants
                                             ¹/₅   ⁴/₅
                                           Equitable
                                       Tenant in Common
Following T selling to V in 1981, and Q selling to T in 1982
P Q R S   on trust for   P   T   R S   V
                              | (replacing Q)   ⁓   (replacing T)
                              | | |
                             ¹/₅   ¹/₅   ¹/₅
                           Tenant   Tenant   Equitable   Tenant
                             in   in   Joint   in
                           Common   Common   Tenants   Common
                                                       ²/₅
Effect of death of R and S (assuming there is no evidence of who died first)
P and Q   P   T   Estate of S   V
Legal   on trust for | | (younger) |
Joint Tenants   ¹/₅   ¹/₅   ²/₅   ¹/₅

Figure 5.4

THE PROBLEM OF CO-OWNERSHIP AND THE HOME

Main Issues

The statutory trust for sale creates special problems where the subject-matter of the trust is a home. It helps to remember that the reason for imposing a trust for sale in all types of co-ownership was to simplify conveyancing by removing dealings between the co-owners from the paper title. To that extent the LPA 1925 was successful. The purchaser of the legal estate need only ensure that the purchase money is paid to the legal joint tenants or the survivors. However, difficulties have arisen with regard to the relationship between the legal joint tenants and the equitable co-owners, particularly over whether a beneficial co-owner has any right of occupation. In addition, the approach taken in some of the cases has created difficulties for purchasers (particularly mortgagees) where occupation by a beneficial co-owner has led to the creation of overriding interests within the Land Registration Act 1925, s. 70(1)(g). The rest of this chapter will suggest how to approach questions involving the matrimonial and quasi-matrimonial home. We will consider:

(a) how a spouse or co-habitee acquires a beneficial interest,
(b) how the extent of that interest is quantified,
(c) the beneficial co-owners' rights of occupation, and
(d) the effect of beneficial interests on third parties.

The initial point to remember is that, because of the imposition of the statutory trust for sale, the beneficial co-owners' interest is in the proceeds of sale and not in the land, by virtue of the doctrine of conversion. This is unlikely to cause a problem where the legal joint tenants are also the equitable co-owners since their legal estate gives them a right of occupation. If one legal joint tenant severs his beneficial joint tenancy, he still remains entitled to possession and the equitable assignee acquires only an interest in the proceeds of sale (see the comments of Russell LJ in *Bedson* v *Bedson* [1965] 2 QB 666 and Megarry (1966) 82 LQR 29). Remember also that where the property is conveyed to the co-owners on express trust for sale, they hold the legal estate in trust for themselves in the proportions declared in the trust and, in the absence of fraud or mistake, this is conclusive (see *Goodman* v *Gallant* [1986] Fam 106).

Difficulties (and for the examiner fruitful sources for questions) arise where the legal estate is vested in one person and another is claiming a beneficial interest. We will consider the ways in which a beneficial interest can be established later and deal first with the question of whether a beneficial co-owner has a right of occupation against the holder of the legal estate. The strict application of the doctrine of conversion would mean that the equitable co-owner would have no right of occupation (see, e.g., *Barclay* v *Barclay* [1970] 2 QB 677 in which a will created a trust for sale of property part of which was occupied by one of the beneficiaries who was unable to establish a right of occupation against the trustees). This obviously creates difficulties where a property is purchased as a home, since the parties clearly think in terms of occupation not in terms of interests in proceeds of sale. This situation was considered by the Court of Appeal in *Bull* v *Bull* [1955] 1 QB 234 where a son purchased a home for himself and his mother, but the mother provided part of the purchase money making her an equitable tenant in common. It was held the mother had a right of occupation which could only be removed by the son making an application to the court under LPA 1925, s. 30, or by his appointing another trustee of the legal estate. The court's test was basically one of intention, i.e., what was the purpose of the trust for sale. In this context clearly it was to provide a home for mother and son. The approach taken in *Bull v Bull* was approved by the House of Lords in *Williams & Glyn's Bank Ltd v Boland* [1981] AC 487 so that it now seems clear that a beneficial co-owner will have a right of occupation provided there is a clear intention that the property is to be used as a home.

We now move to the difficult question of how a beneficial interest can be acquired and quantified. To decide this you must be aware both of case law and statutory intervention as between spouses (there is no statutory intervention between cohabitees). We are only concerned here with property rights during subsistence of the marriage and not the wide powers given to the court on dissolution of marriage by the Matrimonial Causes Act 1973. Whilst marriage or cohabitation subsists, the parties' rights are decided according to traditional land law principles and the imposition of the trust.

Imposition of a Trust

If you are faced with a question where the house is vested in one spouse or cohabitee alone, the first point to consider is whether the other spouse has acquired a beneficial interest by application of ordinary trust principles. A trust can be express, resulting, implied or constructive.

An *express* trust must be in writing to satisfy LPA 1925, s. 53, so that an oral declaration that the house is to be the other spouse's is insufficient (see *Gissing v Gissing* [1971] AC 886).

A *resulting* trust will arise where the beneficiary has contributed the whole or part of the purchase price, in which case the legal estate will be held on trust in proportion to the beneficiaries' respective contributions.

For example, A and B purchase a home for £30,000, A contributing £20,000 and B £10,000. The legal estate is vested in A. Then A will hold the legal estate on a resulting trust for A and B as tenants in common as to two thirds and one third respectively.

This is the most simple illustration and for an example of the difficulties the courts can find themselves in see *Sekhon v Alissa* [1989] 2 FLR 94.

An *implied* trust is found where at the time of acquisition there is evidence of a common intention that the property should be jointly owned and the claimant has acted to his or her detriment. It is this search for the elusive common intention that has caused the courts most difficulty and provides a fruitful source for exam problems. It is useful to bear in mind the words of Mustill LJ in *Grant v Edwards* [1986] Ch 638: 'The time has not yet arrived when it is possible to state the law in a way which will deal with all the practical problems which may arise in this difficult field, consistently with everything said in the cases'.

This evidence of judicial uncertainty is of small comfort to the poor student who has to satisfy the examiner he knows something of matrimonial property. While we cannot hope to deal with all the cases, we will endeavour to extract some principles which may assist in the exam room.

(a)   It must be remembered that the common intention must be present at the time of acquisition not in the light of subsequent events. (See per Lord Templeman in *Winkworth* v *Edward Baron Development Co. Ltd* [1986] 1 WLR 1512 and the guidelines laid down by the Court of Appeal in *Grant* v *Edwards* [1986] Ch 638. See also Warburton [1987] Conv 217 and Sufrin (1987) 50 MLR 94.)

(b)   The court will readily infer an intention when a 'direct' contribution has been made to the purchase price, e.g., paying part of the deposit, regular and substantial contributions to mortgage instalments. For a direct contribution made by a cohabitee see *Stokes* v *Anderson* [1991] 1 FLR 391 in which the Court of Appeal held that payments made by the respondent to the appellant to assist him in acquiring his former wife's share of the house were evidence of common intention.

(c)   'Indirect' contributions are unlikely to be sufficient to show common intention especially in view of the decision in *Lloyds Bank plc* v *Rosset* [1991] 1 AC 107 where the House of Lords thought it unlikely that anything less than a direct contribution would suffice. Consequently the wife who contributes by looking after the home or bringing up the children will have no claim although these factors may be taken into account in dissolution proceedings under the Matrimonial Causes Act 1973.

(d)   Since cohabitees cannot take advantage of divorce legislation (*Mossop* v *Mossop* [1989] Fam 77) it will be extremely difficult for an unmarried person to establish an interest. In *Pettitt* v *Pettitt* [1970] AC 777 Lord Upjohn stated that husband and wife property disputes should be decided on ordinary principles taking into account their relationship in context of the relationship rather than legal status. The courts have taken the view that marriage is evidence of common intention and in that way discriminated against the unmarried, e.g., *Burns* v *Burns* [1984] Ch 317 where the Court of Appeal could find no remedy for a cohabitee who had lived with her partner for 20 years and had borne his two children.

(e)   The claimant must have acted to his or her detriment in reliance on the common intention there should be a beneficial interest see *Midland Bank* v *Dobson* [1986] 1 FLR 171 and dicta of Lord Bridge in *Lloyds Bank plc* v *Rosset*.

(f)   A spouse may be able to take advantage of the Matrimonial Proceedings and Property Act 1970, s. 37, but this is not available to cohabitees unless they have been formally engaged and the engagement broken off (see Law Reform (Miscellaneous Provisions) Act 1970, s. 2(1), and *Bernard* v *Josephs* [1982] Ch 391).

Section 37 of the Matrimonial Proceedings and Property Act 1970 provides that a substantial contribution in money or money's worth by husband or wife to the improvement of real or personal property entitles the contributor to such a share or enlarged share as agreed or, in default, as may seem just in all the circumstances. The section is subject to evidence of contrary intention and applies where either or both spouses are beneficially entitled. The question of what is a substantial improvement is essentially one of fact and consequently is difficult to clarify. For example, in *Re Nicholson* [1974] 1 WLR 476 the wife's payment for central heating led to an increased share, whereas in *Pettitt* v *Pettitt* [1970] AC 777 (a case predating the statute) do-it-yourself activities were insufficient because they were no more than would be done by the normal handyman husband. The essential question is whether any improvement is of a substantial and lasting nature.

A *constructive* trust is found when it is necessary to do so to satisfy the demands of justice and good conscience. Here then the courts should be able to look at all the circumstances irrespective of common intention. While the constructive trust is widely used in other common law jurisdictions it has found little support in the English courts (see *Gissing* v *Gissing* and *Lloyd's Bank plc* v *Rosset*).

In view of the strict approach to contribution and common intention taken by the House of Lords in the *Rosset* case it may be that examiners will find examination of acquisition of beneficial interests less fruitful and be more concerned with the issues of occupation and the effect of beneficial interests on third parties. However, there may still be some scope for discussion of common intention, especially in relation to cohabitees. In *Rosset* the House of Lords was not prepared to find evidence of common intention from the fact that the house was to be acquired as a future matrimonial home, seeming to be more interested in finding what could amount to a commercial agreement. It may be, therefore, that this kind of agreement will be more readily found in the case of cohabitees. In *Hammond* v *Mitchell* [1991] 1 WLR 1127, Waite J was willing to find an express understanding that the beneficial interest in the bungalow should be shared between two cohabitees. Whilst in that case there had been discussions between the parties, that although the property was in the man's name, half would be the woman's when they were married, the judge seemed mainly concerned that the couple had been involved in a number of commercial activities and treated all their property as being part of a commercial joint venture. This case should be contrasted with the decision of Vinelott J in *Ungurian* v *Lesnoff* [1990] Ch 206 where *no* agreement was inferred that there should be an interest in property where the woman hoped to marry the man and have a home for themselves and her children (she did however acquire a life interest under the Settled Land Act 1925).

Once a beneficial interest has been found, other issues you may have to consider are: quantification of the interest, the beneficial owner's rights and the effect on third parties.

Quantification

Where there is an express declaration of trust, the courts are bound by the trusts declared (*Goodman* v *Gallant* [1986] Fam 106). When there is no such declaration the court must examine the evidence to decide whether there was a common intention that the interest should be other than equal and if so the proportions. The court can take into account contributions (direct and indirect) made over the whole period of ownership (for a recent discussion by the Court of Appeal see *Risch* v *McFee* [1991] 1 FLR 105).

Beneficial owners' rights

As we have already seen, the beneficiary will have a right of occupation against the trustee. In addition you may also consider the Matrimonial Homes Act 1983 which is available to spouses but not cohabitees. The Act does not create interests in land but gives the non-property-owning spouse a right of occupation or right to re-enter the matrimonial home. The Act is not dependent upon the finding of a beneficial interest so you may still consider it even if, in a question, you have decided there is no beneficial interest. The right of occupation will bind third parties if registered as a class F land charge (unregistered title) or a notice (registered title). The right remains until determined by divorce or application to the court. Application can be made either by the other spouse or a person deriving title under that spouse, including a purchaser (Matrimonial Homes Act 1983, s. 2(5)). Under s. 1 the court must take into account all the circumstances of the case, which includes the purchaser's circumstances, see per Dillon LJ in *Kashmir Kaur* v *Gill* [1988] Fam 110 in which it was considered relevant that the purchaser was blind and wanted the house because it was smaller and more convenient than his present house.

The holder of the legal estate will only be able to sell the property by appointing a second trustee (*City of London Building Society* v *Flegg* [1988] AC 54) or by making an application to the court under LPA 1925, s. 30. Under s. 30 the court has a discretion to order sale or make such order as it thinks fit on application by any person interested. In exercising its discretion the court will have regard to the underlying intention of the trust for sale. Since in matrimonial cases the purpose of the trust is to provide a home, the issue will be whether the relationship is still subsisting (see *Jones* v *Challenger* [1961] 1 QB 176). The section cannot be used where matrimonial proceedings are pending. It is the only avenue open to cohabitees. The advantage of s. 30 for cohabitees is that the court, as well as ordering or refusing sale, can impose terms which may give a form of protection to cohabitees in possession. In *Re Evers's Trust* [1980] 1 WLR 1327 the Court of Appeal postponed an order for sale until the cohabitee's child attained the age of 16. The court took the view that there was no evidence that the male cohabitee needed the proceeds of sale whereas an order for sale would put the female cohabitee in a difficult position so that the equitable solution was to postpone sale. Similarly in *Dennis* v *McDonald* [1982] Fam 63 the court refused sale but ordered the cohabitee in possession to pay his former cohabitee an occupation rent since it was his conduct towards her and the younger children of the relationship that had caused her to leave the house. In both these cases the needs of children had been of primary importance but the court will also take into account its social responsibility. For example, in *Martin* v *Martin* [1976] Fam 335 an order for sale was refused since there would be insufficient money from the sale to rehouse the separate spouses and the court took into account the difficulty of finding local authority housing. For useful articles on the application of s. 30 see M.P. Thompson [1984] Conv 103 and R. Cocks [1984] Conv 198. Finally remember that where sale is ordered the parties' respective interests must be valued at the date of realisation not at the date the parties last lived together (*Turton* v *Turton* [1988] Ch 542).

Beneficial Co-owners and Third Parties

A typical family property question may require you to discuss whether a beneficial interest binds third parties. To do this, you must be aware of the effect of the three House of Lords' decisions in *Williams & Glyn's Bank Ltd* v *Boland* [1981] AC 487, *City of London Building Society* v *Flegg* [1988] AC 54 and *Abbey National Building Society* v *Cann* [1991] 1 AC 56. These cases have been fully discussed in chapter 3 so we need only now consider their effect on family property. The effect of the decisions would seem to be as follows:

(a) Where the legal estate is vested in a sole trustee, a purchaser of registered land will be bound by the equitable interest of a beneficial owner in actual occupation under LRA 1925, s. 70(1)(g) (*Williams & Glyn's Bank Ltd* v *Boland*).

(b) Where there are two or more trustees of the legal estate, the equitable co-owners' interest will be overreached and consequently not bind a purchaser (*City of London Building Society* v *Flegg*). This, of course, would not affect the beneficial co-owners' right to share in the proceeds of sale but would mean there would be no right of occupation against the purchasers.

(c) An overriding interest must exist at the time of registration of title, but where it is dependent upon actual occupation of the house, the beneficial owner must be in actual occupation at the time the purchase deed takes effect, i.e., the actual time of completion (*Abbey National Building Society* v *Cann*).

The effect of these decisions on the matrimonial home would seem to be that it is now very difficult for a beneficial owner to establish an overriding interest against a mortgage on the purchase of the house. Whilst actual occupation is a question of fact, the House of Lords made it clear in *Abbey National Building Society* v *Cann* that it involves some degree of permanence so that the fact that a person moves into property before the vendor's solicitor actually receives the purchase money and the legal estate is vested in the purchaser would be insufficient. Entry into occupation after exchange of contracts but before completion may be sufficient although this again will be a question of fact and was, unfortunately, not a point pursued by the House of Lords in *Lloyds Bank plc* v *Rosset* [1991] 1 AC 107, although the court did accept that there could be occupation through an agent, e.g., workmen renovating the property. Where a sole legal owner mortgages or remortgages a house, the beneficial co-owner would be in actual occupation and have an overriding interest under *Williams & Glyn's Bank Ltd* v *Boland* provided no deed of postponement or waiver of rights is signed in favour of the new mortgage.

The decisions of the House of Lords related to registered title so there is still some doubt about whether the dicta in *Williams & Glyn's Bank Ltd* v *Boland* apply to unregistered title. In *Caunce* v *Caunce* [1969] 1 WLR 286 it was held that in unregistered title, a mortgagee was not bound by the wife in possession's equitable interest. The correctness of this decision was doubted, *obiter*, in *Williams & Glyn's Bank Ltd* v *Boland*, and the approach taken in *Williams & Glyn's Bank Ltd* v *Boland* was applied to unregistered title by Judge John Finlay QC in *Kingsnorth Finance Co. Ltd* v *Tizard* [1986] 1 WLR 783. There is still no appellate decision directly applying *Williams & Glyn's Bank Ltd* v *Boland* to unregistered title.

Whilst the decisions in *Cann* and *Rosset* have alleviated the problems for mortgagees in relation to beneficial interests in the home, the House of Lords' decision in *Barclays Bank plc* v *O'Brien* [1993] 3 WLR 786 indicates that there are still traps for unwary mortgagees. The facts were that the husband (H) wished to mortgage the matrimonial home, jointly owned with his wife (W), to secure his indebtedness to the bank. H falsely represented the nature of his debt to W and it was not suggested to W that she seek independent legal advice before signing the mortgage. It was held that W could have the transaction set aside as the bank had constructive notice of H's undue influence or misrepresentation which had induced W to enter into the mortgage. The test seems to be that the bank was put on enquiry:

(a) because the transaction was not on the face of it to W's financial advantage; and

(b) that there was a substantial risk that W was persuaded to act as surety by H's undue influence or misrepresentation.

The bank was fixed with constructive notice because it failed to take reasonable steps to ensure W's agreement was properly obtained, i.e., suggesting she sought independent legal advice.

One final point to note is that Lord Browne-Wilkinson made it clear that the principle extends to all other cases where there is *an emotional relationship* between the cohabitees.

The ambit of *O'Brien* was to some extent limited in *CIBC Mortgages plc* v *Pitt* [1993] 3 WLR 802, where it was held that a third party is not put on enquiry where there is no indication that the transaction was anything more than a normal advance to H and W for their own benefit. Possibly a prospective mortgagee should not therefore ask too many questions. The decision in *O'Brien* has given rise to a number of cases where the courts have considered the nature of constructive notice, e.g., *Goode Durrant Administration* v *Biddulph* (1994) 2 FLR 551. A particularly interesting decision is *TSB Bank plc* v *Camfield, The Times*, 7 December 1994, where it was decided that a mortgage cannot be partially enforceable against a wife. Under *O'Brien* Nourse LJ took the view that the wife's remedy was all or nothing; the mortgagee etc. could not be put in any better position than any other third party fixed with constructive notice.

An examiner may be interested in whether you can explore the issue of whether an emotional tie, other than between cohabitees or spouses, might automatically put the mortgagee on enquiry.

SPECIMEN EXAMINATION QUESTION

Ronny and Sheila were married in 1989. Ronny works on an off-shore oil rig one month in two. In 1990 Sheila had a child and they decided to buy a house, 'Chez Nous' (title to which is registered). In view of Ronny's work commitments they agreed that Sheila would deal with all the purchase arrangements. They bought the house for £40,000, Sheila paid £39,000 and Ronny contributed £1,000. The legal title was registered in the sole name of Sheila. They moved in during the autumn of 1990.

Six months later Sheila arranged a mortgage from Getrich Building Society to finance some renovation work. During his shore leave Ronny helped out with the renovation work and decorated the house himself. Ronny also likes to play golf, and he keeps all his golf equipment in the spare bedroom. Sheila paid the mortgage instalments and Ronny paid the household expenses.

In 1991 the couple decided to buy a holiday home, 'Our Patch' in the Lake District (title to which is registered). Once again Sheila dealt with the purchase arrangements and the property was put in her sole name. It was bought with the aid of a mortgage from Getrich. Sheila told Ronny that 'Our Patch' was 'as much his as hers'. Ronny spent much of his leave decorating the holiday home and converting the loft into a spare bedroom, tasks which he particularly enjoyed, having studied interior design at night school.

Unfortunately, last month Ronny lost his job and came home to find that Sheila had run off with Cecil, the milkman, leaving Ronny and the baby.

Ronny has discovered that Sheila has not been paying the mortgage on 'Chez Nous' and Getrich Building Society are threatening possession proceedings with a view to sale.

Ronny is also concerned that Sheila might sell the holiday home.

Advise Ronny. No divorce proceedings are envisaged.

SUGGESTED APPROACH

Commentary

In this question you are asked to advise Ronny in a situation where no divorce proceedings are contemplated. As the legal estate is vested in Sheila alone you will need to discuss 'ordinary trust principles' to decide whether Ronny has a beneficial interest in the houses and then go on to consider whether he has a right of occupation against (a) Sheila and (b) Getrich Building Society. Since there are two houses involved you may approach the problem by dealing with the issues of beneficial interest and occupation to each property in turn.

(a)   Chez Nous

It was accepted in the House of Lords in *Gissing* v *Gissing* and *Pettit* v *Pettit* that beneficial co-ownership will only be established where there is an express, resulting or constructive trust. In order to satisfy LPA 1925, s. 53 an express trust must be made in writing and while the facts mention an agreement, there is no evidence that it was in writing. In order to establish a beneficial interest you would need to consider a resulting or constructive trust. A resulting trust will arise where the beneficiary has made a direct contribution to the purchase price, as in this case where Ronny contributed £1,000 towards the purchase price of £40,000. Assuming this was not a gift or loan, Ronny will have acquired a beneficial interest, albeit a small one. You should therefore consider whether the implied or constructive trust has arisen under the principles established in *Lloyd's Bank* v *Rosset*. You will need to consider whether Ronny and Sheila's discussions showed a common intention that they should have a joint interest in the home and that Ronny had acted to his detriment. Other than the fact that Chez Nous was to be the family home, which was insufficient in *Rosset*, there seems to be no indication of the requisite common intention. Ronny could perhaps argue that he has acquired an increased share in the house by substantial contributions to improvements under the Matrimonial Proceedings and Property Act 1970,

s. 37. Ronny has helped with the renovation work and decorated the house but this would seem unlikely to amount to a contribution to a substantial improvement (see *Pettit* v *Pettit*).

Once you have established whether Ronny has a beneficial interest you will need to advise him of his position in view of the building society's proposed possession proceedings. In *Williams & Glyn's Bank* v *Boland* the House of Lords established that a beneficial interest coupled with actual occupation gives rise to an overriding interest binding on the mortgagee under the Land Registration Act 1925, s. 70(1)(g). The effect of the decision was restricted in *Abbey National Building Society* v *Cann* where the House of Lords held that where an overriding interest is dependent upon actual occupation, the occupation must exist at the date of completion not the date of registration. You need to consider whether Ronny was in actual occupation at the date of completion of the mortgage. According to *Boland* this is a question of fact and according to *Cann* indicates some degree of permanence. We are told that Ronny is away one month in two but does pay household expenses and keeps golf equipment in the house which would seem to indicate some degree of permanence. (On this point *Kingsnorth Finance* v *Tizard* could be considered where a wife leaving some of her clothes in the former matrimonial home was a relevant factor.) If Ronny can establish actual occupation then it would clearly exist before the loan for the renovation work was completed and by binding on the building society.

(b)   Our Patch

Once again you would need to discuss whether Ronny has a beneficial interest and then go on to consider whether he could prevent Sheila selling the holiday home. There is no evidence of an express trust, Sheila's assurance that the house was as much his as hers being insufficient (*Gissing* v *Gissing*). We are not told whether Ronny and Sheila provided a deposit or whether the whole purchase price was raised by the mortgage with Getrich. If Ronny provided the whole or part of any deposit a resulting trust would arise. Alternatively, it may be that Ronny has made a direct contribution by meeting the mortgage repayments. You should also discuss the effect of Ronny's work on Our Patch in the light of Sheila's assurance to Ronny. In *Rosset* the wife's contribution in supervising the renovation work and doing the interior designing was no more than any wife would do — this could perhaps be applied to Ronny as he is said to have enjoyed doing the conversion work.

If Ronny can establish a benefical interest then he will have a right of occupation against Sheila since the object of the purchase was to provide a holiday home for the family (*Bull* v *Bull*). Even if Ronny has no beneficial interest he could register a caution under the Matrimonial Homes Act 1983. Such a registration would make the sale practically more difficult but it could be discharged by application to the court (*Kashmir Kaur* v *Gill*).

Sheila would be able to sell the house by appointing another trustee of the legal estate (*City of London B.S.* v *Flegg*). However, as this is not mentioned in the facts, you would need to consider the effect of an application to the court under LPA 1925, s. 30. Sheila could seek an order for sale which the court could grant, refuse or refuse subject to conditions. You would therefore need to discuss the cases in which the courts have considered the exercise of their discretion, e.g., *Re Evers* and *Dennis* v *McDonald*. From these cases it seems the court will consider the purpose of the trust for sale and whether it has come to an end, whether the applicant needs to realise her capital and the interests of any children. In our question, Our Patch is a holiday home and once Sheila has left Ronny it could be argued that the purpose of the trust has come to an end. Ronny has a home for himself and the baby so the interest of the child does not need protection and Ronny would receive some share of the proceeds of sale. On the facts it seems that an application under s. 30 would be successful.

SUGGESTED ADDITIONAL READING

Co-ownership is dealt with fully in the standard textbooks. The area of matrimonial property is not discussed in any detail and you should consult the following family law texts:

Cretney and Masson, *Principles in Family Law*, 5th ed., 1990 (Sweet & Maxwell).
P. Bromley, *Family Law*, 8th ed., 1992 (Butterworths).
J. Dewar, *Law and the Family*, 2nd ed., 1992 (Butterworths).

6 MORTGAGES

INTRODUCTION

Most people take out a mortgage either to assist them in purchasing their home or in securing capital for their business. The borrower is known as the *mortgagor*, the lender as the *mortgagee*.

Simple! and yet the terminology is again confusing to some students leading them into foolish errors. A mortgage, which can be either legal or equitable, is essentially a transaction where by an *interest* in property, be it a house, land or business etc. is transferred to the mortgagee *as security for a loan*, subject to a right of redemption vested in the mortgagor (*Santley* v *Wilde* [1899] 2 Ch 474).

The terms of a mortgage therefore must be such as to provide security for the mortgagee in respect of the loan he has provided for the mortgagor *and nothing more*. Once the student has grasped this fact then the law of mortgages falls into place.

TYPES OF MORTGAGE

Although there are several types of mortgage available, it is essential to be aware of the two main types. These are:

(a) *The repayment mortgage* (or instalment mortgage as it is sometimes called), which involves periodic repayments to the mortgagee consisting partly of capital and partly of interest.

(b) *The endowment mortgage*. Here the capital sum borrowed (sometimes referred to as the principal sum) is left outstanding during the mortgage term.

The mortgagor makes periodic repayments consisting this time of interest only. The capital sum is repaid at the end of the mortgage term usually by way of an insurance policy taken out at the same time as the mortgage. This matures at the end of the mortgage term. It may be with or without profits but it must produce sufficient to cover the capital sum borrowed.

These two types of mortgages are discussed at this point for the reason that there has been judicial discussion about whether a mortgagor with such mortgages, particularly the endowment type, can benefit from the relief afforded by the Administration of Justice Act 1970, s. 36, and the Administration of Justice Act 1973, s. 8, where a mortgagee seeks possession of the mortgagor's home. This point will be taken up later. Suffice to say here that in view of the decision of the Court of Appeal in *Bank of Scotland* v *Grimes* [1985] 2 All ER 254 it is likely that mortgagors with either type of mortgage will be able to rely on those sections.

Tax relief on Mortgages

This is not something which a student of land law will need to know in detail, but for completeness you should at least be aware that income tax relief is available on the interest the mortgagor pays on up to £30,000 of loans to buy his only or main home.

MAIN ISSUES

The law of mortgages is a vast topic. It can, however, be split into three main areas — all of which are common examination topics. These are:

(a) Creation and discharge.
(b) Rights of the mortgagor.
(c) Rights of the mortgagee.

It is the aim of the rest of this chapter to examine some of the more difficult topics within these three areas and provide revision summaries for the remainder. In addition to the standard texts. The Law Commission Working Paper No. 99 *Land Mortgages*, also provides valuable reading material.

CREATION AND DISCHARGE

This is fairly straightforward and it is unlikely that an examination question will be confined to this topic alone. It may, however, form part of a question overlapping with either or both of the other two areas.

See revision summary 1 for quick reference.

Priority

You will notice that this revision summary divides creation of mortgages into 'mortgages of the legal estate' and 'mortgages of an equitable interest'. This is because since 1925 the correct question to ask yourself is 'Has the legal estate been mortgaged?' not 'Is the mortgage legal or equitable?' Why? Because the protection afforded to a mortgagee and therefore retention of priority over subsequent mortgagees and over later incumbrances, depends upon *notice*. In the case of *a mortgage of the legal estate* notice takes the form of registration of any mortgage not protected by the deposit of the title deeds as land charges. Where the mortgage is a *legal* one it must be registered as a 'puisne mortgage'; if *equitable* as a 'general equitable charge' (see Land Charges Act 1972, s. 2(4)).

No registration is necessary, of course, where the mortgagee has possession of the title deeds (a right of the first mortgagee), for their absence will be *notice* to other persons seeking to deal with the land.

The same principles apply where the title to the land is required to be registered under the Land Registration Act 1925 and as such will be governed by the Land Registration Rules.

Regarding the mortgage of an *equitable interest*, priority again depends upon *notice*. Accordingly the rule in *Dearle v Hall* (1828) 3 Russ 1 (as amended by LPA 1925, ss. 137 and 138) applies, namely, that priority depends upon the *order* in which *notice* of the mortgages is received by the appropriate trustee or trustees. (Remember, being equitable interests they can only exist behind a trust of the legal estate (LPA 1925, s. 1(3)) and as such the legal estate is held by trustees.)

To complete the picture, remember there is a special way of obtaining priority, namely by *tacking*, i.e., by amalgamating a mortgage with another of higher priority. Do not forget that since 1925 this can only be done where the mortgagee makes further advances (LPA 1925, s. 94).

The Charge

By far the most common method of creating a mortgage of the legal estate is the charge. This creates a *legal interest* in favour of the mortgagee (LPA 1925, s. 1(2)(c)) and by s. 87(1), the chargee (i.e., mortgagee) is given the same powers *as if* the mortgage had been created by any other permitted method.

One advantage of the charge is that compound mortgages involving both freehold and leasehold land can be created, even where the lease contains a covenant forbidding underletting without the lessor's consent. The latter is a common covenant in leases.

The charge is also simpler and it allows the mortgagor to retain the legal estate in the land. He may therefore create second and subsequent mortgages (which will, remember, not normally be protected by the retention of the title deeds) to secure further loans. (See above for the protection of such mortgages.)

RIGHTS OF THE MORTGAGOR

The sum total of the mortgagor's rights during the mortgage term are customarily referred to as 'the equity of redemption'. As an aid to revision, these rights are summarised in summary 2.

Right to redeem
Most important is the right of the mortgagor to redeem his mortgage. This is a topic which has led to a considerable amount of case law and one with which all students must be fully conversant. To do this you must distinguish between the common law and equitable rules regarding redemption. These are explained below.

Common law rule
'Redeem on the legal date of redemption or not at all.' In the mortgage deed the mortgagor covenants to repay the capital sum borrowed with interest on a date specified in the deed, e.g., in the case of a classical instalment mortgage there is usually a clause making the capital sum due after some short period, customarily six months from the execution of the mortgage deed, notwithstanding that the mortgage term may be for 25 years or more (see for example *Centrax Trustees Ltd* v *Ross* [1979] 2 All ER 952). This date is termed the 'legal or contractual date of redemption' and at common law once it is passed the mortgagor has no right to redeem (see figure 6.1).

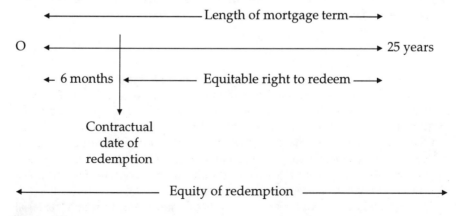

Figure 6.1

Equitable right to redeem
Equity, mellowing the common law, compels the mortgagee to allow redemption at any time *after* the contractual date on receipt of the capital sum, on payment of interest and cost of discharging the mortgage subject to prior notice to the mortgagee. Hence the so-called 'equitable right to redeem'.

Equity of redemption and equitable right to redeem compared
These two expressions, somewhat outmoded but still adhered to, can cause confusion. Their meaning is illustrated in figure 6.1 in relation to a classical instalment mortgage with a six-month contractual date of redemption.

Protection of the Equity of Redemption

This is a common examination area. Bear in mind the following points:

(a) Equity is concerned to ensure that a mortgage provides security for the loan and nothing more; that it shall not be irredeemable and that the mortgagee does not bring improper pressure to bear on the mortgagor. As a result the court is *not* concerned with the reasonableness or otherwise of the mortgage, but whether it is unconscionable, or oppressive, or a 'clog or fetter' on the equity of redemption.

(b) Reconciling case law in this area is not easy, yet this is what most examiners are looking for, particularly from undergraduates. It is useful to bear in mind the reason for this difficulty, namely, that this equitable doctrine runs contrary to the common law doctrine of 'sanctity of contract', i.e., bargains are made to be kept, not broken.

(c) A further factor to consider when attempting to reconcile cases is whether the mortgagor and mortgagee are of equal bargaining strength. The doctrine after all is equitable. It developed to protect the *weak* mortgagor as against the strong and unscrupulous mortgagee. Consequently, where the parties are of equal bargaining power and have voluntarily entered into a mortgage agreement there is no need for equity to intervene. 'Any other result would place an unfortunate restriction on the liberty to contract of competent parties who are at arm's length' (Court of Appeal in *Knightsbridge Estates Trust Ltd* v *Byrne* [1939] Ch 441).

Equitable Rules

Equity looks to the substance of the agreement and not the form
This has the effect that equity will treat as a mortgage any transaction that is in substance intended to give security for a loan, whatever name the parties put on it (*Grangeside Properties Ltd* v *Collingwood Securities Ltd* [1964] 1 WLR 139).

Attempts to exclude redemption will be void
For example, any term in the mortgage granting an option to the mortgagee to purchase the mortgaged property, as in *Samuel* v *Jarrah Timber & Wood Paving Co. Ltd* [1904] AC 323. The House of Lords 'reluctantly' declared the mortgage void in that case because it was a 'fair bargain between people who knew what they were doing'. Yet not to have done so would have been seen as a 'serious weakening' of the equitable doctrine (but compare *Reeve* v *Lisle* [1902] AC 461 where an option granted subsequent to the mortgage was valid).

Equity will not allow the right of redemption to be postponed to such an extent that the right would be rendered nominal or illusory
The rationale behind this rule was explained by the Judicial Committee of the Privy Council in *Fairclough* v *Swan Brewery Co. Ltd* [1912] AC 565 by saying that 'the mortgage for all practical purposes was irredeemable since on redemption the effective value to the mortgagor of an almost expired lease would be minimal', thus holding that a 20-year mortgage only redeemable six weeks before the termination of the lease was invalid.

Relevance of the restraint of trade doctrine
Do not forget that if postponement is coupled with a 'tie' between mortgagor and mortgagee which is void as being in restraint of trade, then the postponement will also be void. See Heydon (1969) 85 LQR 251, who discusses amongst other things the application of the doctrine to mortgages and the case of *Esso Petroleum Co. Ltd* v *Harper's Garage (Stourport) Ltd* [1968] AC 269. There the owner of a petrol station mortgaged it to an oil company, agreeing to take supplies from the company throughout the term of the mortgage and not redeem the mortgage for 21 years. The House of Lords held the restraint unreasonable in duration and therefore would not enforce it. A postponement for a lesser period coupled with a tie may therefore be valid. See also *Alec Lobb (Garages) Ltd* v *Total Oil GB Ltd* [1983] 1 All ER 944 for a further possible restriction on the doctrine.

Equity permits collateral advantages
Equity permits advantages over and above repayment of the loan with interest, provided:

(a)   they are not unconscionable or oppressive (see *Cityland & Property Holdings Ltd* v *Dabrah* [1968] Ch 166), and
(b)   they do not extend beyond the term of the mortgage (see *Noakes & Co. Ltd* v *Rice* [1902] AC 24).

Rate of interest as a collateral advantage

Bear in mind that the terms of the mortgage deed will indicate the rate of interest to be paid.

It is a possibility that part of an examination question will require a discussion of the validity of such a term. What an examiner will be looking for, once again, is an appreciation of the conflict between the common law and equitable doctrines, backed up by judicial guidance as found in reported cases. A brief consideration of the applicability or otherwise of the Consumer Credit Act 1974 (discussed below), where relevant, will also show the examiner that you are aware of the implications of statutory intervention in this important area. For judicial guidance students should consider the case of *Cityland & Property Holdings Ltd* v *Dabrah* [1968] Ch 166. There the court showed itself willing to come to the rescue of the oppressed mortgagor by declaring that a mortgagee is only entitled to a reasonable sum by way of interest. What will be reasonable, of course, will depend on the facts in a given case.

This approach should be compared with that taken in later cases such as *Multiservice Bookbinding Ltd* v *Marden* [1979] Ch 84. Here the linking of mortgage payments consisting of part capital and part interest, to the exchange rate of the Swiss franc was held to be lawful even though the pound sterling fell to a third of its original value against the Swiss franc, causing considerable hardship to the mortgagor. It may be unreasonable said Browne-Wilkinson J, but 'it was *not* unfair or unconscionable in that the terms had [not] been imposed in a morally reprehensible manner'. Furthermore again note that the parties were of equal bargaining strength and had received the benefit of independent legal advice. For these reasons, as well as that of public policy, the common law doctrine of sanctity of contract prevailed. Similarly, in *Nationwide Building Society* v *Registry of Friendly Societies* [1983] 1 WLR 1226 the court declared valid a building society scheme to index-link capital repayments to the UK general index of retail prices.

Relevance of the Consumer Credit Act 1974 to Mortgage Terms

This is something which many students forget to cover in their answer.

Sections 137 to 140 are particularly important as they apply to all mortgages including building society mortgages. The effect of these sections is to enable the court to reopen an 'extortionate credit bargain', i.e., one which requires payments which are 'grossly exhorbitant' or which 'grossly contravene ordinary principles of fair dealing' — where the interest rate is exceedingly high perhaps? In deciding whether a bargain is extortionate, however, the court will consider the degree of risk accepted by the mortgagee having regard to the value of the security provided. In *A. Ketley Ltd* v *Scott* [1981] ICR 241, for example, the High Court declared that a credit agreement fixing 48 per cent annual rate of interest was not extortionate due, among other factors, to the high risk involved.

Do not forget this Act, especially the provisions relating to extortionate credit bargains, and remember that the financial limit of £15,000 (SI 1983 No. 1878) does not apply to these provisions.

RIGHTS OF THE MORTGAGEE

For a summary of these rights see revision summaries 3 and 4 dealing with legal and equitable mortgagees respectively. From an examination point of view the most important rights are the right of a legal mortgagee to take possession, the right to sell and the right to foreclose, particularly in view of the recent increase in mortgage arrears.

Right to Take Possession

Usually this right is not exercised unless the mortgagor is in default with his mortgage payments. Where it is exercised it is either to protect the mortgagee's security by carrying out repairs or prevent vandalism as in *Western Bank Ltd* v *Schindler* [1977] Ch 1, or more commonly as a prelude to exercising the power of sale (see [1979] Conv 266). You must remember, however, that, subject to an agreement to the contrary in the mortgage deed, the mortgagee does have the right to possession even if there is no default (*Four-Maids Ltd* v *Dudley Marshall (Properties) Ltd* [1957] Ch 317). This applies even if the mortgagor has a counter-claim or right of set-off exceeding the amount of the mortgage debt (see *National Westminster Bank* v *Skelton* [1993] 1 All ER 242).

Limitations on the exercise of this right are provided by the Administration of Justice Act 1970, s. 36, and the Administration of Justice Act 1973, s. 8. These statutory limitations give the court discretionary power to adjourn or postpone proceedings for possession of a dwelling-house for such periods as the court thinks reasonable. To do so the court must, however, be of the opinion that the mortgagor is likely to be able 'within a reasonable period to pay any sums due under the mortgage or to remedy a default'. The courts take a very limited view of 'reasonable period' and it seems that it must be almost certain that the default will be remedied. See *Citibank Trust Ltd* v *Ayivor* [1987] 1 WLR 1157 in which the court refused to give weight to the fact that a possible counterclaim by the mortgagor against the mortgagee might bring in a substantial sum. The more recent case of *First National Bank plc* v *Syed* [1991] 2 All ER 250 seems to indicate that the Administration of Justice Act 1970, s. 36, should only be used sparingly even where some attempt at remedying the default can be made. In that case the Court of Appeal was of the opinion that courts should not stay or suspend possession orders on the basis that payments were to be made towards arrears of instalments if the instalments were either beyond the borrower's means or if payments within his means would not clear the arrears within a reasonable time and at the same time cover current instalments. The effect of this would, in most cases, seem to be that in the absence of an agreed sale or remortgage, the mortgagor will find it almost impossible to rely on s. 36. Similarly in *Britannia Building Society* v *Earl* [1990] 2 All ER 469 the Court of Appeal refused to use s. 36 to assist tenants of property which had been let to them by the mortgagor in default of his mortgage covenants. While the court accepted that, as against the mortgagor they were statutory tenants within the Rent Act 1977, they could not rely on the Administration of Justice Act 1970, s. 36, since a statutory tenancy is not an estate or interest in land and in any event the only way the mortgagor could remedy the default in the mortgage was by removing the tenants, which was the object of the mortgagee's possession proceedings.

It is worth considering whether the effect of the recession raising the number of possession cases may have occasioned the courts to take a more pragmatic view of the enforcement of mortgagees' rights. For example, in *Target Homes Ltd* v *Clothier* [1994] 1 All ER 439, the Court of Appeal deferred a possession order even though there was no evidence that the mortgagors were likely to discharge the sums due under the mortgage within a reasonable time and it was unlikely that the ongoing mortgage commitments would be met. The house had been put up for sale and the court felt that it was more likely that a purchaser would be found if the property was occupied. Possession was deferred for three months after which the mortgagees would be entitled to possession unless the indebtedness had been discharged.

Whether a court will be pragmatic is not certain. An alternative stance was in fact taken by the Court of Appeal in *Palk* v *Mortgage Services Funding plc* [1993] Ch 330. Here the court exercised its discretion to order sale under LPA 1925, s. 91(2), even though the sale price was insufficient to discharge the mortgage. In the court's opinion this would produce the best financial outcome for the mortgagor; the alternative being to allow the mortgagee to take possession and decide the time of sale during which period the mortgagor's indebtedness would continue to increase.

To what extent these decisions are intended to deal with the current economic situation is unclear, although the *Palk* decision has been extended to commercial mortgages in *Arab Bank plc* v *Mercantile Holdings Ltd* [1994] 2 WLR 307. It is something which students should consider however.

Operation of the Administration of Justice Act 1973, section 8

In view of its importance, s. 8(1) of the Administration of Justice Act 1973 is reproduced below:

Where by a mortgage of land which consists of or includes a dwelling-house, or by any agreement between the mortgagee under such a mortgage and the mortgagor, the mortgagor is entitled or is to be permitted to pay the principal sum secured by instalments or otherwise to defer payment of it in whole or in part, but provision is also made for earlier payment in the event of any default by the mortgagor or of a demand by the mortgagee or otherwise, then for purposes of section 36 of the Administration of Justice Act 1970 ... a court may treat as due under the mortgage on account of the principal sum secured and of interest on it only such amounts as the mortgagor would have expected to be required to pay if there had been no such provision for earlier payment.

You will find it helps to understand this section if it is divided into two limbs:

(a)   'permitted to pay the principal sum [i.e., capital sum] by instalments', and
(b)   'permitted ... to defer payment [of the capital sum] in whole or in part'.

This is a common examination area and students, especially undergraduates, must be able to discuss the ambit of this section and recognise the problems of interpretation.

Some Problems Identified

Bank overdrafts secured by a charge on a dwelling-house cause a problem, a harsh line having been taken in the case of *Habib Bank Ltd* v *Tailor* [1982] 1 WLR 1218, in which the Court of Appeal construed the phrase 'to defer payment', in limb (b), to mean 'to defer until *after* the sum becomes due'. As a result the mortgagor in that case could not avail himself of the relief provided by s. 8, for the agreement was to 'repay the capital sum on the bank's written demand'.

To understand the rationale behind that decision reference can be made to the judgment of Cumming-Bruce LJ, who said that *if* s. 8 had applied then it would deprive bankers, who use the usual charge for securing an overdraft, of any right of enforcement so long as the debtor (i.e., the mortgagor) continued to pay interest on the capital sum.

You should contrast the more liberal approach taken in *Centrax Trustees Ltd* v *Ross* [1979] 2 All ER 952 and followed in *Bank of Scotland* v *Grimes* [1985] 2 All ER 254. In the *Centrax* case it was stated that 'section 8 should receive a reasonably liberal interpretation'. Different fact situations perhaps led the courts in these two cases to give such a liberal interpretation and you may wish to reconcile or distinguish them from the *Habib Bank* case, e.g., by arguing along the lines that the mortgage in *Centrax* required the capital sum to be paid on a *specific date*, but it was clear on a true construction of the agreement that the parties had contemplated an indefinite loan with the right of redemption being kept alive indefinitely in equity, unless the mortgagee took foreclosure proceedings, and in the *Bank of Scotland* case the mortgage was of an endowment type. (See an article by Stephen Tromans [1984] Conv 91 for further discussion.)

Assuming possession is obtained of the mortgaged property then usually the mortgagee will exercise his power of sale. Always remember that although the *mortgagee is not the trustee of his power of sale,* he *is* the trustee of the proceeds of sale. When answering a question involving the power of sale students must make this quite clear, explaining that the consequence of this rule is to cause the mortgagee to act in good faith and with reasonable care to ensure that he gets the best price reasonably obtainable for the mortgaged property. Any attempt to authorise the mortgagee to sell in such manner and on such terms and for such consideration 'as he thinks fit' is subject to the duty of care and does not exempt liability for loss arising from failure to take reasonable care to obtain a proper price. See *Bishop v Bonham* [1988] 1 WLR 742 (although this was a case on the mortgage of shares the Court of Appeal applied the decision in *Cuckmere Brick Co. Ltd v Mutual Finance Ltd* [1971] Ch 949). You should be clear that the duty of care imposed on a mortgagee is not the same as the duty of care imposed in the law of tort, so that the mortgagee does not owe a duty to third parties with a beneficial interest in the property. In *Parker-Tweedale v Dunbar Bank plc* [1991] Ch 12 the Court of Appeal made it clear that the mortgagee's duty arises in equity not tort so that no duty was owed to a former husband with a beneficial interest in his former wife's property which was sold by a mortgagee in possession. Even if the duty did arise in tort the decision would seem to follow from the more restrictive view of tortious duty adopted by the House of Lords (reversing the Court of Appeal) in *Murphy v Brentwood District Council* [1991] 1 AC 398. You should remember a mortgagee cannot sell to himself (*Farrar v Farrar Ltd* (1888) 40 ChD 395) but in *Tse Kwong Lam v Wong Chit Sen* [1983] 1 WLR 1349 it was held a mortgagee may sell to a company in which he has an interest provided he gets the best price and the dealings are at arms length.

Foreclosure

Any question seeking knowledge of the mortgagee's remedies will undoubtedly require a student to be aware of the right of the mortgagee to foreclose. It is always useful to preface any such discussion with the statement that 'Foreclosure is done by order of court, not by any persons', thus indicating to the examiner that you understand the Draconian impact of exercising such a remedy where the effect is to destroy the mortgagor's equity of redemption and transfer the fee simple or the term of years to the mortgagee. The mortgagor in fact loses all, but only on the court's say-so. (For protection for the mortgagor see LPA 1925, s. 91(2).)

In undergraduate courses you are most likely to be concerned with knowledge of the mortgagee's rights to possession and sale. In a professional course questions may be of a more general nature and you should be aware of the mortgagee's right to appoint a receiver and remember that it is open to the mortgagee to sue in contract on the mortgagor's personal covenant to repay. Consequently, even if the property is sold for less than the amount outstanding on the mortgage, the mortgagee can still try to recover the balance by an action in contract. You should also be aware of other rights of the mortgagee such as the right to the title deeds and the right to insure (see post at revision summary 3).

SPECIMEN EXAMINATION QUESTION

Typical questions on mortgages for undergraduates often take the form of problems, although essays have been set, e.g., ' 'The equity of redemption is inviolable.' Discuss.'

Those taking professional examinations are likely to be faced with more basic but practical questions such as: 'What is meant by the equity of redemption?' or 'Explain tacking and consolidation in relation to mortgages', or 'Outline methods of mortgaging the legal estate'.

Problem Questions

It is always useful to have a plan in mind on how to tackle a problem question. It makes it much easier to identify the issues in the problem and helps you to approach it in a logical way.

Suggested Plan

(a)   Identify the mortgagor and mortgagee — remember there may be more than one.

(b)   Identify the mortgage (or mortgages):

(i)   Is it of a dwelling-house? ——— Yes ———▸ Administration of
                                                                Justice Acts 1970 and
                                                                1973 will apply.

(ii)   Is it a business mortgage? ——— Yes ———▸ Above Acts will *not*
                                                                apply.

Remember again there may be two or more mortgages, e.g., a first mortgage of a dwelling-house with a building society and a second mortgage with a bank etc.

(c) (i) Is the mortgagee private, e.g., a bank or private individual or company etc? —— Yes ——▶ Consumer Credit Act 1974 may apply in part.

(ii) Is mortgagee a building society? —— Yes ——▶ In addition Building Societies Act will apply.

(d) Identify the terms of the mortgage — itemise them.

(e) Are these terms:

(i) Unconscionable or oppressive? —— Yes ——▶ Void.

(ii) A clog or fetter on the equity of redemption? —— Yes ——▶ Void.

(iii) Coupled with a 'tie'? —— Yes ——▶ The restraint of trade doctrine will apply.

At this point it will be necessary to discuss the equity of redemption and the conflict between that doctrine and the common law doctrine of sanctity of contract, linking it with the question being answered.

(f) Assuming the terms are valid, is the mortgagor in breach? —— Yes ——▶ Consider remedies open to mortgagee.

Discuss the most likely remedy (or remedies) available in the circumstances, perhaps if relevant commenting that others are available, not forgetting to link with (b) above, i.e., if the mortgage is of a dwelling-house and the mortgagee is relying on his remedy of possession and sale then the mortgagor may find relief provided by the Administration of Justice Acts 1970 and 1973.

(g) Is there evidence of undue influence or misrepresentation? —— Yes ——▶ Mortgagee's remedies may be restricted (see under recent developments below).

(h) Is there more than one mortgage? If so does the question require discussion of priority? —— Yes ——▶ Registration, tacking, and consolidation are important.

(i) Conclusion. It is always important to end any answer, whether an essay or an answer to a problem, with a well constructed conclusion. A good way of doing this is to go back to the question, i.e., read it and pull together your main findings.

Question

In 1983 Shady was granted overdraft facilities with a limit of £4,500 by Easilend Bank. He intended to use the facility to prepare his yacht for the 1984 Round Britain Race. By the end of 1983 the overdraft was approaching £4,000 and Shady agreed to charge his house 'Cuckoo's Nest' as security. It was agreed that the interest rate would vary according to the strength of the US dollar and Shady would pay the bank £100 a month. It was further agreed Shady would take out an assurance policy on his own life for the sum of £5,000 which he has failed to do. Shady failed to make regular payments and has now been badly injured after his yacht foundered off the coast of Cornwall. He is due to receive a prize of £2,000 for winning a small boats race around the Isle of Wight prior to the Round Britain Race. Easilend now wish to obtain an order for possession of 'Cuckoo's Nest' with a view to sale.

Answer

Following the suggested plan, any answer would incorporate the following points:

(a)   Mortgagor: Shady, Mortgagee: Easilend Bank.

(b)   It is a mortgage of a dwelling-house named 'Cuckoo's Nest' for the wording of the question is '[He] agreed to charge his house'. The Administration of Justice Acts 1970 and 1973 may therefore apply.

(c)   A bank is providing the mortgage by way of an overdraft. It is therefore a 'private mortgage' and the Consumer Credit Act 1974 may apply.

At this point it is open to you to show your understanding of the relevance of the Act and make the point that the mortgage may be caught within the financial limit (£15,000) *and* there may be a possibility of an 'extortionate credit bargain' whereupon the court has the power to reopen such an agreement under ss. 137 to 140. *A. Ketley Ltd* v *Scott* [1981] ICR 241, illustrating the risk element, should be mentioned. Considering the facts, however, you may conclude it unlikely that the agreement in question is extortionate.

(d)   The terms of the mortgage are:

(i)   The interest rate to vary with the US dollar.
(ii)   To pay the bank £100 per month.
(iii) To take out an assurance policy on the mortgagor's own life for the sum of £5,000.

(e)   Are the terms unconscionable etc? This requires a general discussion of the protection of the mortgagor's equity of redemption and the competing philosophies of the common law and equity, followed by *specific* examples.

Term (i) indicates that the examiner is looking for an understanding of cases such as *Multiservice Bookbinding Ltd* v *Marden* [1979] Ch 84; *Cityland & Property Holdings Ltd* v *Dabrah* [1968] Ch 166 and *Nationwide Building Society* v *Registry of Friendly Societies* [1983] 1 WLR 1226.

Terms (ii) and (iii) appear not to be unconscionable, not being clogs or fetters or in restraint of trade etc. You should explain clearly that the question of reasonableness does not concern the court.

(f)   Assuming the terms are valid, which seems likely, the mortgagor is nevertheless in breach:

(i)   he has failed to make regular payments, and

(ii)   he has failed to take out the required assurance to cover the overdraft.

The particular remedy sought by the mortgagee in this question is a possession order in respect of Cuckoo's Nest, with a view to sale. As this is a dwelling-house then a discussion of the Administration of Justice Act 1970, s. 36, and particularly s. 8 of the 1973 Act is called for. The differing approach taken in *Habib Bank Ltd* v *Tailor* [1982] 1 WLR 1218 and *Centrax Trustees Ltd* v *Ross* [1979] 2 All ER 952 and more recently in *Bank of Scotland* v *Grimes* [1985] 2 All ER 254 should be fully explored. Remember that in order to exercise its discretion the court must be of the opinion that the mortgagor will be able to repay any arrears in a reasonable time. Here Shady is due to receive a prize of £2,000 for winning the small boats race. You may wish to consider whether that will be sufficient to indicate an ability to repay.

(g)   There is no evidence of undue influence or misrepresentation.

(h)   There is only one mortgage in this question so the issue of priority does not arise.

(i)   *Conclusion.* Finally you should round off your discussion of the problem with a short conclusion, something to the effect that:

It appears that the terms of the agreement between Easilend Bank and Shady are valid in view of the approach taken by the court in the *Cityland* case. The parties here, however, are not of equal bargaining strength and the court may therefore step in to prevent Easilend getting more than a reasonable sum by way of interest. Shady will, however, be able to rely on s. 8 of the Administration of Justice Act 1973 even though the mortgage is by way of overdraft, since the House of Lords in the *Bank of Scotland* case gave a liberal interpretation to that section.

Easilend will consequently find it difficult to obtain a possession order as a prelude to sale of Cuckoo's Nest. If Easilend do obtain such an order, however, they must act in good faith when exercising the power of sale and ensure that they got the best price reasonably obtainable for the property

(*Tse Kwong Lam* v *Wong Chit Sen* [1983] 1 WLR 1349), for they are trustees of the proceeds of sale. Furthermore these proceeds must be employed strictly according to the order laid down in LPA 1925, s. 105.

Recent Developments

In any answer to any examination question you should ensure that you are up to date with recent developments and case law. Often there is more scope to display your knowledge on recent developments in essay-type questions: for example, if the question asked you to discuss the rights of the mortgagor, a good answer would include a discussion of the ambit of the Administration of Justice Act 1970, s. 36, and s. 8 of the 1973 Act as illustrated by recent case law. In particular, *First National Bank plc* v *Syed* [1991] 2 All ER 250 and *Britannia Building Society* v *Earl* [1990] 2 All ER 469 ought to be discussed in depth and the point made that as far as the appellate courts are concerned it now appears that their discretion under the legislation will be exercised but rarely.

Direct your Answer to the Question

You must be very careful that your answer is always directed to the question and does not go off at tangents. For example, if the question asks you to 'discuss remedies available to the mortgagee', then *all* the remedies need to be mentioned, with emphasis placed on the more important ones commonly relied upon, together with their effectiveness. Therefore the limitations on them and relief afforded to mortgagors is relevant. What you must *not* do is merely discuss *one* of the remedies to the exclusion of all the others.

Conversely if you are asked to discuss the right of the mortgagee to possession and sale, confine yourself to those rights and do not go off at tangents on remaining ones.

It helps if you constantly keep referring back to the question and so keep reminding yourself of what the examiner wants.

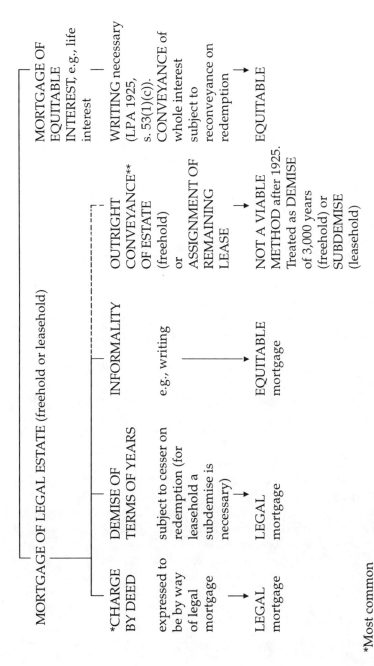

MORTGAGE OF LEGAL ESTATE (freehold or leasehold)

*CHARGE BY DEED

expressed to be by way of legal mortgage

LEGAL mortgage

DEMISE OF TERMS OF YEARS

subject to cesser on redemption (for leasehold a subdemise is necessary)

LEGAL mortgage

INFORMALITY

e.g., writing

EQUITABLE mortgage

OUTRIGHT CONVEYANCE** OF ESTATE (freehold) or ASSIGNMENT OF REMAINING LEASE

NOT A VIABLE METHOD after 1925. Treated as DEMISE of 3,000 years (freehold) or SUBDEMISE (leasehold)

MORTGAGE OF EQUITABLE INTEREST, e.g., life interest

WRITING necessary (LPA 1925, s. 53(1)(c)). CONVEYANCE of whole interest subject to reconveyance on redemption

EQUITABLE

*Most common

**Subject to reconveyance on redemption (freehold) or reassignment (leasehold)

Figure 6.2

REVISION SUMMARIES

1   Creation of Mortgages after the 1925 Legislation

See figure 6.2.

2   Rights of Mortgagor

(a)   **Right to redeem**, i.e., bring the mortgage agreement to an end on repayment of the sum advanced together with the interest due and the mortgagee's proper costs. The mortgagor will also be released from all the conditions of the mortgage. For rights of spouse of mortgagor see Matrimonial Homes Act 1983.

(b)   **Right to enjoyment** of the property.

(c)   **Right to grant leases**. Normally a mortgagor will require the mortgagee's permission to grant leases unless to do so is *expressly* granted in the mortgage deed or otherwise in writing. The mortgagee will usually impose conditions on their consent, in particular requiring the mortgagor to serve a valid notice on the tenant prior to the letting to ensure that the mortgagee can obtain possession should the mortgagor fall into arrears. (See case 11 requirements of the Rent Act 1977 as amended by the Housing Act 1980.)

(d)   **Right to accept surrender of leases** (LPA 1925, s. 100).

(e)   **Right to bring actions** (LPA 1925, s. 98), e.g., aginast trespassers or neighbours causing a nuisance etc.

(f)   **Right to inspect** and make copies of or abstracts from the documents of title (LPA 1925, s. 96).

(g)   *Right to require the mortgagee to transfer the mortgage to a third party* (LPA 1925, s. 95(1)).

3   Common Rights of Legal Mortgagee

(a)   *Rights to investigate the title* offered by a would-be mortgagor before granting a mortgage.

(b)   First mortgagee's *right to retain the title deeds* for the duration of the mortgage (LPA 1925, s. 85(1)). Where the land has registered title the charge certificate is deposited at the land registry.

(c)   *Right*, if in possession, or if a receiver has been appointment, *to grant and accept surrender of leases* on the same terms as could a mortgagor (LPA 1925, ss. 99 and 100).

(d)   *Right to insure the mortgaged property against fire* at the mortgagor's expense (LPA 1925, s. 101).

(e)   *Right to tack* — a way of obtaining priority for a mortgage (see LPA 1925, s. 94(2) as amended).

(f) *Right to consolidate* — one example of equity restricting the mortgagor's right to redeem instead of expanding it! For a really good explanation see Megarry and Wade, *The Law of Real Property,* 6th ed.

(g) *Powers to realise security:*

(i) *Right to sue on the mortgagor's personal covenant.* Subject to the Limitation Act 1980, ss. 5 to 8 (right to recover capital sum barred after 12 years; interest in arrears after six years).

(ii) *Right to take possession* (LPA 1925, s. 94(5)).

(iii) *Right to sell mortgaged property* (LPA 1925, ss. 101 to 103).

(iv) *Right to foreclose,* subject to Limitation Act 1980, ss. 88 and 89(2). This is the most Draconian and a court order is essential. Action is commenced in the High Court Chancery Division.

(v) *Right to appoint a receiver* (LPA 1925, s. 101). The receiver is the agent of the mortgagor although appointed by the mortgagee.

4 Rights of Equitable Mortgagee

(a) *Right to sue* mortgagor for recovery of money due.

(b) *Right to foreclose* (in the same manner as the legal mortgagee, therefore a court order will be necessary).

(c) *Right to sell* mortgaged property. This is available only if the equitable mortgage was made by *deed* (LPA 1925, s. 101).

(d) *Right to appoint a receiver* — again only if the mortgage was made by deed. In other cases a receiver can be appointed by the court.

There is no right to take possession or to collect rents or profits in the absence of an express agreement to this effect in the mortgage.

SUGGESTED ADDITIONAL READING

In addition to the discussion in the general textbooks there are a number of specialist books which may be consulted:

Fisher and Lightwood, *Law of Mortgages,* 10th ed., 1988, updated supplement 1994 (Butterworths).

7   EASEMENTS AND PROFITS À PRENDRE

INTRODUCTION

Easements and profits à prendre are dealt with together in this chapter as this is the way they are dealt with in most textbooks. You would be well advised to study this area of law because no matter whether you are studying land law as part of a law degree or for a professional examination, it is extremely likely that one or both of these topics will appear on the examination paper. Easements provide a most fertile area enabling examiners to set 'interesting' problems aimed at testing students' ability to apply the law they have learned. If you have prepared well such questions should be welcomed as they enable you to show off your skills, and thus high marks can be gained *provided* you answer the question given and do not write 'all you know about easements'.

Unfortunately students tend to get lost in the detailed provisions of the law of easements and as a result cannot organise their answers as well as they might. This is often due to the fact that some students cannot 'see the wood for the trees' — consequently they are unable to organise their material and identify the important landmarks or legal principles. The aim of this chapter is to do just that — to guide you through the labyrinth of the law on easements (this being the more important of the two topics) so that you can confidently identify the important legal principles and use them as landmarks to assist you in tackling questions on easements logically and thoroughly.

TERMINOLOGY

Easement
A right over land for the benefit of other land, such as a right of way, right of storage, right of light.

Profit à prendre
A right to take something from another's land, e.g., right to pasture cattle or take fish or gravel.

Remember that both can only exist as legal interests in land within LPA 1925, s. 1(2), if the interest is:

(a)   held for an interest equivalent to a fee simple absolute in possession or a term of years absolute *and*
(b)   has been created either by deed, will, statute or prescription.

If it is not created by the correct method then an easement can only be equitable. Even if created by deed it will only be equitable if it is for life or in tail. Similarly if an easement is not under seal it cannot create a legal easement but if made for value may create an equitable easement (*May* v *Belleville* [1905] 2 Ch 605). Equitable easements will not bind the whole world, remember, not being rights *in rem*, and will (if title to the land is unregistered) need to be registered as Class D (iii) land charges in order to bind a subsequent purchaser of the legal estate for money or money's worth (Land Charges Act 1972, s. 4, LPA 1925, s. 199).

It is not quite as simple as stated above. The case of *E.R. Ives Investment Ltd* v *High* [1967] 2 QB 379 suggests that there may be two sorts of equitable easement:

(a)   those equitable before 1925, e.g., arising by virtue of estoppel or acquiescence and not created by deed;
(b)   those that could have been legal prior to 1925 but are now equitable by virtue of LPA 1925, s. 1(2), i.e., easements for an interest not equivalent to a fee simple absolute in possession or a term of years absolute.

The case suggests that only the latter are subject to registration as land charges, the former probably remaining subject to the old doctrine of notice (see chapter 3).

To complicate matters, where *title* to the land is registered then any easement should be entered on the property register as a minor interest (see *Celsteel Ltd* v *Alton House Holdings Ltd* [1986] 1 WLR 512). See the interesting article by A.M. Prichard, 'Easements and profits as overriding interests' [1987] Conv 328.

The above points are all too often forgotten by students in the examination. Too many fail even to consider whether the easement in question is legal or equitable and consequently fail to be credited with marks they could easily have gained. Similarly take note of whether the question indicates whether the land has registered or unregistered title.

Dominant and Servient Tenements

This terminology often leads to confusion. At the outset draw yourself a diagram like figure 7.1 and you will realise to what these terms refer.

Dominant tenement
The land which is to benefit from the easement (the right of way shown in figure 7.1) owned by B.

Servient tenement
The land over which the easement is exercised, owned by A.

The terms 'quasi-dominant' and 'quasi-servient' tenement and quasi-easement are sometimes used. This is to distinguish the situation in figure 7.1 from figure 7.2 where both pieces of land are owned by the same person, say A, and A uses the path to the road. Use of this path is, of course, merely use of *his own land* and cannot be classed as an easement. However, if A sells Whiteacre to B then use of the path may pass to B on sale under the rule in *Wheeldon* v *Burrows* (1879) 12 ChD 31 or LPA 1925, s. 62 (discussed later).

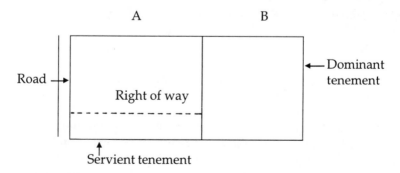

Figure 7.1

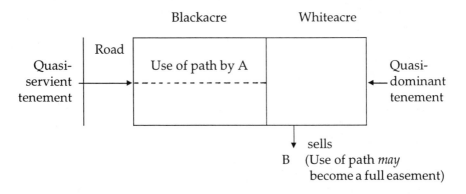

Figure 7.2

As a general rule it is a good idea to get used to drawing diagrams as it helps with problem questions and helps to understand the ways in which an easement can be acquired.

MAIN ISSUES

Questions on the law of easements usually fall into three parts:

    (a)   The characteristics of a valid easement.
    (b)   The means by which an easement may be acquired.
    (c)   Extinguishment of easements.

CHARACTERISTICS OF A VALID EASEMENT

An easement, like any interest in land is said to 'lie in grant', i.e., no right can exist as an easement unless it could have been granted by deed (LPA 1925, s. 51). Consequently the initial approach to an examination question in the form of a problem is to identify the rights claimed and ascertain whether they are rights capable of being treated as easements.

    Points to emphasise in any answer include:

    (a)   While most easements fall within well-known categories, e.g., rights of way or support, the courts are prepared to accept the possibility of new categories emerging.

(b) It is extremely difficult to decide what rights will be accepted as easements, e.g., a right of support is well established as an easement but in *Phipps* v *Pears* [1965] 1 QB 76 the Court of Appeal refused to recognise a right of protection from the weather for one building from another as being an easement. Lord Denning MR took the view that to decide otherwise would be to put an undue restriction on a person's use of his land, even though the required objective could be achieved by a suitably drawn covenant (for a criticism of the decision see (1964) 80 LQR 321).

(c)   What can be said with certainty is that no right will be recognised as an easement unless it satisfies the general characteristics of an easement. In *Miller* v *Emcer Products Ltd* [1956] Ch 304 Romer LJ, in recognising the right to use a neighbour's lavatory as an easement, said:

In my judgment the right had all the requisite characteristics of an easement. There is no doubt as to what where intended to be the dominant and servient tenements respectively, and the right was appurtenant to the former and calculated to enhance its beneficial use and enjoyment.

On this point, examiners would be looking for comments on the effect of the decision in *Re Ellenborough Park* [1956] Ch 131 in which it was held that the right to use an open space in connection with the occupation of a home could exist as an easement. It could, for example, be pointed out that at first sight the decision appears to be contrary to the general rule, outlined above, which does not recognise a right to an open space as capable of existing as an easement. (See the suggestion by Russell LJ in *Dowty Boulton Paul Ltd* v *Wolverhampton Corporation (No. 2)* [1976] Ch 13 to the effect that 'A tendency in the past to freeze the categories of easements has been overtaken by the defrosting operation in *Re Ellenborough Park*'.) However, it must be remembered that Evershed MR in *Re Ellenborough Park* made it clear that there must be sufficient nexus between the dominant and servient tenements, a requirement which the facts of the case satisfied, and that the decision was based upon the use of the park as a communal garden for the residents of the adjoining houses. It could be suggested, therefore, that the decision is not a departure from the general rule at all and should not be extended beyond its facts.

(d)   A final point concerns the question of joint use of the servient tenement. It is generally said that a claim to joint use of land is beyond the scope of an easement, see *Copeland* v *Greenhalf* [1925] Ch 488. However, the case seems inconsistent with other decisions. In *Wright* v *Macadam* [1949] 2 KB 744 the Court of Appeal had held that the right to store coal in a shed was an easement (a decision not cited in *Copeland* v *Greenhalf*) but a possible distinction between the two was suggested by Brightman J in *Grigsby* v *Melville* [1972] 1 WLR 1355 where the issue was whether the defendant had the right to store articles in a cellar beneath the plaintiff's drawing-room floor. Brightman J, rejecting the claim, suggested that a claim to the whole beneficial use of land cannot be an easement but something less than exclusive use may. To enhance an answer requiring the discussion of the possibility of a right amounting to an easement, reference should be made to any articles on the point and any comments in textbooks. For example, enlarging on the possibility of an easement of storage and the cases relating to the problem of joint user of land, mentioned above, you could comment as follows:

Megarry and Wade (p. 840) point to an unreported decision of Megarry V-C in *Newman* v *Jones* (22 March 1982) holding that a right to park cars on the forecourt of a block of flats passed as an easement under LPA 1925, s. 62(2). The Vice-Chancellor said that: 'In view of *Wright* v *Macadam*, which was not cited in *Copeland* v *Greenhalf*, I feel no hesitation in holding that a right for a landowner to park a car anywhere in a defined area nereby is capable of existing as an easement'. D.J. Hayton (1973) 37 Conv (NS) 60, 62 had earlier commented on the issue of a 'defined area' by pointing out that on this basis:

... it would appear, for example, that a right to park a car in a particular defined space amounts to a claim to whole beneficial user of the servient space and so cannot rank as an easement, whilst a right to park a car anywhere in a large area does not amount to a claim to whole beneficial user of any servient area and so can rank as an easement.

For a further discussion on car-parking see the Court of Appeal decision in *London and Blenheim Estates* v *Ladbroke Retail Park* [1994] 1 WLR 31.

ACQUISITION OF EASEMENTS

In addition to the characteristics of an easement, many questions on easements will require a discussion of acquisition. To be a legal interest the easement must be for a term equivalent to a fee simple or term of years absolute and must be created by statute, deed or prescription. If these requirements are not satisfied, there may be an equitable easement or licence. Easements can be acquired by:

(a) Statute.
(b) Express grant or reservation.
(c) Implied grant or reservation.
(d) Estoppel or acquiescence.
(e) Presumed grant (i.e., long user).

Examination questions may be worded generally, requiring a critical analysis of *all* the various methods listed above, or the question may provide you with certain facts and ask you to advise whether or not an easement has been acquired in the circumstances given. To answer the latter you will need first to ascertain that the right exercised has the characteristics of an easement as described at the beginning of this chapter. Then you will need to be able to identify one or more methods of acquisition relevant to the given facts and apply the legal principles to those facts. Be selective in your material. That does not mean that you must limit yourself to discussing one method of acquisition only, however, as there may be more than one possibility. It means only discuss the methods which are relevant to the facts given. For example, if the question mentions 20 years' or more enjoyment of a particular right, your answer will concentrate on the acquisition of an easement by presumed grant. Conversely if the right has not been exercised for 20 years, it will be pointless to describe the method of acquiring an easement by presumed grant. Another method or methods will be relevant. If there is a quasi-easement, for example, then a discussion of both the rule in *Wheeldon* v *Burrows* and the operation of LPA 1925, s. 62, may be called for, especially if there has been a conveyance. In addition if the servient owner led the dominant owner to believe the use could be enjoyed, the principle of estoppel or acquiescence may also be relevant and will need to be brought into the discussion. Read the facts, therefore, and sift through the various methods of acquisition in order to ascertain which are relevant.

The rest of this chapter is aimed at helping you to understand the various methods of acquisition and overcome any problems and pitfalls in applying the legal principles involved.

Statute

The method of acquiring an easement by statute is of limited application and can be dispensed with quickly as it is usually public utilities such as electricity and water boards etc., which are granted easements in this way. It will therefore be abundantly clear in any problem question whether or not this method is relevant.

Express Grant or Reservation

Easements can be created by express grant or reservation under LPA 1925, s. 52, i.e., by deed. Express grant arises where the owner of the servient tenement gives a right over his property to the owner of the dominant tenement. Reservation arises where on a sale of part of his land the vendor retains some right over the part sold (see figure 7.3).

Express grant

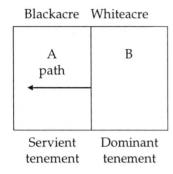

Blackacre   Whiteacre

Servient   Dominant
tenement   tenement

A expressly grants an
easement of a right of
way to B by deed across
Blackacre.

Express reservation

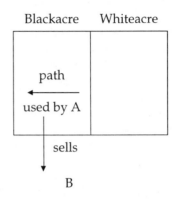

A (original owner of both plots)

Blackacre   Whiteacre

sells

B

A expressly reserves the use of
the way across Blackacre to
himself, by deed, on the sale of
Blackacre to B.

Figure 7.3

In any examination problem it will therefore be necessary to read the question carefully to ascertain whether there has been an express grant or reservation made. If there has then it will be a matter of construction — i.e., construing the words of the deed in order to give an opinion on the *extent* of the easement — for example, if a right of way is granted or reserved is this a right *to walk* across the servient tenement or does it extend to vehicles crossing, and if so what type of vehicle? A point which is often forgotten is that where an easement has been expressly reserved the terms will be construed against the *grantee,* not the grantor as is usual. This is historical and is due to the fact that before LPA 1925, s. 65, simplified the procedure by which an easement could be reserved, this was done by way of a grant of the easement, followed by a regrant. Thus the current grantee was in fact the grantor. (This view was upheld in *St Edmundsbury and Ipswich Diocesan Board of Finance* v *Clark (No. 2)* [1973] 1 WLR 1572, but for a differing view see *Cordell* v *Second Clanfield Properties Ltd* [1969] 2 Ch 9.)

Implied Grant or Reservation

In addition to express grants and reservations, or if there is no evidence of such, in certain circumstances grants and reservations may be implied out of necessity. Grants are more easily implied than reservations on the basis that if a person wishes to retain a right for himself he must do so expressly. A grant is implied either out of necessity or in order to give effect to the parties' common intention, e.g., to have a shared driveway. Reservations are only implied out of necessity on the basis that the land would otherwise be unusable, e.g., when the land would be landlocked without implication of a right of way. Where a reservation is claimed by implication, the issue is one of construction based upon the parties' intentions at the time the grant was made. Reference here can usefully be made to *Nickerson* v *Barraclough* [1981] Ch 426 where the Court of Appeal, in reversing Megarry V-C at first instance, made it clear that reservation is *not* based upon a rule of public policy that land should not be allowed to be made sterile, but upon common intentions of the parties.

Where an implied grant is claimed the rule in *Wheeldon* v *Burrows* (1879) 12 ChD 31 and the operation of LPA 1925, s. 62, are particularly relevant.

The Rule in Wheeldon v Burrows

Wheeldon v *Burrows* (1879) 12 ChD 31 is based upon the rule of non-derogation from grant, i.e., a grantor cannot give with one hand and take away with the other. It is concerned with the extent to which a quasi-easement can be enlarged into a full easement on the grant of part of a piece of land. The rule is:

> On the grant of *part* of a tenement there would pass to the grantee as easements all quasi-easements which were continuous and apparent or were necessary for the reasonable enjoyment of the land granted and were used by the grantor for the benefit of the part granted.

This is an important rule and you should be conversant with it. Its effect can be illustrated and explained by the situation shown in figure 7.4.

When A sells Whiteacre to B, B will, by virtue of the rule in *Wheeldon* v *Burrows*, acquire not only Whiteacre but the right of way across Blackacre as a full easement provided A used the way 'continuously' and its presence was 'apparent'. Continuous = permanent without the necessity for constant use. Apparent = capable of disclosure by useful inspection (see, e.g., *Pyer* v *Carter* (1857) 1 H & N 916, an underground drain into which water ran from the eaves of a house was continuous and apparent; and *Hansford* v *Jago* [1921] 1 Ch 322, a track to the rear of several houses used as a means of access to the highway was also continuous and apparent).

Faced with a question containing facts which give rise to a quasi-easement, therefore, you should be alerted to the possibility that it could be enlarged into a full easement under the rule in *Wheeldon* v *Burrows*.

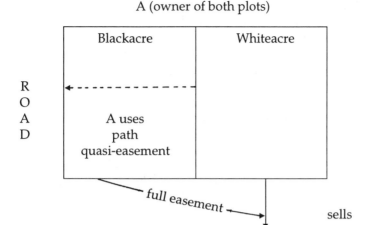

Figure 7.4

Law of Property Act 1925, section 62 (General Words Implied in Conveyances)

LPA 1925, s. 62, applies on a conveyance of land (subject to a contrary intention) and passes all 'liberties, privileges, easements, rights, and advantages whatsoever, appertaining or reputed to appertain to the land or any part thereof, or, at the time of the conveyance, demised, occupied, or enjoyed with, or reputed or known as part or parcel of or appurtenant to the land or any part thereof'.

This section has taken over much of the area formerly governed by the rule in *Wheeldon v Burrows*, but the effect of this so-called 'general words' section is wider in that, subject to contrary intention, not only does it have the effect of passing to any grantee of land the benefit of existing easements, but under certain circumstances has the effect of creating entirely new easements out of many kinds of quasi-easements, rights or privileges etc. existing at the date of the conveyance. For example, in *Wright v Macadam* [1949] 2 KB 744 a right of a tenant to use a shed for storing coal passed under s. 62 on the grant of a new tenancy, Jenkins LJ taking the view that the fact that the use was originally permissive rather than and of right was irrelevant.

The distinction between the rule in *Wheeldon v Burrows* and LPA 1925, s. 62 may be summarised as follows:

Wheeldon v *Burrows*	Section 62
Must be continuous, apparent or reasonably necessary for enjoyment of the land *and* at time of grant used by the grantor for the benefit of the land granted.	Only requirements are that the right must have been enjoyed with the land conveyed (subject to contrary intention).
Conveyance unnecessary.	Conveyance necessary. It does not apply where the dominant owner obtains his interest without a conveyance, as by will or under a contract (e.g., *Borman* v *Griffith* [1930] 1 Ch 493).
Diversity of occupation unnecessary.	Diversity of occupation required (see *Sovmots Investments Ltd* v *Secretary of State for the Environment* [1979] AC 144, criticised in [1978] Conv 449).

Faced with a question where it is clear there has been a conveyance of the dominant tenement, therefore, you should be prepared to discuss the ambit of s. 62 and its limitations. As the requirement that there must have been some diversity of occupation prior to the conveyance often confuses students, the case of *Sovmots Investments Ltd* v *Secretary of State for the Environment* [1979] AC 144 will be dealt with below for in this case the House of Lords considered both the rule in *Wheeldon* v *Burrows* and s. 62.

Sovmots Investments Ltd v *Secretary of State for the Environment*

The Greater London Council let a site to Sovmots Investments Ltd who built a large complex of offices topped by 36 residential maisonettes, known as 'Centre Point'. A compulsory purchase order was made by the London Borough of Camden to acquire the maisonettes. The question was whether certain ancillary rights over and in respect of other parts of the complex, not part of the order, but without which the maisonettes could not be used as housing accommodation, passed on conveyance: namely the right of support from the building below, and the right of passage for water, electricity, gas etc. from below. Lord Wilberforce, after outlining both the rule in *Wheeldon* v *Burrows* and the words of LPA 1925, s. 62, commented first on *Wheeldon* v *Burrows* stating that:

The rule is a rule of intention, based on the proposition that a man may not derogate from his grant. He cannot grant or agree to grant land and at the same time deny to his grantee what is at the time of the grant obviously necessary for its reasonable enjoyment. To apply this to a case where a public authority is taking from an owner his land without his will is to stand the rule on its head.

He continued to explain that, for the rule to apply, there must be actual and apparent use and enjoyment at the time of the grant. But no such use or enjoyment had taken place at all at Centre Point for the maisonettes had never been occupied.

Equally, he explained, s. 62 does not fit the case.

The reason is that when land is under one ownership one cannot speak in any intelligible sense of rights, or privileges, or easements being exercised over one part for the benefit of another. Whatever the owner does, he does as owner and, until a separation occurs, of ownership or at least of occupation, the condition for the exercise of rights, etc., does not exist.

Applying this point to the case, remember the maisonettes had been unoccupied, Lord Wilberforce explained:

A separation of ownership, in a case like the present, will arise on conveyance of one of the parts (e.g., the maisonettes), but this separation cannot be projected back to the stage of the compulsory purchase order so as, by anticipation to bring into existence rights not existing in fact.

For a criticism of the case see for example P. Smith [1978] Conv 449, which poses the question 'What is left after *Sovmots*?'

Acquisition by Presumed Grant (i.e., Long User)

A further area which may be popular with examiners is acquisition by prescription, particularly in professional examinations where knowledge of the Prescription Act 1832 is useful. Prescription can arise either at common law, or under the doctrine of lost modern grant or under the Prescription Act. It must be remembered that the basis of all forms of prescription is *presumed grant* and consequently the following prerequisites must be satisfied:

(a) Use of land as of right (*nec vi, nec clam, nec precario*) without force, without secrecy, without permission.

(b) User in fee simple. Remember a tenant can grant an easement binding on his limited interest in the land, but one tenant cannot obtain an easement by prescription against another tenant holding under the same landlord since it is not available to holders of estates less than fee simple (see Fox LJ in *Simmons* v *Dobson* [1991] 1 WLR 720).

(c)   Continuous user.

When answering a question involving the possibility of long user, it is important to establish these prerequisites at the *outset*. See, for example, *Goldsmith* v *Burrow Construction Co. Ltd* (1987) *The Times*, 31 July 1987, in which it was emphasised that before establishing whether there was an interruption within the meaning of the Prescrition Act 1832, s. 4, it was first necessary to examine the nature of the user and whether but for any interruption it was capable of subsisting as an easement. In this case, although the defendants or their predecessors in title had not given the plaintiffs permission (either expressly or impliedly) to use a pathway, on the evidence there had not been acquiescence in the user by the defendants or their predecessors. Rather, they had tolerated the plaintiffs' user. The fact that the defendants had interfered with the user by locking a gate from time to time for substantial periods demonstrated that the plaintiffs' user could *not have been as of right*. However in *Mills* v *Silver* [1991] Ch 271 Dillon LJ was of the opinion that mere acquiescence or tolerance of user could not prevent the user being 'as of right' since it was not use by permission. It would therefore seem that for the use to be permissive there must be some overt act by the servient owner. In *Mills* v *Silver*, the Court of Appeal restricted prescriptive rights by holding that a prescriptive right does not allow the dominant owner to make improvements which would benefit his own land to the detriment of the servient land. If an improvement goes beyond repair it amounts to trespass on the servient land for which the servient owner has a remedy in damages.

The Law Reform Committee's 14th Report (Cmmd 3100, 1966) criticised the law of prescription as being 'unsatisfactory, uncertain and out of date' and in need of extensive reform. While part of the Committee were in favour of total abolition, there was a suggestion for replacement by a 12-year period of user (in line with the requirement for adverse possession), a suggestion which may come into force in the light of present proposals regarding covenants.

Faced with a question showing 20 or more years user of a right, you should be alerted to the probability of an easement being acquired by this method. When tackling such a question, remember that there are three methods of acquiring an easement by prescription:

(a)   Prescription at common law.
(b)   Prescription under the doctrine of lost modern grant.
(c)   Prescription under the Prescription Act 1832.

Remember:

(a)   A claimant may establish his claim by any one or more of these methods.
(b)   The difference between them lies in the *period* of enjoyment which must be shown to establish a claim.

(c)   To establish an easement by long user at common law it must be shown that the right has been exercised continuously since 1189 (time immemorial). Although the courts adopt a working rule of 20 years or more, or use as far back as living memory, remember it can be defeated by showing that the right could not have existed in 1189.

(d)   Acquisition by the doctrine of the lost modern grant, i.e., the fiction that there was a grant of an easement made at some time and this has been lost. Once again, 20 years' user is generally sufficient, but a claim can be defeated by showing that there was no one capable of making a grant during the relevant period (e.g., *Neaverson* v *Peterborough Rural District Council* [1902] 1 Ch 557).

(e)   The most common method is to rely on the Prescription Act 1832 which lays down two statutory periods of 20 and 40 years and divides easements into general easements and easements of light.

Section 2 of the Prescription Act 1832 deals with general easements and the problem of the inability to show user since time immemorial. It provides that a period of 20 years' use as of right and without interruption cannot be defeated by proof that use began after 1189, though it can be defeated by the existence of oral or written consent. Forty years' use is 'absolute and indefeasible' unless enjoyed with written consent (by s. 1 the respective periods for profits are 30 and 60 years).

It must be noted that, under the Act, a period of use does not create any right until an action is brought questioning the right, e.g., until an alleged right of way is obstructed. The period of use must continue up to the time of action (s. 4) so that a long period of use, in itself, is of no assistance, e.g., a claim beginning in 1960 is of no assistance if it ceased in 1981.

The alleged use must be 'without interruption' which has a special meaning under the Act. Where a right is obstructed a successful action can still be brought provided there has not been acquiescence for one year after the obstruction and the person responsible for it was known (s. 4). The question of acquiescence is one of fact (e.g., see *Davies* v *Du Paver* [1953] 1 QB 184 per Morris LJ where it was held that the erection of a fence did not amount to an interruption because it had been objected to — this despite the fact that after the initial protest the claimant was silent).

Bear in mind the effect of the meaning of an interruption within the Act, discussed above. It enables a claimant who has enjoyed a right continuously for 19 years and 1 day before some act of interference is encountered still to succeed in claiming an easement provided legal proceedings are commenced on *the first day of the twenty-first year*. The reason being that on this day the claimant can show 20 years' user immediately before the action is brought and the interference will not amount to an interruption at law since it is *one day less* than a year. A claim commenced on the following day will be too late.

If a claim is commenced earlier, the claimant cannot show 20 years' user. This has led to the maxim '19 years and a day is as good as 20 years'. A maxim which is sometimes quoted by examiners for discussion, especially in professional external examinations.

Easements of Light

Should an examination question require consideration of whether an easement of light has been acquired, two issues will have to be dealt with:

(a) Are the requirements of the Prescription Act 1832, s. 3, met?
(b) How much light has been acquired?

Taking them in turn, under the Prescription Act 1832, s. 3, 20 years' enjoyment of *access to light* to a home, workshop or other building, without interruption makes the right absolute and indefeasable unless enjoyed with written consent or agreement. Note:

(a) Only one period is mentioned, i.e., 20 years.
(b) Access to light is all that is required. There is no need for the light to be enjoyed as of right (*Colls* v *Home & Colonial Stores Ltd* [1904] AC 179).
(c) Only access to light to a building can be acquired as an easement.
(d) The enjoyment must be without interruption.

Whilst the same principles regarding an interruption apply to both general easements and easements of light, as described above, there are special provisions specific to light which must not be forgotten, namely those contained in the Rights of Light Act 1959. Section 2 of that Act enables a servient owner to register a 'light obstruction notice' as a local land charge. This notice obviates the need for an actual physical obstruction. By s. 3, such a notice is deemed to amount to an obstruction of access of light as if the obstruction had been both known to and acquiesced in by all concerned.

Consequently, the notice must identify the servient land, the dominant building and the size of the obstruction to which the notice is intended to be equivalent. It remains in force for one year unless it is cancelled or it expires. While in force, the dominant owner may sue for a declaration claiming cancellation or variation of the obstruction.

How Much Light has been Acquired?

Several recent cases have dwelt on this question. A leading case is *Allen* v *Greenwood* [1979] 1 All ER 819 (discussed in [1984] Conv 408 by A.H. Hudson) which suggests that the amount of light which can be acquired by prescription is measured according to the nature of the building and the purpose for which the building is normally used. In this case, after a greenhouse had been in use as an ordinary domestic greenhouse for more than 20 years, the defendants erected a fence on their adjoining property. This left sufficient light in the greenhouse for working in it, but insufficient light for growing plants (tomatoes etc.). The plaintiffs sought injunctions to restrain the defendants from causing a nuisance by diminution of the greenhouse's access to light. The Court of Appeal, in granting the injunction, held that the light required for the normal use of a greenhouse is 'ordinary' but that a right to a specifically high degree of light may also be acquired by prescription. A similar view was taken in the case of *Carr-Saunders* v *Dick McNeil Associates Ltd* [1986] 2 All ER 888 in which it was stated that the question is not how much light has been taken but how much is left. The amount left must be sufficient to leave the premises adequately lit for ordinary purposes for which they might reasonably be expected to be used.

SPECIMEN EXAMINATION QUESTION

Guidelines to Answering a Problem

(a)   Identify the properties concerned and the parties by drawing a diagram illustrating the facts given.

(b)   Ascertain whether the right claimed has the characteristics of an easement.

(c)   If it has the necessary characteristics, consider by what method or methods the easement can be acquired.

(d)   Having decided on the possible methods, comment on whether the easement acquired will be legal or equitable.

(e)   If relevant, consider possible remedies if the easement acquired has been infringed.

Question

Edwin is the registered proprietor of the fee simple estate in Whiteacre. In 1970 Edwin gave Fred, the owner of the neighbouring property, Blackacre, permission to park Fred's car in Edwin's garage during the bad weather. In 1973 Fred started to use Edwin's garage all the time. In 1990 Edwin allowed Gertrude to live in a cottage on Whiteacre and whilst living there Gertrude, rather than use the direct access to the cottage from the road, used a short cut across Whiteacre. In 1991 Edwin granted Gertrude a lease of the cottage for seven years.

Earlier this year Fred sold Blackacre to Harold and, despite Harold's objections, Edwin has not allowed him to park his car in the garage. Edwin has also told Gertrude to stop using the short cut.

Advise:

(a) Harold whether he can insist on parking his car in Edwin's garage, *and*
(b) Gertrude whether she can continue to use the short cut.

Commentary

In questions concerning easements it is essential to identify the respective properties and parties as stated in the guidelines mentioned above. You could therefore at the outset of your answer draw a sketch of various transactions as in figure 7.5.

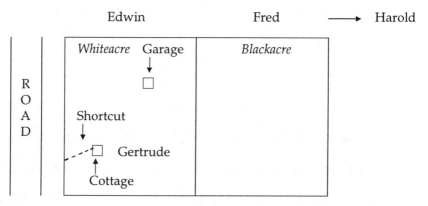

Figure 7.5

In this particular question you are asked to advise both Harold and Gertrude. It would be convenient to deal with them separately and consider whether the respective rights claimed have the characteristics of easements and the means by which they may have been acquired. You could then conclude your answer by considering the potential remedies available to Harold and Gertrude.

(a) Harold

Harold is a successor in title of Fred so that it may be necessary to consider whether the use of the garage has passed to him. This may depend upon whether the right claimed is legal or equitable.

We must first consider whether the use of the garage has the characteristics of an easement laid down in *Re Ellenborough Park*. There are dominant and servient tenements, i.e., Blackacre and Whiteacre, which are adjacent to each other and in separate ownership and possession (Harold and Edwin). The major difficulties for Harold are whether a right to use a garage is within the general nature of easements and, if so, whether the use of the garage amounts to a claim to exclusive possession which is outside the scope of an easement (*Copeland* v *Greenhalf*). You could begin your discussion by making the general point that the categories of easements are never closed and the courts will recognise new kinds of easements providing they fall within the general nature of an existing easement (*Miller* v *Emcer Products Ltd*). The courts have accepted that a right of storage can amount to an easement and this has been extended to car parking spaces in *Newman* v *Jones* and *London and Blenheim Estates* v *Ladbroke Retail Park*. You could therefore argue by analogy that the use of a garage amounts to storage for car parking purposes.

If Harold can establish that the use of the garage is within the nature of an easement, he may have difficulty with regard to the exclusive use. We are told that Fred's use was originally only in bad weather but that Fred had used the garage all the time since 1973. If, therefore, Edwin is excluded from using the garage then Harold's claim would be beyond the scope of an easement as was the case in *Copeland* v *Greenhalf*. In addition the *Ladbrooke* case seemed to indicate that a right to car parking would only be considered an easement where there was a general right to park not a right to a specific space.

Although it seems that there would be a difficulty for Harold establishing the right as an easement, you should still consider the means by which a right could be acquired. Clearly acquisitions by statute is unapplicable here and we are not told of any express grant by deed. In this particular question you should consider implied acquisition or possibly estoppel. The use of the garage is not essential for Harold's enjoyment of Blackacre so that an easement of necessity need not be discussed. Harold may argue acquisition under the rule in *Wheeldon* v *Burrows*, LPA 1925, s. 62 or prescription.

Under *Wheeldon* v *Burrows* it must be shown that there was a quasi-easement which was continuous and apparent or reasonably necessary for the enjoyment of the dominant land. If Edwin had a car and had used the garage then it could be argued that there was a quasi-easement. Continuous means regular, not incessant, use but in the facts we have no evidence of this. Apparent means that the use must be indicated by careful inspection of the land which may be a problem here for Harold. Having a garage to park a car may be beneficial to the individual car owner but it is difficult to say that it is reasonably necessary for the enjoyment of the land.

You would therefore conclude that a claim under *Wheeldon* v *Burrows* is unlikely to succeed and you would therefore consider LPA 1925, s. 62. Under this section all rights, easements and privileges appertaining, or reputed to be appertaining to land, will pass in a conveyance unless a contrary intention appears in the deed. We are told that Fred sold Blackacre to Harold so we may assume there was a conveyance and we are not told of any contrary intention in the deed. You should therefore consider whether the right to use the garage was appertaining to the land. In *Wright* v *Macadam* it was held that a right to use a coal shed passed under s. 62 even though the use was originally permissive. We are told that Fred was originally given permission to use the garage by Edwin so that Harold could argue that s. 62 is applicable here. In considering s. 62 you should also bear in mind the House of Lords decision in *Sovmots Investments Ltd* v *Secretary of State for the Environment* where it was said that s. 62 is only applicable where there was a diversity of ownership and possession prior to the conveyance, which is satisfied here.

The final means of implied acquisition is by prescription either at common law, lost modern grant or the Prescription Act 1832. All three methods are dependent upon a period of continuous long use — a minimum of two years — which would appear to be satisfied here. Prescription cannot be relied upon unless it was shown that the use was as of right, i.e., without the use of force, without secrecy and without needing to seek permission. The facts show that Fred was given permission to use the garage in 1970 which may exclude prescription. However, the original use was restricted to periods of bad weather, whereas since 1973 the garage has been used all the time. Harold may try and argue that permission was not sought for this extended use and the prescription period could run from 1973. Edwin could clearly defeat a claim at common law by showing that the garage did not exist at some point between now and 1189. Harold may be more successful by claiming under lost modern grant or the Prescription Act but if using the latter Harold must show that there has been no interruption for more than a year.

(b) Gertrude

Again you would need to look at the characteristics and means of acquisition but we can deal with them more briefly than in Harold's case.

Once again there is a dominant and servient tenement — Whiteacre and Gertrude's cottage. A short cut as a right of way would fall within the general nature of an easement. However, it could be argued that the short cut is more of a personal benefit to Gertrude then being of benefit to the cottage, but this is unlikely.

The main points for discussion as regards Gertrude relate to acquisition. Again statute does not apply and we are not told of any deed of grant. Since Gertrude has only used the short cut since 1990, she cannot claim a right acquired by prescription. You should therefore consider the possibility of the right arising under *Wheeldon* v *Burrows* or LPA 1925, s. 62. There is a direct access to the cottage from the road so the right would not arise out of necessity.

With regard to *Wheeldon* v *Burrows*, we are not told whether Edwin ever occupied the cottage or used the short cut, so it may be difficult for Gertrude to show a quasi-easement. For a right of way to be apparent there must be some indication of a path, e.g., a worn track in *Hansford* v *Jago*. The facts of the question give no guidance as to whether any path exists. If the short cut was frequently used before Gertrude occupied the cottage it may be that there is some sort of path or track.

To advise Gertrude with regard to s. 62 you will need to consider whether there has been a conveyance. Although Gertrude was originally allowed to use the cottage, she was granted a seven year lease in 1991. In order to create a legal estate the lease would need to be by deed (LPA 1925, s. 52) but we are not told whether Edwin executed a deed in Gertrude's favour. However, the facts state that Edwin granted a lease which would seem to indicate a deed was entered into. A lease by deed is a conveyance within LPA 1925, s. 205 so that s. 62 would be satisfied on this point. Assuming the lease was by deed, the facts would seem to fall within the ambit of *Wright* v *Macadam* so that Gertrude could claim an easement to use the short cut.

Alternatively, Gertrude could argue that Edwin's acquiescence in allowing her to use the short cut from 1990 would amount to estoppel — for the principles see the dicta of Lord Scarman in *Crabb* v *Arun District Council* [1976] Ch 179. However, it should be remembered that estoppel would create an equitable, not a legal, easement.

Remedies
In examinations you are rarely given the information or the time to discuss remedies fully. For the sake of completeness you would indicate that if easements were established possible remedies would be abatement, injunction or damages with a note of their effects.

REVISION SUMMARIES

1 Modes in which Easements may be Extinguished

(a) Statute, e.g, Commons Registration Act 1965.

(b) Unity of seisin, i.e., where the dominant and servient tenement pass into possession and ownership of one and the same person, provided that the tenements are held in the same capacity (*White* v *Taylor* [1969] 1 Ch 150).

(c) Express or implied release.

(i) Express release needs a deed at common law, but in equity an informal release may be upheld.

(ii) Implied release. Although nonuser or demolition of a building which enjoys an easement does not imply a release they are evidence from which it can be inferred that the dominant owner has the necessary intention to release (see *Tehidy Minerals Ltd* v *Norman* [1971] QB 528).

However, see *Benn* v *Hardinge* (1992) *The Times*, 13 October 1992 where it was stated that there must be a clear intention to abandon. In that case non-user for 175 years was not sufficient to show abandonment on the facts.

2 Remedies for Infringement of Easements

(a) Injunction.
(b) Damages or declaration.
(c) Abatement using reasonable force.
(d) Right of access — access order. The Access to Neighbouring Land Act 1992, which came into force in January 1993, allows a landowner to apply to court for an 'access order' to adjoining land, e.g., to enable work to be carried out in accordance with an easement, but which can only be done by entering the servient land. Such an order is *not* an overriding interest and must be protected (where the land has registered title) be way of notice or caution, see Access to Neighbouring Land Act 1992, s. 5.

SUGGESTED ADDITIONAL READING

In addition to the general texts, there are two leading specialist works:

Gale, *The Law of Easements*, 15th ed., 1986 (Sweet & Maxwell).
Jackson, *Law of Easements and Profits*, 1978 (Butterworths).

8   RESTRICTIVE COVENANTS

INTRODUCTION

> All law students find some areas of law incomprehensible, and as a rule become lawyers without being informed by their lecturers that this incomprehension is a result of the woeful state of the law and not the students' intellect. The body of doctrine known as 'restrictive covenants' seems to be one of these areas. (Phillip Kenny (1983) 80 LS Gaz 2494.)

The body of law relating to restrictive covenants is complex and 'in a woeful state'. Despite this, students should not be depressed. On the contrary this is an area commonly encountered in practice and it is worth spending the time coming to grips with it. The majority of examination papers will contain a question on this topic for that reason. Furthermore it is an area, similar to easements, where it is possible to gain high marks and even enjoy doing so. Preparing for and answering a question on covenants are akin to playing a game of chess:

(a)   Learn the existing rules.

(b)   Prepare a 'battle plan', i.e., design a logical plan to cover all contingencies so that the rules can be applied in any situation.

(c)   Once (a) and (b) are mastered, *then* further develop your understanding of the interrelationship between case law and statute, so important in this field, by reading the standard texts and various articles.

The object of this chapter will be to help you to feel confident with all those issues.

TERMINOLOGY

Once again the first hurdle is terminology.

A covenant is a promise under seal by which A (covenantor) promises B (covenantee) that he will perform a certain duty. This duty may be of a *positive* nature, e.g., to maintain fences, to clean a ditch etc., or of a *negative* (or *restrictive*) nature, e.g., not to construct more than x houses on a plot of land, to restrict the use of the land to residential use only, not to keep more than one dog etc.

This promise (or indeed sometimes mutual promises) is contained in a deed under seal, usually in a conveyance, or lease, often on sale of part of a piece of freehold land. For instance the vendor may wish to regulate the purchaser's use of that land (the *servient* land) for the benefit of the part retained (the *dominant* land). This is illustrated in figure 8.1, which shows B, the original owner of Blackacre, having sold part (plot 1) to A, retaining plot 2. A covenants with B not to build more than one house on plot 1.

This terminology is very simple yet it is amazing how many students still make careless errors. When this happens, students are often completely thrown off the correct path and their answers become confused and muddled. So the message is: 'Get the terminology correct. It will save you time and help make your way clear'.

MAIN ISSUES

Although the law relating to covenants is complex it can be split into three main areas, all possible examination areas. These are:

(a)   Enforceability of the covenant.
(b)   Modification and discharge.
(c)   Reform, especially since the January 1984 Law Commission Report No. 127 on positive and negative covenants and the Condominium Law Working Group's report on freehold flats and ownership (1987: Cm 179).

The aim of the rest of this chapter is to consider these three areas, especially enforceability which is probably the most important — it is difficult to envisage any examination question not requiring a detailed understanding of this area. In addition to standard texts, you should consult Phillip Kenny's excellent article 'Restrictive covenants — the state of the art', (1983) 80 LS Gaz 2494.

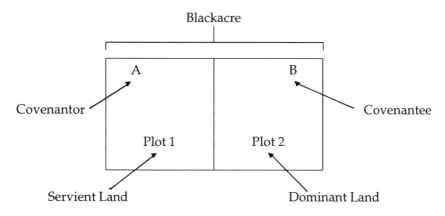

Figure 8.1

ENFORCEABILITY

As a first step in deciding whether the dominant owner can enforce a covenant (be it positive or restrictive) against the servient owner, consider the *relationship* between the parties. Whether the land concerned is freehold or leasehold the fundamental question is: Is there *privity of contract*? In other words, are the parties involved the *original* covenantor and *original* covenantee? Is B (original covenantee) trying to enforce the covenant against A (original covenantor)? For remember, as between the original parties, any covenant will be enforceable under the law of contract even if the covenantor has parted with his land *unless*:

(a) the covenant is against public policy as being in restraint of trade, as in *Esso Petroleum Co. Ltd* v *Harper's Garage (Stourport) Ltd* [1968] AC 269 per Lord Hodson; or

(b) the deed containing the covenant expressly limits the covenantor's liability to his period of ownership and he no longer retains ownership of the land.

A third party, i.e., a successor in title to either A or B will, of course, not be able to enforce under this doctrine. Where a third party is involved, therefore, you must look to further doctrines (described below).

If the land is *leasehold* then the next question to ask is: Is there *privity of estate*? This means that there is tenure between the parties, i.e., that the relationship of landlord and tenant exists between them (*Manchester Brewery Co.* v *Coombs* [1901] 2 Ch 608 at 614). For example, if landlord L grants a lease to tenant T for 20 years and then T assigns it to A after only five years the position is as shown in figure 8.2. T will still remain personally liable to L for any breach of covenant by A by reason that there is privity of contract between T and L. There is privity of estate, however, between L and A, and L may prefer to sue A for the breach (*Spencer's Case* (1583) 5 Co Rep 16a).

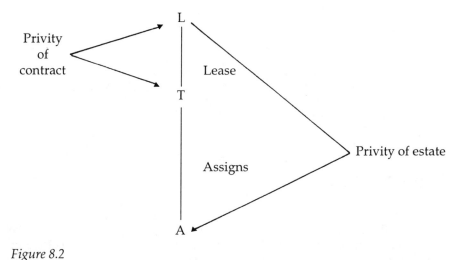

Figure 8.2

The following points should be remembered:

(a)   Although two different persons are liable for one breach of covenant, T by privity of contract and A by privity of estate, these are *alternative* liabilities and the landlord may only gain satisfaction from one.

(b)   Similar principles apply where L assigns the reversion of the lease to X (see figure 8.3). L will remain liable on the covenants for the whole term by reason of LPA 1925, s. 141 (benefit) and s. 142 (burden).

(c)   To be enforceable under this doctrine, i.e., the doctrine of estate, the covenant must 'touch and concern the land', or, as stated in LPA 1925, ss. 141 and 142, have 'reference to the subject-matter' of the lease. There is no definition of the meaning of these phrases. Generally a good guide is that the covenant must affect the value of the land and not be merely of a personal nature. A considerable list of examples is provided in Megarry and Wade, *The Law of Real Property* (in the 5th edition these are at p. 744 — see now 6th ed.).

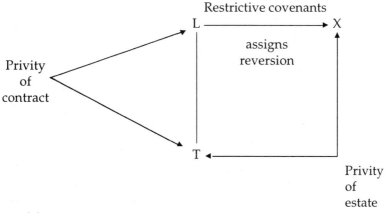

Figure 8.3

If the land is *freehold* and there is no privity of contract then the liability of the servient owner to observe a covenant depends on strict rules laid down by common law and in equity. Any examination question will require a detailed understanding of these rules and an ability to apply them. The examiner will expect the student to be aware, not only that the common law and equitable rules differ concerning covenants, but also that there are different rules on the *running of the benefit* of the covenant to the covenantee's successors in title enabling a successor to sue for breach of the covenant, and on the *running of the burden* of the covenant, i.e., the passing of the burden of the covenant to the covenantor's successors in title, enabling a successor to be held liable for any breach. This is illustrated in figure 8.4.

Before C can initiate action against D for breach of covenant, the *benefit* of the covenant must have passed to C and the *burden* must have passed to D.

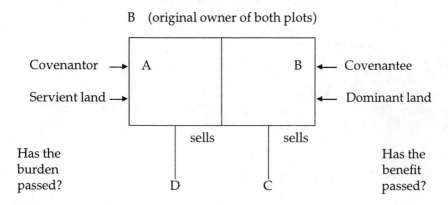

Figure 8.4

Rules on Passing the Burden

At common law, the burden of a covenant will *not* pass. Authority for this is to be found in the case of *Austerberry* v *Oldham Corporation* (1885) 29 ChD 750 in which the Court of Appeal held, by way of opinion, that the burden of a covenant never runs with the land at law except between landlord and tenant. There are indirect devices which can be utilised (see later), none of them, in the opinion of the Law Commission, providing an effective general solution.

In equity, only the burden of *restrictive* covenants may pass (*Tulk* v *Moxhay* (1848) 2 Ph 774). Lord Templeman reaffirmed this rule in the recent House of Lords case *Rhone* v *Stephens* [1994] 2 All ER 65. The facts were as follows. In 1960 the freehold owner of Walford House sold part of the property which became known as Walford Cottage. The conveyance contained the following positive covenant:

> the vendor covenants for himself and successors in title to maintain to the reasonable satisfaction of the purchaser and their successors in title such part of the roof of Walford House aforesaid as lies above the property conveyed in wind and watertight condition.

Since 1960 both properties had been sold more than once and on each occasion the covenant had been expressly assigned. In 1984 when severe leaks developed in the roof of Walford House the issue arose as to whether the burden of the covenant had run with the land. The House of Lords affirmed the rule in *Tulk* v *Moxhay* that only restrictive covenants can run and that the rule of privity of contract is not affected by LPA 1925, s. 79. An example is shown in figure 8.5, A covenants with B to maintain a ditch between plots 1 and 2 and not to erect any buildings on plot 1 other than one dwelling-house. A sells plot 1 to D. Can B enforce the covenant against D? This will depend upon whether the burden has passed to D. The positive element of the covenant (i.e., to maintain the ditch) will be unenforceable, whereas the restrictive element may be enforceable.

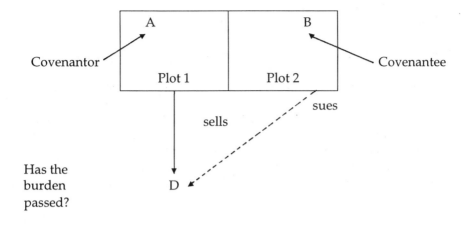

Figure 8.5

Points to Remember

(a)   Where a covenant such as the one in the example above contains both positive and restrictive elements, the positive element may be *severed*, leaving the restrictive element to be enforced (*Shepherd Homes Ltd* v *Sandham (No. 2)* [1971] 1 WLR 1062).

(b)   The test of a restrictive covenant is a test of substance, and is not related to the phrasing of the covenant. For example:

(i)   a covenant 'not to allow the property to fall into disrepair' is in substance a positive covenant as it implies the need to maintain; whereas

(ii)   a covenant 'to use the premises for residential purposes only' is in substance a restrictive covenant implying that it may not be used for any other purpose.

(c)   D will not be liable if the covenant is worded such that it is intended to bind the original covenantor only and *not* his successors in title. As Pennycuick J put it in *Re Royal Victoria Pavilion, Ramsgate* [1961] Ch 581: 'A deed which is obviously personal on the face of it is not to be construed as passing the burden to the covenantor's successors in title'.

In the absence of any express intention to the contrary, LPA 1925, s. 79, presumes the covenant was made on behalf of the covenantor, his successors in title and persons deriving title under him or them.

Indirect Devices to Enable the Burden of Positive Covenants to Pass at Common Law

As only the burden of a restrictive covenant may pass and only then in equity, it is worth remembering that there are several indirect devices enabling the burden of positive covenants to pass at law. Students often forget these, and, whilst it is the opinion of the Law Commission in its recent report that they do not provide a generally satisfactory solution, you may gain extra marks if you have considered one or all of them where it is relevant to do so, i.e., where the question of the passing of a positive covenant is involved.

Detailed descriptions of these devices are contained in the major texts, see especially Megarry and Wade, *The Law of Real Property*, 6th ed. The two main methods are:

(a) A chain of indemnity covenants.
(b) The benefit and burden principle.

You may find the following comments helpful:

(a) A chain of indemnity covenants is weakened in practice by the death or disappearance of the original covenantor or the interruption of the chain. The only remedy available is damages, whereas what is usually required is an injunction.

(b) The principle of benefit and burden, namely, that a person who wishes to take advantage of a continuing service or facility (the benefit) must accept the continuing burden that goes with it, is discussed along with the relevant cases of *Halsall* v *Brizell* [1957] Ch 169 and *Tito* v *Waddell (No. 2)* [1977] Ch 106 by E.P. Aughterson [1985] Conv 12 and more recently by J. Snape (1994) *Gazette* 91/23 at p. 22. You will find these helpful additional reading as the two aspects of the principle are discussed: the pure principle and the conditional benefits principle (the former being disapproved by the House of Lords in the recent case of *Rhone* v *Stephens* [1994] 2 All ER 65).

Rules Relating to Passing of Benefit at Common Law

There is no problem at common law regarding the passing of the benefit. Providing the following conditions are satisfied the benefit will run with the land:

(a) The covenant must touch and concern the land.
(b) The covenant must have been entered into with the owner of the legal estate. After 1925 the person seeking to enforce the covenant need not, however, have the same estate as the original covenantee (*Smith and Snipes Hall Farm Ltd* v *River Douglas Catchment Board* [1949] 2 KB 500).

(c)   There must be an intention that the benefit will run with the land. Since 1925 this is presumed as a result of LPA 1925, s. 78, which states that 'A covenant … shall be deemed to be made with the covenantee and his successors in title and the persons deriving title under him or them, and shall have effect as if such successors and others were expressed'.

Consider the situation shown in figure 8.6. B sells part of his land, plot 1, to A who enters into a covenant with B. B sells plot 2 to C. Can C enforce the covenant against A? This depends on whether the benefit has passed to C. Provided it complies with the criteria outlined above, the answer is yes, it will pass to C at common law enabling him to sue A.

Rules Relating to Passing of Benefit in Equity

The benefit of a covenant may also pass in equity. You must consider these equitable rules particularly where the servient land (plot 1 in figure 8.6) has been sold, so that the passing of the *burden* of the covenant depends upon the equitable doctrine laid down in *Tulk v Moxhay* (1848) 2 Ph 744, as in figure 8.7.
   Equity permits the benefit to pass to successors in title in three ways. You should know these methods and when they apply:

(a)   *By annexation* which can be:

   (i)   express,
   (ii)   implied from circumstances,
   (iii)   as a result of LPA 1925, s. 78 (sometimes referred to as statutory annexation).

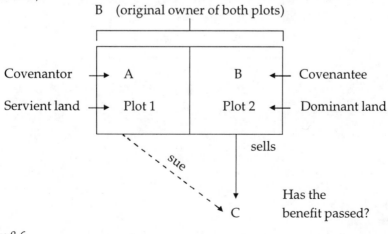

B   (original owner of both plots)

| Covenantor | A | B | Covenantee |
| Servient land | Plot 1 | Plot 2 | Dominant land |

sue

sells

Has the benefit passed?

C

Figure 8.6

(b) *By assignment:*

   (i)   express,

   (ii) as a result of LPA 1925, s. 62.

(c) *By a scheme of development.*

Detailed discussion of these methods is available in the standard texts. It is therefore intended only to point out some important features of each to enable you to recognise them.

Express Annexation

The main point to remember is that express annexation confers the benefit of the covenant upon the *land* and not persons, i.e., the right to sue for breach, or indeed to prevent a breach of the covenant attaching itself to the land thereby resembling an 'incumbrance' such as an easement.

Whether this 'right' attaches itself in this way will depend upon the wording of the deed of covenant. An example would be: 'with intent that the covenant may enure to the benefit of the vendors, their successors and assigns and others claiming under them *to all or any of their lands adjoining'* (*Rogers* v *Hosegood* [1900] 2 Ch 388). The emphasised words refer to the *land* to be benefited, i.e., the dominant land. This is essential. Wording which omits any reference to the land, such as a covenant 'with the vendors, their successors and assigns', would be inadequate. Similarly, wording to the effect that the covenant be made for the benefit of a particularly large estate, such as 'for the benefit of the Chickwickbury estate' (of about 690 hectares) would be inadequate (*Re Ballard's Conveyance* [1937] Ch 473) because, despite the fact that the land has been identified, it is unrealistic to expect the whole of it to be benefited by the covenant. Consequently it is usual to add the words 'or any part thereof' when identifying the land, although not strictly necessary for it can be inferred from circumstances.

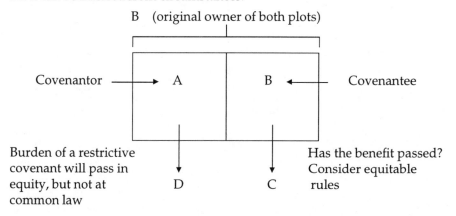

Figure 8.7

Implied Annexation

In the absence of express annexation a covenant will be impliedly annexed where to ignore it would not only be an injustice but a departure from common sense (*Marten* v *Flight Refuelling Ltd* [1962] Ch 115 at p. 133) e.g., a covenant 'not to let down the surface of overlying land'. See also *Shropshire County Council* v *Edwards* (1982) 46 P & CR 270.

Statutory Annexation

Here we have a dramatic development in the area of restrictive covenants. Dramatic because of the way in which the courts have begun to interpret the dormant 'word-saving' provisions of LPA 1925, in particular s. 78.

Many articles have been written on this interesting area and examiners will be looking to see whether students, particularly undergraduates, have read around this area and are able to comment on it and even provide constructive criticism and/or informed opinion. They should be aware of the differing views of various academic writers. See, for example, D.J. Hurst, 'The transmission of restrictive covenants' (1982) 2 Legal Stud 53; David Hayton, 'Revolution in restrictive covenants law?' (1980) 43 MLR 445; G.H. Newsom, 'Universal annexation?' (1981) 97 LQR 32 and 'Universal annexation? A postscript' (1982) 98 LQR 202; and P.N. Todd, 'Annexation after *Federated Homes*' [1985] Conv 177.

The leading cases are *Federated Homes Ltd* v *Mill Lodge Properties Ltd* [1980] 1 WLR 594 and *Roake* v *Chadha* [1983] 3 All ER 503.

In an examination, time is of the essence. In most cases you only have about 35 minutes to supply an answer. Consequently, unless the question specifically requires the facts of these cases it would be a waste of time to reproduce them, especially as they are quite complex. However, you should make sure that you have read these cases in full, not just the headnote. An examiner will not only be looking for the decisions in these cases, which are regarded as fundamentally important but also for the reasons behind these decisions and informed comment. For example, you may explain that s. 78 was never regarded as anything but a 'word-saving' provision, operating only to pass the benefit of a covenant when a valid express or implied annexation had *already* been established by the methods described above. The section merely rendered it unnecessary to name the covenantee's successor in title. However, the Court of Appeal in *Federated Homes Ltd* v *Mill Lodge Properties Ltd* took a different view, deciding that the effect of s. 78 was to annex the covenant to the land *automatically*, providing it was intended to benefit the land in question. A narrower view was taken in *Roake* v *Chadha*, the High Court emphasising that for s. 78 to operate there must be an intention that the covenant will run with the land. In that case it was expressly stated that 'this covenant shall not enure for the benefit of any owner or subsequent purchaser unless the benefit of this covenant has been expressly assigned'. It had *not* been expressly assigned and so clearly there was no intention that the covenant should run; unlike the *Federated Homes* case which was silent on the question of intention, enabling such intention to be inferred from the facts.

Time permitting, you could draw the examiner's attention to the courts in which these cases were decided, namely the Court of Appeal and High Court, Chancery Division, respectively, and then pose the question, 'Will these decisions be followed?', or 'Is it likely that the House of Lords will at some future date overrule the *Federated Homes* decision?' Certainly you ought to point out that the issues raised by the Court of Appeal are 'live issues', which have yet to be finally settled. If the case is followed, albeit restricted to some extent by *Roake* v *Chadha*, some writers believe that the law on covenants will have been revolutionised and the common law and equitable rules concerning the passing of the benefit will be swept away. Note, however, that *Federated Homes Ltd* v *Mill Lodge Properties Ltd* will not apply to pre-1926 covenants (see per Morritt J in *J. Sainsbury plc* v *Enfield London Borough Council* [1989] 1 WLR 590).

Express Assignment

The difference between annexation and assignment is that express assignment confers the benefit of a covenant on *persons*, unlike annexation which attaches the covenant to the land.

Whereas, once a covenant is annexed to the dominant land it passes automatically with that land for ever, assignment is only effective to confer the benefit on the immediate assignee. The covenant needs to be assigned afresh with every subsequent transfer of the land. Consequently, a person other than the original covenantee, seeking to enforce a covenant will need to show a complete chain of assignments down to him. Remember it is not unusual for there to have been five, six or even more subsequent purchasers of the dominant land. If this fails then, apart from trying to show annexation, there are two other arguments available. Being somewhat controversial, students often forget to include them in their answers. They are:

(a) On the first *express* assignment the benefit becomes annexed to the dominant land and from then on passes automatically with the land, i.e., assignment effects delayed annexation, per Ungoed-Thomas J in *Stilwell* v *Blackman* [1968] Ch 508 at 519.

(b) LPA 1925, s. 62, may operate in the same way as s. 78 to assign the benefit of the covenant automatically on transfer of the land, i.e., statutory assignment. By LPA 1925, s. 62, a conveyance of land shall be deemed to include all rights, privileges and advantages etc. appertaining or reputed to appertain to the land. The question you should consider is this: 'Is a covenant a right appertaining or reputed to appertain to land?' If it is then there is no reason why s. 62 should not produce statutory assignment. An examiner will be looking out for students who have considered this issue. The issue was also considered in *Roake* v *Chadha* [1983] 3 All ER 503 at p. 509, Judge Paul Baker QC, however, deciding on the facts that the covenant in question was not such a right because it had been precluded from passing with the land except on express assignment, which had not occurred. He continued to comment generally:

> On whether the benefit of a covenant not annexed can ever pass under s. 62, I share the doubts of Farwell J. Counsel for the defendants suggested, and there may well be something in this, that the rights referred to in s. 62 are confined to legal rights rather than equitable rights. . . . But again I place it on construction.

Clearly the issue is undecided, but see the comments of Browne-Wilkinson V-C in *Kumar* v *Dunning* [1989] QB 193 where he seemed to be of the opinion that s. 62 can only apply where the covenant has in some way been annexed to the land, otherwise it cannot be said to be appurtenant to land. He thought that if covenants could pass under s. 62 without prior annexation the whole modern law of restrictive covenants would have been established on an erroneous basis.

Scheme of Development

Such schemes are relatively easy to identify as they are normally found in housing estates where the aim is to maintain a certain standard for all the residents. The overriding criterion is *common intention*. Parker J first laid down the means of establishing that intention in *Elliston* v *Reacher* [1908] 2 Ch 374:

(a)   The land should be laid out *in lots*.
(b)   The lot in question to be sold to a purchaser by a *common vendor*.
(c)   Covenants were to be *for the benefit of all* the lots sold and the original purchasers must have known the covenants were for the benefit of the land.

These are still an initial aid to identification although examiners will be looking to see whether students are aware that the courts have moved towards a more flexible approach. In *Baxter* v *Four Oaks Properties Ltd* [1965] Ch 816, for example, a common vendor did *not* set out land in lots but sold each purchaser the amount of land they required. Nevertheless Cross LJ held that there was sufficient evidence of common intention. See also *Re Dolphin's*

Conveyance [1970] Ch 654. It should be remembered, however, that there is a limit to this flexibility. In *Kingsbury* v *L.W. Anderson Ltd* (1979) 40 P & CR 136 the court refused to find a common intention where the covenants in question varied, despite the fact that there had been a common owner and the land had been divided into lots. The reason given was that the lack of similar covenants on all the lots showed a lack of reciprocity of obligation and lack of intention to create such reciprocity, which is a fundamental requirement in equity for the establishment of a building scheme.

You might also refer to the Privy Council decision in *Emile Elias & Co. Ltd* v *Pine Groves Ltd* [1993] 1 WLR 305 where Lord Browne-Wilkinson was of the opinion that the imposition of non-uniform covenants on plots of a similar nature showed that there had been no intention to create reciprocally enforceable rights. The case thus confirmed that while the courts may now be more flexible, the general principle laid down in *Elliston* v *Reacher* remains the basis of the law.

Effect of LPA 1925, section 56

Although questions involving the effect of LPA 1925, s. 56, do not seem to occur often, depending on your course they may occasionally arise. The operation of the section is not as difficult as some students seem to think. What this section does is to allow an adjoining landowner to take the benefit of a covenant, albeit that he was not a named party to the original deed, provided:

(a)   He was alive and identifiable at the time the covenant was made. This is because he is being treated as an original covenantee.

(b)   It is clear, from the circumstances of the case, that it was intended that he could benefit from the covenant (see *Stromdale & Ball Ltd* v *Burden* [1952] Ch 223).

In figure 8.8, A and B are adjoining landowners. A sells part of his land to C. C covenants with A and owners for the time being of adjoining plots of land not to build more than one house on his plot. B *can* rely on LPA 1925, s. 56, to enforce the covenant against C, there being intention that he be treated similarly to A, the original covenantee. If B sold his land to D, however, D could *not* rely on s. 56 for it was made clear by the House of Lords in *Beswick* v *Beswick* [1968] AC 58 that the benefit of a covenant can only pass by one of the methods already described. You may also wish to draw the examiner's attention, where applicable, to the argument that this section does not necessarily, on the basis of the House of Lords decision, abrogate entirely the doctrine of privity of contract.

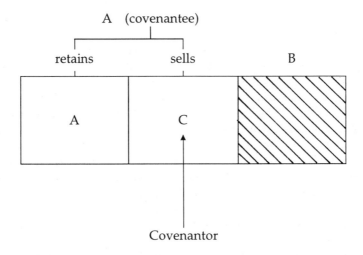

Figure 8.8

DISCHARGE AND MODIFICATION

Professional courses are more likely than undergraduate ones to be concerned with the detail of this topic. An examination question, may, for example, quite straightforwardly ask for a description of a method, or methods of discharge and modification. Provided the student has learned these, this should pose no problem. By way of revision, remember there are two methods:

(a)   By the Lands Tribunal which is empowered by LPA 1925, s. 84(1), as amended by LPA 1969, s. 28 and sch. 3, to discharge or modify *restrictive* covenants with or without compensation, provided one of the grounds listed in s. 84 can be established. This power does *not* extend to positive covenants. For useful examples refer to Riddall, *Introduction to Land Law*. Lands Tribunal decisions tend to turn on their facts, however, and consequently do not follow precedent. Any case you cite therefore will only be of use as an example and will not be authoritative. Appeal from the Tribunal lies to the Court of Appeal (*Ridley* v *Taylor* [1965] 2 All ER 51).

(b)   Discharge by seisin, i.e., when both the dominant and servient land come under the same occupation. If the dominant and servient land come into common ownership and then become severed again, the covenant binding the servient land will not revive unless a scheme of development is in existence as there was in *Texaco Antilles Ltd* v *Kernochan* [1973] AC 609 (a Privy Council case) followed in *Re Tiltwood, Sussex* [1978] Ch 269.

REFORM

The rule that positive covenants do not run with the servient land has long been recognised as leaving a gap in the law. It is all the more anomalous because positive covenants in leases *do* bind successors in title of both the landlord and tenant. The Law Commission report, No. 127 (1984), entitled *Transfer of Land: The Law of Positive and Restrictive Covenants*, recommended the end of that anomaly (as did an earlier report, No. 92, in 1967). The 1984 report contained a Land Obligations Bill. Students should therefore be aware of its recommendations and those of the Condominium Law Working Group's Report published in July 1987, entitled *Commonhold: Freehold Flats and Freehold Ownership of Other Interdependent Buildings* (Cm 179). On 12 July 1991 the government announced plans to legislate as soon as possible to introduce a new scheme for land and property ownership called 'commonhold'. As part of the scheme it is also proposed to give long-leaseholders in a block of flats the right to buy the freehold interest in the block. To date only the latter has been implemented in the Leasehold Reform, Housing and Urban Development Act 1993. See a useful article on this Act by M. Davey (1994) 57 MLR 773.

SPECIMEN EXAMINATION QUESTIONS

This area of the law tends to lend itself mostly to problem questions. Consequently brief guidelines to answering problems are suggested below. These are not intended to be exhaustive but merely to help you to design your own 'battle plan' in line with your lecture notes etc.

Brief Guidelines to Answering Problems

(a)   By way of introduction, *ascertain all potential plaintiffs and defendants* (a diagram helps), e.g., plaintiffs = original covenantee and any successors in title, defendants = original covenantor and any successors in title.

(b)   Is there privity of contract or privity of estate between covenantor and covenantee? Remember that there is privity of contract between the *original* covenantor and *original covenantee*. Therefore, unless the covenant is specially worded the original covenantor will remain liable at common law even if he has parted with the land affected.

(c)   Identify the covenant. Is it restrictive or positive? Remember it is possible to sever the positive part if necessary, leaving the restrictive part to be enforced (*Shepherd Street Homes Ltd* v *Sandham (No. 2)* [1971] 1 WLR 1062).

(d)   If the answer to point (b) is no, then *ask yourself whether the burden has passed to the defendant* (where the defendant is not the original covenantor) enabling the defendant to be held liable for breach of the covenant.

In order to ascertain this:

(i)   Consider the *common law* rules, which are briefly that the burden *cannot* pass (*Austerberry* v *Oldham Corporation* (1885) 29 ChD 750).

(ii)   Consider the *equitable rules*, which allow the burden of restrictive covenants to pass under the doctrine of *Tulk* v *Moxhay* (1848) 2 Ph 744 namely, that a restrictive covenant can be enforced against a later purchaser unless the burdened land was bought without notice of the covenant. Since the Land Charges Act 1925 (now 1972), notice depends on registration of the restrictive covenant as a Class D(ii) land charge. If not registered it is void as against a subsequent purchaser of the legal estate for money or money's worth even if he has notice. (There is no exception for building scheme covenants.) However, restrictive covenants entered into before 1925 or contained in a lease are not registrable and the doctrine of notice will still apply to them.

(iii)   If necessary, i.e., where the covenant is positive, consider any *indirect* means by which the burden may have passed (e.g., *Tito* v *Waddell (No. 2)* [1977] Ch 106). See Aughterson [1985] Conv 12.

(e)   *Ask yourself whether the benefit has passed to the plaintiff* (where the plaintiff is not the original covenantee), thus enabling the plaintiff to sue for breach of the covenant.

In order to ascertian whether the benefit has passed:

(i)   Consider *common law* rules.

(ii)   Consider *equitable* rules, which are briefly that the benefit *can* pass provided:

(1)   The covenant touches and concerns the land of the covenantee.

(2)   There is land to be benefited. Once it has all been parted with, the benefit will not pass in equity.

If persons other than the original covenantee (i.e., the covenantee's assigns) wish to sue on the covenant, the benefit must have passed to them in one of three ways:

(i)   *Annexation*, which can be:

(1)   Express.

(2)   Implied for circumstances.

(3)   As a result of LPA 1925, s. 78 (see *Federated Homes Ltd* v *Mill Lodge Properties* [1980] 1 WLR 594 and *Roake* v *Chadha* [1983] 3 All ER 503.

(ii)   *Assignment* (see above cases).

(iii) *Scheme of development (Elliston v Reacher* [1908] 2 Ch 374). See also *Baxter v Four Oaks Properties Ltd* [1965] Ch 816 and *Re Dolphin's Conveyance* [1970] Ch 654 which suggest a more flexible approach being taken by the courts.

(f) Assuming the covenant is enforceable, consider the appropriate remedy required by the plaintiff. The remedy available at common law is damages. In equity an injunction may be granted but may be refused if the court considers that the covenant is obsolete, or the plaintiff acquiesced in previous breaches thereby waiving his rights or if it would be inequitable to enforce the covenant (e.g., in *Wrotham Park Estate Co. Ltd* v *Parkside Homes Ltd* [1974] 1 WLR 798 houses had been constructed in breach of covenant: damages awarded in lieu of mandatory injunction requiring demolition). By LPA 1925, s. 84 (as amended), the Lands Tribunal has power to modify or discharge a restrictive covenant, with or without compensation, on various grounds, e.g., if the character of the neighbourhood has changed so much that the covenant has become obsolete.

(g) *Conclusion.* Sum up your answer briefly, pointing out why you think the covenant is, or is not as the case may be, enforceable. It may also be appropriate to comment briefly on possible reform suggested by the Law Commission, for example, if the problem involves a positive covenant.

Question

Amelia was the owner in fee simple of one acre of land known as Pinkacre Meadow. In 1978 she sold and conveyed one half of the Meadow to Belinda and in the deed of conveyance both Amelia and Belinda entered into mutual covenants to the effect that they would each erect and maintain a fence along one half of the boundary between their respective plots and would construct no buildings other than one dwelling-house on those plots.

Last year Amelia sold and conveyed her plot to Chloe and Belinda sold and conveyed hers to Drusilla. Drusilla has since commenced a small market garden business on her plot and has recently embarked upon the construction of several large greenhouses and potting sheds. In retaliation, after several heated exchanges over the boundary fence, Chloe has refused to carry out any further repairs to her part of that fence following recent storm damage. This has not caused Drusilla to refrain from further construction work and Chloe now seeks your advice on whether she is entitled to bring an action on the covenant contained in the original conveyance between Amelia and Belinda.

Advise Chloe.

Following the suggested plan, any answer should incorporate the following points (a)–(e):

(a) The diagram in figure 8.9 illustrates the position outlined in the problem.

(b) There is no privity of contract between Chloe and Drusilla for they are successors in title to Amelia and Belinda, the original parties. Neither is there privity of estate, since there is no landlord-tenant relationship between them.

(c) Type of covenant. Here there are *mutual* covenants, both Amelia and Belinda agreeing:

(i) To erect and maintain a fence — positive.

(ii) To construct no buildings other than one dwelling-house on these plots — restrictive.

Chloe (Belinda's successor in title) is interested in enforcing the restrictive element and so preventing Drusilla (Amelia's successor in title) from constructing greenhouses etc. on the servient land. The positive element, therefore, may be severed, enabling the restrictive part to be enforced.

(d) Has the burden of the restrictive element of the covenant passed to Drusilla? Yes, in equity under the doctrine of *Tulk* v *Moxhay*. However, we are not told whether the covenant has been registered as a D(ii) land charge. As the covenant was entered into in 1978 this is a necessary prerequisite to enforcement, for if it is not registered it will be void as against Drusilla even if she has notice of it, providing she purchased the servient land 'for money or money's worth'. You are not asked to concern yourself with the positive element, although you may wish to comment briefly that Drusilla could not force Chloe to maintain the fence unless it could be shown that the burden had passed to Chloe by one of the indirect methods. Perhaps the doctrine of mutual benefit and burden of *Halsall* v *Brizell*, discussed in *Tito* v *Waddell (No. 2)* could be relevant here, both Amelia and Belinda having entered into mutual covenants. It would, however, be a mistake to go too far down this road as the question does not demand it.

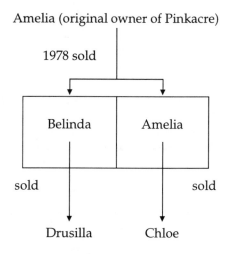

Chloe is the potential plaintiff.
Drusilla is the potential defendant.

Figure 8.9

(e)   Has the benefit of the covenant passed to Chloe? Here the equitable rules are to be considered as the burden has passed to Drusilla in equity.

The benefit can pass in several ways, by annexation, assignment or via a scheme of development. The latter here is of no relevance, neither is there any express wording to be able to identify any express annexation or assignment. This leaves the possibility of statutory annexation by virtue of the decisions in *Federated Homes Ltd* v *Mill Lodge Properties Ltd* [1980] 1 WLR 594 and *Roake* v *Chadha* [1983] 3 All ER 503, which held that the effect of LPA 1925, s. 78, is to annex the covenants automatically to the dominant land, provided there is no contrary intention. There is no contrary intention indicated in the question.

Alternatively, it could be argued that LPA 1925, s. 62, will operate in the same manner and result in statutory assignment of the benefit of the covenants to Chloe on conveyance. This is a controversial issue and was doubted in *Roake* v *Chadha*. You may here wish to refer to articles you have read in this area, briefly commenting on them and pointing out the creative interpretation put on ss. 78 and 62, which could, if followed, result in the common law and equitable rules being dispensed with altogether.

Assuming the covenant was registered as a D(ii) land charge, Chloe can seek an injunction to restrain any construction work in breach of the 1978 covenant. Expanding on this point you could, for example, explain:

An injunction is an equitable remedy, however, and the court may refuse it on the grounds that Chloe is refusing to maintain the fence. This is despite the fact that Chloe could not be held liable for refusing to carry out these positive obligations due to the present inability of positive covenants to run with the land. This may change if the draft Land Obligations Bill recommended by the Law Commission becomes law (although this now seems unlikely as the proposals were made in 1984). The Bill contains proposals to create new legal interests in land, to be called 'land obligations', which would have the effect of making the burden of positive covenants run with the land.

Essay-type Questions

It may be that you are faced with an essay-type question. This type of question is fairly common, especially in professional examinations, and may ask for a general discussion such as:

Explain with examples what is meant by 'covenants running with the land'.

Or the question may be seeking to ensure that you have an understanding of differing types of property interests and can distinguish between them. For example:

Distinguish an easement from a restrictive covenant.

In answering these questions, and essay-type questions in general, read the question carefully and decide exactly what the examiner requires before you put pen to paper. A brief plan outlining the structure of your answer helps and prevents you from going off at tangents into irrelevant areas not asked for.

Consider the first question. A plan could be along the following lines:

(a) Introduction — definition of a covenant — distinction between positive and negative or restrictive covenants — examples of both.

(b) Explanation of the phrase given — emphasise the intervention of equity modifying contract principles.

(c) To be capable of running, the covenant:

    (i)   must be restrictive,

    (ii)   must touch and concern the dominant land,

    (iii) must satisfy the rules relating to the passing of the benefit and the burden of the covenant.

(d) Notice requirements.

(e) Conclusion.

Expanding on the above. Your introduction could give the general definition of a covenant and distinguish between positive and negative or restrictive covenants as this is an important issue to be taken up later in the essay. For example:

> A covenant is simply an agreement under seal. Covenants relating to land may be either negative, i.e., restrictive in nature, whereby the covenantor (person making the promise and therefore assuming the obligation) undertakes to restrict the use of his own land for the benefit of the neighbouring land, e.g., that he will not keep more than 10 dogs or 10 cats, or they can be positive. In this case the covenantor undertakes a positive obligation, e.g., to keep the premises in repair.

This could be developed in your next point which is to explain the meaning of the phrase given. For example:

> The main difference between positive and restrictive covenants is that restrictive covenants are more than personal agreements, binding in contract. As Michael Harwood in *Modern English Land Law* says: 'Equity has intervened to allow [such contractual] agreements to be stamped with the character of a property interest'. For restrictive covenants are property interests capable of binding third parties, namely, successors in title, providing the requirements explained below are complied with. Thus they are capable of running with the land and are not confined by the principles of privity of contract.

The overall requirements, i.e., of the need for a dominant and a servient tenement and the need for the covenant to touch and concern the dominant land, logically fall to be considered next, as they are overall requirements. Remember, the covenant must benefit land (compare perhaps the similar requirement in respect of an easement). There are several cases which you could cite to illustrate the meaning of this phrase, but probably the judgment of Farwell J in *Rogers v Hosegood* [1900] 2 Ch 388 is the most useful. If you can remember it, quote from the judgment: '[A] covenant must either affect the land as regards mode of occupation, or it must be such as *per se*, and not merely from collateral circumstances, affects the value of the land'. Expand if you have time, giving examples such as *Newton Abbot Co-operative Society Ltd v Williamson & Treadgold Ltd* [1952] Ch 286 in which it was held that the dominant property (an ironmongers') was sufficiently touched and concerned by a covenant, intended to prevent competition, not to carry on a similar business in the covenantor's premises across the road.

Attention then can be turned to the common law and equitable rules relating to the passing on of the benefit and the burden of restrictive covenants, which has been outlined earlier in this chapter, and will therefore not be discussed here. One point you should emphasise, however, is the importance of the intervention of equity, for it is only in equity that the burden of a restrictive covenant can pass (*Tulk* v *Moxhay*).

Finally, the requirement of notice should not be omitted. Remember a restrictive covenant is an equitable interest, therefore in order for it to run and be capable of binding successors in title it must be registered either as a Class D(ii) land charge, where title to the land is unregistered (this includes covenants created since 1925 and not made between lessor and lessee) or as a 'notice' if title to the land is registered under the Land Registration Act 1925.

To draw the essay to a close, provide a brief conclusion, perhaps referring back to the question and commenting briefly on possible reform. This would show the examiner that you have understood the question and also are abreast of any such suggested reforms. For example:

Restrictive covenants are capable of running with the land, as shown above, and are therefore more than contractual interests. However, it must be remembered that they may retain many contractual characteristics, e.g., the original parties to the covenant remain liable in respect of the agreement even after the land has been parted with. Various committees have suggested reforms, the most recent being the Law Commission Report No. 127 in 1984, entitled *Transfer of Land: The Law of Positive and Restrictive Covenants* and the Condominium Law Working Group's report, published in July 1987, entitled *Commonhold: Freehold Flats and Freehold Ownership of Other Interdependent Buildings* (Cm 179). Whilst the government has not gone as far as was recommended in the report, the Leasehold Reform, Housing and Urban Development Act 1993, which came into force in November 1993, does give leaseholders the right collectively to buy the freehold of their block of flats and the right of an individual leaseholder to extend their lease.

SUGGESTED ADDITIONAL READING

There is a specialist book in this area, Preston and Newsom, *Restrictive Covenants Affecting Freehold Land*, 8th ed., 1991 (Sweet & Maxwell). Another useful book for this area is McKenzie and Phillips, *A Practical Approach to Land Law*, 5th ed., 1994 (Blackstone Press) which places the law of covenants in context and in that way assists understanding.

9 LICENCES

INTRODUCTION

It is only in fairly recent times that the topic of licences has been dealt with in any great detail, other than to show the distinction between licences and leases. Most recent textbooks have fairly large chapters devoted to licences but for examination purposes the issues are fairly narrow as will be shown in this chapter.

For many years licences were viewed as merely personal privileges conferring no interest in the land on the licensee (see Vaughan CJ in *Thomas v Sorrell* (1673) Vaugh 330). The present importance of licences is due to a line of mainly Court of Appeal decisions dealing with contractual licences and proprietary estoppel. Such is the effect of these cases that the 5th edition of Megarry and Wade's *The Law of Real Property* stated: 'The courts appear to be well on their way to creating a new and highly versatile interest in land which will rescue many informal and unbusinesslike transactions, particularly within families, from the penalties of disregarding legal forms.'

Why should the law be developing along these lines? You should stop and consider, for a moment, living arrangements between family and friends. These are often informal, loose arrangements, much more so than arrangements made between strangers. More often than not they are oral, vaguely expressed and open to misinterpretation. The net result is that when things go wrong and relationships become strained the courts find it difficult to fit the arrangement within the traditional categories relating to the law of contract and the law of property. As a result the courts have attempted to

adapt the concepts of licence, equity and constructive trust in order to deal
with the legal implications of loosely based family arrangements.

The difficulty therefore from the student's point of view, is to find a
common thread running through what appears to be a number of conflicting
cases. It is intended in this chapter to concentrate on contractual licences and
estoppel, on the basis that these are most likely to cause pitfalls for the
student. Consideration will be given also to the use of the constructive or
resulting trust as a means of providing a remedy. It may also be useful to
remember the link with matrimonial property so that licences may be used
to give a remedy where a beneficial tenancy in common cannot be
established. See for example *Ungurian* v *Lesnoff* [1989] 3 WLR 840 where
Vinelott J found a constructive trust creating a life interest although he was
unable to find the requisite common intention for co-ownership.

Licences can also arise where the requisite formalities for the creation of an
easement have not been complied with, e.g., if there is no intention to create
an interest in land as in *Fitzgerald* v *Firbank* [1897] 2 Ch 96. The principles
relating to bare licences and licences coupled with an interest are reasonably
clear and will only be referred to in so far as they bear upon contract and
estoppel. The distinction between leases and licences and the effect of the
House of Lords decision in *Street* v *Mountford* [1985] AC 809 will be dealt with
in the following chapter on leases.

TERMINOLOGY

For once this is not a problem. A licence can be simply defined as permission
given by one person (the licensor) allowing another (the licensee) to enter
upon land. Just remember not to confuse the licensor and the licensee. The
licensor grants the licence. The licensee is the recipient of the licence.

MAIN ISSUES

As we said in the introduction, the issues for examination purposes in this
area tend to be fairly narrow. They can be identified as follows:

(a)   Classification of the types of licences.
(b)   Relationship between contractual licences and licences based on the
doctrine of estoppel.
(c)   Binding nature of licences on third parties.

This, amongst other things, raises the issue as to whether licences are purely
personal arrangements or akin to proprietary interests in land. See the
revision summary at the end of this chapter. Licences are a fertile area for
examination purposes, not least because, as has been said above, the courts

use this area to rescue informal and loose family arrangements, often protecting cohabitees. This can result in an overlap with co-ownership and matrimonial property law (discussed in chapter 5).

Furthermore, cases are difficult to reconcile, judges often agreeing on a particular remedy but for different reasons. Examiners are therefore not looking for a 'right answer', but for an answer which demonstrates that the student both knows and understands the underlying issues in this area of law which M.P. Thompson [1983] Conv 50 calls a 'vexing subject'.

Whilst the three main issues outlined above can be identified and the majority of examination questions will encompass all of them, it cannot be stressed enough that to really understand this area and be able to discuss it confidently and so impress the examiner, students should read articles in addition to the standard texts. Also the recent case of *Ashburn Anstalt* v *Arnold* [1989] Ch 1 is most instructive and is one of those cases which reward the reader who takes time to study the judgments. Although this case has been over-ruled by the *Prudential Assurance* case [1992] 3 WLR 273, it was on other grounds and so does not affect the comments made by the Court of Appeal in *Ashburn* or licences.

Some articles of particular interest are: A. Briggs, 'Licences: a return to basics' [1981] Conv 212; M.P. Thompson, 'Licences: questioning the basics' [1983] Conv 50; A. Briggs, 'Contractual licences: a reply' [1984] Conv 285; P.N. Todd, 'Estoppel licences and third-party rights' [1981] Conv 347; P. T. Evans, 'Choosing the right estoppel' [1988] Conv 346 and an earlier article, but nonetheless instructive, A.J. Oakley, 'Has the constructive trust become a general remedy?' (1973) 26 CLP 17.

CLASSIFICATION OF LICENCES

Licences may be Classified as Follows:

(a) Bare licences.
(b) Licences coupled with an interest.
(c) Contractual licences.
(d) Licences giving rise to an estoppel.

Contractual Licences

A bare licence — the simplest form of licence, merely negating trespass — is freely revocable by the licensor, so the first question for you to consider is whether consideration (in the contractual sense) makes any difference. If there is a contract between the parties then the licensor's revocation may amount to breach of contract. The issue then is whether the licensee must be satisfied with common law damages or whether he can prevent revocation by the equitable remedy of injunction. From the licensee's point of view the equitable remedy is preferable since it would allow him or her to remain in possession of the land until completion of the contract. Examiners will expect students to compare the courts' initial reaction, which was to confuse contractual principles with interests in land and say that a contractual licence was not irrevocable (see *Wood* v *Leadbitter* (1845) 13 M & W 838), with the development of equitable remedies, first by the Court of Appeal in *Hurst* v *Picture Theatres Ltd* [1915] 1 KB 1 and ultimately by the House of Lords in *Winter Garden Theatre (London) Ltd* v *Millennium Productions Ltd* [1948] AC 173. In this latter case the House of Lords made it clear that the issue of revocability is one of *construction* of the contract. Only if, on its true construction, the contract is irrevocable will breach be prevented by use of an injunction. In dealing with the issue of revocability you must remember you are dealing with the parties' intentions and the length of occupation. Relief granted will vary with the circumstances, e.g., a spectator at a football match will be entitled to remain for the duration of the game but where the contract is of indefinite duration, it can only be revoked after a reasonable period has been allowed for withdrawal. The approach of the House of Lords in the *Winter Garden Theatre* case was followed by Megarry J in *Hounslow London Borough Council* v *Twickenham Garden Developments Ltd* [1971] Ch 233. In that case the plaintiff and defendant were disputing the defendant's commission for work on the plaintiff's property. The plaintiff sought an injunction to restrain the defendant from entering on to the plaintiff's property pending settlement of the dispute. The court held that, while the work was being carried out, there was a contractual licence subject to an implied obligation that the plaintiff could not revoke it. The judgment of Megarry J should be read in full as it reviews the law relating to contractual licences.

As well as preventing breach by injunction, equity may also enforce a right of entry by specific performance. A useful dictum to quote is that of Lord Denning MR in *Verrall* v *Great Yarmouth Borough Council* [1981] QB 202:

> Since the *Winter Garden* case, it is clear that once a man has entered under his contract of licence, he cannot be turned out.... On principle it is the same if it happens before he enters. If he has a contractual right to enter, and the licensor refuses to let him come in, then he can come to the court and in a proper case get an order for specific performance to allow him to come in.

The result is that even where equitable relief is not available, the licensee will be able to bring an action for assault in the event of being forcibly ejected or refused entry. Even at common law there are dicta to suggest that although a licensor has a *power* to evict a licensee he has no *right* to do so. Consequently an action for assault will lie where there is forcible eviction (see *Hounslow London Borough Council* v *Twickenham Garden Developments Ltd*).

Licences by Estoppel

It is, at this stage, intended to consider estoppel licences and then to consider their relationship with contractual licences and the effect of both on third parties. It is this area of licences which has caused most contention and is likely to be of interest to examiners. It is also one of the areas where you will benefit from considering the articles mentioned on page 10 and 11. Faced with the need to classify a licence, you will be able to put forward the opposing arguments of Briggs and Thompson along the following lines:

> Briggs in his article, places great importance on the need to classify a licence. He claims that a licence can either be contractual, in which case it will not bind a third party, or have its basis in the doctrine of estoppel, in which case it will be so binding. It cannot, however, be both. Thompson replying to Briggs, disagrees, considering that it is not easy to distinguish between these two types of licences (see *Errington* v *Errington* [1952] 1 KB 290), nor is it desirable. He is of the opinion that a licence can display features of both. Consequently in such cases he considers rigid classification unnecessary and attempts to establish a common basis by which contractual and equitable licences can bind successors in title to the licensor.

It has long been accepted that a licensor is estopped from revoking a licence where he has acquiesced to or encouraged the use of land. The present approach of the courts is best illustrated by Lord Kingsdown's dissenting judgment in *Ramsden* v *Dyson* (1866) LR 1 HL 129 in which he said:

> If a man, under a verbal agreement with a landlord for a certain interest in land, or, what amounts to the same thing, under an expectation, created or encouraged by the landlord, that he shall have a certain interest, takes possession of such land, with the consent of the landlord, and upon the faith of such promise or expectation, with the knowledge of the landlord, and without objection by him, lays out money upon the land, a court of equity will compel the landlord to give effect to such promise or expectation.

The elements of this dictum have been used in a number of subsequent cases; see, e.g., *Crabb* v *Arun District Council* [1976] Ch 179; *Inwards* v *Baker* [1965] 2 QB 29. The important thing to remember about this type of estoppel is that it can give rise to a cause of action and create rights. It must, therefore, always be distinguished from promissory estoppel which can only be used as a defence (see *Combe* v *Combe* [1951] 2 KB 215). The dictum of Lord Kingsdown has been extended by subsequent decisions so that it is no longer necessary to show expenditure of money. It is sufficient that the licensee has suffered detriment arising from activity or lack of activity by him. The modern approach seems to be for the courts to consider whether the assertion of the licensor's strict legal rights would be unconscionable in all the circumstances (see Oliver J in *Taylors Fashions Ltd* v *Liverpool Victoria Trustees Co. Ltd* [1982] QB 133).

This flexible approach has enabled the court to find remedies where there might be none at common law and this has been particularly useful in domestic situations in which it might be difficult to find a contract. The approach to be taken by the court was formulated by Scarman LJ in *Crabb* v *Arun District Council*: the court must analyse and assess the parties' conduct and then consider three questions:

(a) Is there an equity established?
(b) What is the extent of the equity, if established?
(c) What is the relief appropriate to satisfy the equity?

While this leads to great flexibility the difficulty for the student is to anticipate how the estoppel will be applied in any given situation. As the long-suffering student will be well aware, there are many apparently conflicting decisions, particularly by the Court of Appeal and an authoritative statement is still awaited from the House of Lords. The cases are numerous but a couple of examples may show how the difficulties can be faced.

In *Pascoe* v *Turner* [1979] 1 WLR 431 the Court of Appeal ordered a transfer of the fee simple where a man's mistress had spent money on repairing and improving a house in the belief that it was to be hers. Although there was an imperfect gift of the house, which could not be perfected by the court, an estoppel arose by the acquiescence and encouragement of the man. It was held that the minimum equity required was a transfer of the fee simple; otherwise the mistress would have no security to improve the house and be protected from acts of the plaintiff. The outcome was that the woman acquired a house worth £16,000 for an outlay of about £1,000. The court was influenced towards this conclusion by the fact that the plaintiff was a relatively rich man who had shown himself 'determined to pursue his purpose of evicting [his mistress] by any legal means with a ruthless disregard of the obligations binding on conscience' (per Cumming-Bruce LJ).

On the other hand, in *Dodsworth* v *Dodsworth* (1973) 228 EG 1115, the plaintiff invited her brother (together with his wife) to live in her bungalow. They spent £700 on improvements in the belief, encouraged and induced by the plaintiff, that they and their successors would be able to remain as long as they wished. The Court of Appeal found an equity but held it could be satisfied by allowing the defendants to remain until their expenditure was reimbursed.

Note that there are clear distinctions between the two cases which resulted in the estoppel being applied differently in each case to give effect to the equity or 'fairness' each fact situation demanded.

Despite the difficulties of application, however, estoppel has great advantages over contractual licences. The remedies are potentially much more flexible than contract, not being confined to damages or injunctions. More important, perhaps, is the fact that estoppel can both bind and benefit successors in title and is not subject to rules of privity of contract. It is, therefore, necessary to consider how estoppel is distinguished from contract and to what extent licences can be considered interests in land.

RELATIONSHIP BETWEEN ESTOPPEL AND CONTRACTUAL LICENCES

In many cases, a licence will be created either in contract or estoppel and it may be that the ultimate decision will depend upon the remedy thought desirable (but see the articles by Briggs and Thompson cited on page 160). A good example is *Re Sharpe* [1980] 1 WLR 219 where it was held that an aunt's licence in respect of her nephew's home was binding on his trustee in bankruptcy. Browne-Wilkinson J thought the licence binding 'whether it be called a contractual licence or an equitable licence or an interest under a constructive trust' — a decision in sympathy with Thompson's argument. There was, in that case, an element of estoppel in view of the nephew's assurances that the aunt could stay due to the loan given by the aunt to the nephew to enable him to buy the house. Notwithstanding issues of contractual intention, there would appear to have been ample consideration for a contract. However, in order for the contract to bind successors, Browne-Wilkinson J thought a constructive trust necessary because an interest in land cannot depend solely on an oral undertaking. It is this element of constructive trust which makes estoppel more attractive than contract. In the absence of such a trust, the traditional view would be that a contract does not bind successors (see *King* v *David Allen & Sons, Billposting Ltd* [1916] 2 AC 54). Consequently where there is no evidence of a constructive trust, estoppel will be necessary before third parties will be bound. Although constructive trusts are largely a question of intention, the court may not always be able to find such intention and may then fall back upon estoppel. A contract may, however, be binding on a volunteer or where the licence was irrevocable during the licensor's lifetime (see *Re Sharpe* and *Errington* v *Errington* [1952] 1 KB 290).

The courts do now seem to favour the constructive trust approach and in *Re Basham* [1986] 1 WLR 1498 it was said that proprietary estoppel is a form of constructive trust and that the belief encouraged in A by B did not have to relate to an existing right or to particular property. In *Ashburn Anstalt* v *Arnold* [1989] Ch 1, Fox LJ expressed his preference for the use of the constructive trust as a solution to the problem. His judgment is also useful on the issue of contractual licences binding on third parties and his criticism of the approach taken in *Errington* v *Errington*.

The difficulty for students is that judges may agree on the remedy to be granted but disagree on whether there is contract or estoppel. A good example is *Hardwick* v *Johnson* [1978] 1 WLR 683, in which a mother bought a house for her son and daughter-in-law asking them to pay £7 a week. When the son left his wife the Court of Appeal held she had a right to remain in the house provided she kept up the payments. Lord Denning MR based his judgment on estoppel but Roskill and Browne LJJ found a contractual licence although it was admitted there was no contractual intention. This flexible approach can be illustrated in the situation where the courts have sought to find a means of protecting cohabitees. There is an obvious overlap here with co-ownership and matrimonial property and for this reason alone the subject is popular with examiners. Three cases may be used to demonstrate the courts' flexibility in achieving the result it thinks desirable. In *Eves* v *Eves* [1975] 1 WLR 1338 a constructive trust was used to grant a remedy where a mistress had moved into a house on the basis that it was to be the parties' future matrimonial home and she had done a considerable amount of work in modernising the house. In *Tanner* v *Tanner* [1975] 1 WLR 1346 the facts were broadly similar but without any intention to marry. The Court of Appeal held in this case that there was nothing on which to find a constructive trust but found consideration for a contractual licence in that the mistress had given up a rent-controlled flat and had provided furniture for the new flat. Lord Denning MR was prepared to go further and say that Tanner owed a legal and moral obligation to provide for the girl and the children she had by him.

A point worth noting is that in both these cases the premises had been vacated after the county court judgment and the only issue for the Court of Appeal was whether to make an award of damages. In the third case, *Horrocks* v *Forray* [1976] 1 All ER 737 the Court of Appeal (without Lord Denning) were unable to find either a constructive trust or a contractual licence. The case concerned a widow's claim to possession of a house from a mistress in order to sell and save the estate from insolvency. The court held that to find a contract there must be consideration and a common intention, neither of which were present in the case. Unlike the situation in *Tanner* v *Tanner* the mistress had given up nothing and there was nothing to show a contract other than natural love and affection. It may be, however, that the courts' true intention was to protect the 'legitimate' interest of the wife against the mistress!

These cases can be used to illustrate how broadly similar facts can lead to diverse results. It also illustrates how fertile an area this is for exam purposes. The difficulty for the student is not so much in distinguishing cases on their facts but in anticipating how the courts will respond to a given situation.

NATURE OF LICENCES

Before attempting to consider a specimen examination question, one final issue to discuss is the extent to which licences can now be said to be interests in land. Clearly estoppel licences bind third parties whether they be volunteers or purchasers (see Lord Denning MR in *Inwards* v *Baker* [1965] 2 QB 29). Subject to the limitations discussed previously, contractual licences bind third parties as equitable interests; a point accepted without discussion in *Midland Bank Ltd* v *Farmpride Hatcheries Ltd* (1981) 260 EG 493. The ultimate test is whether, once created, the benefit of these licences can be transferred to third parties. There is no English authority on this point but in *Hamilton* v *Geraghty* (1901) 1 SR (NSW) Eq 81 the Supreme Court of New South Wales held that the benefit of estoppel based on acquiescence was capable of assignment. It can be said that the equity created in *E.R. Ives Investments Ltd* v *High* [1967] 2 QB 379 would have been capable of transfer and it may be that the English courts are now prepared to recognise the assignability of an estoppel licence. However, it must be remembered the interest in *Ives* (a right of way) could have existed at law.

SPECIMEN EXAMINATION QUESTIONS

Problem

> Maud owned the freehold estate in Tottering Towers. She intended to convert the property into flats and allocated the conversion work to her son, Claud, who had recently started a general builders' business. Maud agreed to allow Claud's girlfriend, Ann, to occupy the ground floor during conversion work since she was to carry out the redecoration of the flats.
>
> Claud has fallen behind schedule with the conversion work because of the pressure of other business. Maud has told Ann that she can carry on occupying the ground floor for as long as she wishes despite the delays in the work. Claud and Ann have had a number of disagreements with the result that Ann has said she has no intention of redecorating the flats and has been told by Maud that she must leave Tottering Towers immediately.
>
> Discuss.

Brief Guide

Before applying the principles to a particular problem we should perhaps first consider the general issues in the subject of licences. Generally the parties involved will be clear so that a plan will probably be unnecessary provided you are clear about who is licensor and who is licensee. This will be straightforward because, even if a third party is involved in the problem, the issue will be whether they are bound by such licence as may exist. Having identified the parties you will then need to decide on the type of licence created, i.e., bare, coupled with an interest, contractual or estoppel. It may then be necessary to discover the effect of the licence on the parties and possibly third parties, which will be a matter of construction. For example, if the licence is contractual, is it revocable by the licensor? Can it bind a third party in view of the doctrine of privity? Remember that ultimately the effect of the licence will depend on its type, so that you must have the principles (such as they are) clear in your own mind and be able to apply them. The cases are so difficult to reconcile that you should not be looking for a 'right answer' but one that will demonstrate an understanding of the issues and ability to apply the law.

Commentary

The initial question here is whether Ann has any interest binding on Maud. From the facts it seems clear that no legal estate or interest (e.g., a lease) has been conferred on Ann by deed. It seems therefore that any right conferred on Ann is a licence, the issues then being the type of licence and whether it is revocable by Maud.

Clearly, at worst, Ann has a bare licence to occupy the ground floor. The difficulty for Ann is that such a licence is freely revocable upon Maud giving notice. The issue that must be considered is whether Ann has a licence which will be of more lasting benefit to her. The best approach, therefore, is to consider each type of licence in relation to the facts of the problem and then come to a conclusion.

First, there is nothing in the facts to suggest that Ann has a licence coupled with an interest in the land, so that she must try to argue either contract or estoppel. Is there a contract? Cases such as *Hardwick* v *Johnson* [1978] 1 WLR 683 and *Horrocks* v *Forray* [1976] 1 All ER 737 have made it clear that there must be both contractual intention and consideration. Here, although there is a close relationship between Ann and Claud, it would not seem to be such a family relationship as to prevent contractual intention between Ann and Maud. It would, for example, have been different had Ann been Claud's wife. Since Ann was to carry out the redecoration work, there would not appear to be any difficulty in establishing consideration. Ann would appear to have a contractual licence and the next issue to be decided is whether it can be revoked by Maud. In *Winter Garden Theatre (London) Ltd* v *Millennium Productions Ltd* [1948] AC 173 it was said that revocability is a question of construction of the contract and it could perhaps be argued here that the contract could not be revoked during the redecoration work. In *Hounslow London Borough Council* v *Twickenham Garden Developments Ltd* [1971] Ch 233, Megarry J held that the fact that the licensor was purporting to repudiate a construction contract did not allow revocation of the licence until determination of the legality of the repudiation. However, in this case, Ann, the licensee, has repudiated the agreement without just cause; unless it could be said that her arguments with Claud have been concerned with the conversion work and she has effectively been prevented from carrying out her contract. It would seem that Maud would be justified in treating the contractual licence as having been revoked by Ann. If this is the case, then Ann must try to argue that she has a licence by estoppel. The first issue is whether there has been any encouragement or acquiescence by Maud so as to make it 'unconscionable' to deny an equity (*Crabb* v *Arun District Council* [1976] Ch 179). Maud told Ann that she could continue to occupy the premises for so long as she wished. This would seem to be encouragement, but since Ann has incurred no expense as a result, would it be 'unconscionable' for Maud to deny the equity? Since Ann's occupation was originally connected with the redecorating work and this has been effectively prevented by Claud's delays, it could be argued that the work and occupation are no longer connected and if there is reliance by Ann on Maud's promise an equity may arise. It seems from the decision in *Greasley* v *Cooke* [1980] 3 All ER 710 that there is no onus on the licensee to prove reliance, so that it would be for Maud to establish that there was no reliance by Ann.

If estoppel is established, the next thing to decide is the equitable remedy required by the facts of the case. In *Pascoe* v *Turner* [1979] 1 WLR 431 it was said the question must be what is the minimum equity necessary to do justice between the parties. Clearly, there is no question of the court ordering a transfer of the fee simple (*Pascoe* v *Turner*) or a right to occupy for life (*Inwards* v *Baker*). If estoppel is established here it will be an illustration of what was described in *Chandler* v *Kerley* [1978] 1 WLR 693 as 'the supportive role of equity'. It may well be that the 'equity' required here will be reasonable notice after completion of the conversion work. This, however, leads to one final problem, that is, whether an estoppel can be lost, once established, by virtue of the licensee's conduct. There is no conclusive authority on this, but it was considered in both *Hardwick* v *Johnson* [1978] 1 WLR 683 and *Williams* v *Staite* [1978] 2 All ER 928. In *Williams* v *Staite* Lord Denning MR was prepared to say that gross misconduct could result in an estoppel being lost, although the licensor should first explore any other remedies he may have, e.g., in trespass or nuisance. Cumming-Bruce LJ thought that equity cannot be revoked unless conduct is such as to render enjoyment of property impractical. Goff LJ thought that once established an equity cannot be brought to an end unless it is for a limited period or determinable upon condition. In *Hardwick* v *Johnson*, Lord Denning MR was of the opinion that a change in circumstances or failure to pay agreed instalments would be sufficient. However, Roskill and Browne LJJ decided the case on the basis of contract and said that grave misconduct may amount to a breach of an implied term and prevent the licensee relying on equity to restrain revocation.

Applying these cases, it appears that only Lord Denning MR is prepared to say that estoppel can be lost by conduct and then only in very exceptional circumstances. In Ann's case it could be argued that Maud envisaged Ann's occupation as being solely connected with the decorating work so that in refusing to do the work her misconduct could be described as 'gross' with the subsequent loss of her equity. However, there is little support for Lord Denning's view and the equity would probably remain, unless it could be argued it was subject to an implied condition that she would carry out the work (per Goff LJ in *Williams* v *Staite*).

Essay Questions

Although the topic of licences lends itself to problems, the fact that it is a controversial and constantly changing area lends itself equally to essay questions. A typical example of this could be:

'The effect of proprietary estoppel is to create an equity to remain and no more.' Discuss.

A question like this gives you the opportunity to display both your understanding of the subject and evidence of wide reading of cases and articles. To answer this question adequately you have to be able to display a knowledge of the basic requirements of estoppel as already discussed and then build upon the basics to display your own view of the law. Merely recounting lecture notes on tutorial material will not obtain a really good mark; you need to be able to go further and discuss relevant principles, drawing your *own* conclusions from them. Consequently, it is the well-prepared student who benefits from this type of question rather than one who is only adequately prepared. The essential thing to remember is to discuss the law rather than merely to state it. While you will obviously be given some credit for knowing the legal principles at issue, you will only have answered the question when you go beyond this and discuss the implications.

An approach to this particular question may therefore be to state initially what proprietary estoppel is and how it may arise, e.g., the view of Lord Kingsdown in *Ramsden* v *Dyson* (1866) LR 1 HL 129 followed by Lord Scarman's criteria in *Crabb* v *Arun District Council* [1976] Ch 179. It would be useful at an early stage to make it clear that proprietary estoppel can create rights as this is essential to further discussion (a useful guide to this can be found in Spencer, Bower and Turner in *The Law Relating to Estoppel by Representation* where they emphasise estoppel arising out of acquiescence can always found an action, unlike promissory estoppel which is a shield and not a sword). Once you have established the basic framework you should consider the cases illustrating how different fact situations can lead to different remedies being awarded by the court, e.g., compare *Pascoe* v *Turner* [1979] 1 WLR 431 and *Dodsworth* v *Dodsworth* (1973) 228 EG 1115, and add your own critical appraisal. Having demonstrated the wide variety of remedy available, discuss whether the equity can bind third parties and whether it is capable of transfer. If there is authority to support the binding effect of estoppel on third parties then it could be argued that it gives more than a right to remain, e.g., *Errington* v *Errington* [1952] 1 KB 290; *Inwards* v *Baker* [1965] 2 QB 29 (discussed earlier in the chapter). Once you have disussed the issues and shown your understanding of the academic discussion, end the essay with your own conclusions.

One difficulty in the area of licences is that its controversial nature has led to a large number of academic articles over the last few years. Unfortunately, by the very nature of the subject, many of these articles, although very useful when written, have been overtaken by subsequent cases. It is not therefore possible for us to give much guidance on articles, except to say that case notes are extremely useful because of the complexity of the cases. On a more general level, try to keep up to date with recent articles, especially those concerned with third-party rights and the status of licensees.

REVISION SUMMARY

Type of licence	Description	Revocability	Whether binding on third parties	Nature of licence
Bare	Pure permission to enter land	Freely revocable on reasonable notice	Not binding	Personal
Licence coupled with an interest	A licence as an adjunct to a validly created in-terest in land	Irrevocable while interest lasts	Binding only while interest lasts	Not in itself of proprietary force, see (1953) 69 LQR 466

Contractual licence	A licence supported by:			
	(a) Consideration	(a) Revocable at common law with reasonable notice	Not binding	Personal
	(b) Contractual intention	(b) Irrevocable during period of contract in equity, but depends upon construction	Possibly binding (see *Errington* v *Errington* and doubts expressed in *Ashburn Anstalt* v *Arnold*)	Trend towards recognition as a proprietary interest
Estoppel	Based on: Acquiescence or encouragement by licensor	Flexible approach, based on the facts, to find the relief that is appropriate to satisfy the equity		

SUGGESTED ADDITIONAL READING

This is an area where there is considerable overlap in standard land law, family and equity texts. In addition to the land law and family law books previously referred to, you will find discussion of this area in:

P. Pettit, *Equity and the Law of Trusts*, 7th ed., 1993 (Butterworths).
Edwards & Stockwell, *Trusts and Equity*, 1991 (Pitman).

10 LEASES

INTRODUCTION

The topic of leases is in itself a vast one and frequently on law degrees is treated as an option in its own right. Treatment of leases in land law courses is diverse: some courses do not consider them at all, whilst others (particularly professional courses) deal with the whole area including all aspects of residential, business and agricultural tenancies. In this chapter, we intend to steer a middle ground by looking at the creation of leases and obligations imposed on landlord and tenant but without considering usual covenants in leases in detail or any of the forms of security of tenure. We hope to deal with those areas most commonly found in land law courses and indicate some likely examination issues. A specimen examination question concerns the usual covenant prohibiting assignment or parting with possession because that is a topic commonly included in examinations set by some institutions.

TERMINOLOGY

A lease is the remnant of the old feudal system: land is granted by one to the other for a specific period in return for a rent service. Consequently, the person granting the lease is called the landlord, the person occupying the land and paying the rent is the tenant. Alternatively, the landlord may be referred to as the lessor and the tenant the lessee. A tenant may create a lease out of his own term of years which is known as a sublease, the tenant becoming the sublessor (see figure 10.1).

A lease is a legal estate in land if it falls within the definition of term of years absolute in LPA 1925, s. 205(1)(xxvii), i.e., a term for less than a year, or for a year or years and a fraction of a year or from year to year. It can exist for *any* period provided it is for a certain length of time or is capable of being made certain at the outset. A lease which does not comply with this requirement is void (see *Lace* v *Chantler* [1944] KB 368 in which it was held that a lease granted for the duration of the war was uncertain and such a term could not be created). The decision in this case was reviewed and applied by the House of Lords in *Prudential Assurance Co. Ltd* v *London Residuary Body* [1992] 3 WLR 279. This is an interesting case as it confirms that the certainty rule applies to both fixed term and periodic leases. In the *Prudential* case the agreement stated that 'the tenancy shall continue until the land is required by the Council for the purpose of road widening'. Consequently the duration of the lease was uncertain and hence void. The case also explains how a periodic tenancy can arise in such circumstances and the terms of that tenancy. A yearly tenancy arose in the *Prudential* case by virtue of the tenants' possession and payment of a yearly rent. This yearly tenancy 'is saved from being uncertain because each party has power by notice to determine at the end of any year' (per Lord Templeman at page 285). It is now clear that such a tenancy will not incorporate any provisions for determination set out in the void lease which are inconsistent with the periodic tenancy. (Compare the decisions of *Re Midland Railway Co.'s Agreement* [1971] Ch 725 which had been applied in *Ashburn Anstalt* v *Arnold* [1989] Ch 1, both overruled by the *Prudential* decision.) Consequently, a term of years can exist for a fixed period of years or a shorter periodic term, e.g., weekly or monthly. As well as satisfying the definition in s. 205 a lease will only be legal if it satisfies the formal requirements and exclusive possession of the property is given.

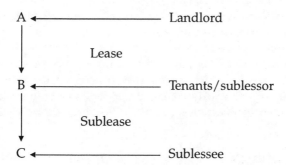

Figure 10.1

Although a legal estate, a lease is less than a fee simple absolute in possession so that on determination of the lease, possession of the land reverts to the landlord. This is the freehold reversion which can be sold by the landlord subject to the tenant's interests, the rent then becoming payable to the new freeholder.

MAIN ISSUES

Examination questions on leases are usually in the form of problems rather than requiring essays and tend to fall into identifiable categories:

(a)   The distinction between a lease and a licence. Such questions involve knowing the formalities required to create a lease and understanding the need for exclusive possession, a prerequisite to the formation of a lease.

(b)   Implied obligations of landlord and tenant, i.e., implied both by statute and at common law.

(c)   Usual covenants expressly incorporated into leases, including repairing covenants and covenants preventing assignment or otherwise parting with possession.

(d)   Protection accorded to residential tenants by the Rent Act 1977 and the Housing Act 1988.

Questions in this area are more common in examinations set by professional bodies than in law degree courses but it depends on the syllabus.

If you are studying this area in detail remember that following the Housing Act 1988, which came into force on 15 January 1989, only two types of tenancy are possible after that date: the new-type assured (no relation to the tenancy of that name under the Housing Act 1980) or the assured shorthold. No longer can protected tenancies under the Rent Act or shorthold or assured tenancies under the Housing Act 1980 be created.

The 1988 Act allows in particular for a market rent rather than a fair rent and has limited security of tenure provisions.

It should be remembered that this Act is *not retrospective* and those who became tenants prior to 15 January 1989 having the benefit of the Rent Act 1977 will continue to do so. Hence a two-tier system will exist for some time.

A useful summary of the provisions, and indeed residential tenancies as a whole, is contained in *Blackstone's Guide to the Housing Act 1988* by Stuart Bridge.

DISTINCTION BETWEEN A LEASE AND A LICENCE

Formalities

To vest a legal estate in the tenant, a lease must be created by deed (LPA 1925, s. 52). Any attempt to create a lease orally or in writing is void at law unless the lease is for less than three years, takes effect immediately in possession and is at the best rent reasonably obtainable without taking a premium (LPA 1925, s. 54). Although a lease not under seal is void at law, it may be effective in equity.

At common law, if a person enters into possession under a void legal lease, he is a tenant at will and his tenancy may be terminated by notice. However, if the tenant pays rent on a regular basis he may acquire a periodic tenancy, based on the period by which the rent is measured (see *Alder* v *Blackman* [1953] 1 QB 146). Thus a valid legal periodic tenancy may arise since being for less than three years it does not need to be created by deed (see LPA 1925, s. 54). But note that it was held in *Jarad* v *Aqil* [1991] 1 All ER 243 that even if payments are made the tenancy will not be converted into a periodic tenancy unless the details of the lease have been agreed. In equity, an imperfect legal lease could be treated as a contract to grant a lease. This led ultimately to the decision in *Walsh* v *Lonsdale* (1882) 21 ChD 9. The effect of the decision was that an agreement for a lease which was specifically enforceable would be regarded in equity as a lease on the terms of the void legal lease. It is the effect of this decision which should be clearly understood as giving rise to a popular exam topic in both degree and professional examinations.

In considering the issue of *Walsh* v *Lonsdale* you must now be aware of the Law of Property (Miscellaneous Provisions) Act 1989, s. 2, which repeals LPA 1925, s. 40, for contracts coming into force after September 1989. In dealing with a problem question in this area you must take careful note of whether any dates are given in the question: if the agreement is before September 1989 you must discuss s. 40; if after September 1989 you must discuss s. 2. As time goes on, it is less likely s. 40 will be relevant and if there are no dates referred to in the question you are probably safe to discuss only s. 2 but a passing reference to s. 40 would show the examiner you are aware of the importance of the date of the contract.

The principal difference between the two sections is that under s. 40 no action could be brought under a contract for the sale of land or an interest in land unless it was in writing or evidenced in writing or there was a sufficient act of part performance. Under s. 2 the contract must be in writing with the terms set out in the contract itself or in some other document(s) identified in the contract and signed by the parties. Under s.2 there is no possibility of part performance but there is nothing in the section to prevent an interest arising out of estoppel. According to Hoffmann J in *Spiro* v *Glencrown Properties Ltd* [1991] 2 WLR 931 the intention of s. 2 is to prevent disputes about whether the parties had entered into an agreement and its terms but that the means of exercise of the agreement is outside s. 2, so that an option to purchase land must be in writing but a notice exercising that option need not be. It seems likely s. 2 will continue to cause difficulties in practice especially in modern conveyancing practice where exchange of contracts frequently takes place by telephone but the written records of the exchange may not match (for an illustration of the problem see *Record* v *Bell* [1991] 1 WLR 853). It might also be useful to consider the case of *Pitt* v *PHH Asset Management Ltd* [1984] 1 WLR 327 when the Court of Appeal considered the use of the 'lock out' agreement. In this case the vendor of a piece of land agreed not to offer the land for sale to anyone else provided the purchaser exchanged contracts within a specified period. The court took the view that the agreement was not a contract for the sale of any interest in land and was not therefore subject to the provisions of s. 2. Although this case was concerned with freehold land, the principle would be applied if a prospective tenant was given a specified period within which to sign a formal lease. However, it should be remembered that the agreement still requires the essentials of a contract, particularly consideration. Two useful articles on the abolition of s. 40 are Pettit, 'Farewell to section 40' [1989] Conv 431 and Rank. 'Part performance: a requiem' (1990) 134 SJ 72.

In order to understand the principle, it may be useful to look at a problem question:

> Trollope was the owner in fee simple of Banchester Towers Estate. On 1 May 1994 he, orally, let Silver Cottage on the estate to Jones for two years at £5 a week rent. On 1 August 1994 Trollope signed an agreement, not under seal, whereby he agreed to let Wilton House on the estate to Smith for 15 years at £1,000 per annum. Both Jones and Smith entered into possession and have since paid their rent regularly. Trollope has now sold the entire Banchester Towers Estate to John who knew of Jones and Smith's rights. How far is John bound by these?
> (Ignore the Rent Act 1977 and Housing Act 1988.)

Commentary

This question requires discussion of whether Jones or Smith have a legal estate. If they have then John is bound by their tenancies. If not, the question arises whether there is any equitable remedy. Clearly in neither case has a deed been drawn up so that the requisite formality is absent and alternative arguments must be considered. Since there are different issues to be considered in relation to Jones and Smith it is better to discuss the two tenancies separately.

Jones

The first point to notice here is that the agreement is oral. The letting is for a period of two years and consequently may be created informally. LPA 1925, s. 52, allows a tenancy for less than three years (which clearly applies here) to be created informally provided it takes effect in possession and is at the best rent obtainable without a premium. The lease takes effect in possession, Jones's only obligation is to pay the rent and there is no premium. The only difficulty for Jones is to be able to show that £5 a week is the best rent obtainable. If it is, then John is bound by a two-year lease. However, it could be argued that £5 a week is a very low rent even for a short tenancy and that a more economic rent could easily have been obtained. If this is the case, s. 52 will not apply and it becomes necessary to consider the effect of Jones's entry into possession. By entering into possession with Trollope's consent, Jones becomes a tenant at will whose tenancy could be terminated at any time by notice. However, the facts tell us that Jones has paid his rent regularly and the effect of this will be to make him a periodic tenant (see *Adler* v *Blackman* [1952] 2 All ER 41).

The question then to be considered is what type of periodic tenancy has been created. In the absence of express agreement a periodic tenancy is referred to the period by which the rent is measured and not necessarily according to the frequency of payment, e.g., a rent of £260 per annum creates a yearly tenancy even though paid at £5 per week. The likelihood here is that Jones would have a weekly tenancy although this would be varied if there was evidence of a contrary intention. If Jones only has a weekly tenancy John could determine it with a week's notice, except that in the case of dwelling-houses a minimum of four weeks' notice is required under the Protection from Eviction Act 1977.

Smith

The situation here is somewhat different in that the agreement is for a 15-year lease so that there is no possibility of LPA 1925, s. 52, being complied with as the agreement is not in the form of a deed.

The discussion should focus on three issues:

(a)   the possibility of a tenancy arising at common law;

(b)   whether s. 2 of the Law of Property (Miscellaneous Provisions) Act 1989 applies enabling Smith to seek specific performance of the agreement entered into with Trollope which is binding on John the new owner; and

(c)   whether Smith could argue an interest in Wilton House by way of proprietary estoppel.

(a)   As explained above, entry into possession with Trollope's consent creates a tenancy at will. Smith has paid his rent regularly and will therefore have a yearly tenancy. If this is the case, then John could only determine the tenancy by serving six months' notice (i.e., 182 days).

(b)   From Smith's point of view it may be better for him to argue that as the agreement between himself and Trollope was in writing and signed, it complies with the requirements of s. 2 of the Law of Property (Miscellaneous Provisions) Act 1989. The answer must point out that this may not be the case as the 1989 Act requires not only that the agreement, but the terms of the agreement, be in writing and both parties should have signed it — which is not clear from the question. Taking both possibilities, explain the effect of each, i.e., if s. 2 is satisfied then Smith could take action seeking specific performance of the contract. The advantage of doing this is that specific performance is an equitable remedy and since equity 'looks on that as done which ought to be done' Smith, if successful, would become an equitable tenant under the contract, hence have a 15-year equitable lease. Of course it should also be pointed out that specific performance being an equitable remedy is discretionary, and a person seeking an equitable remedy 'must come with clean hands'. Check the question therefore to ascertain whether the claimant has behaved correctly and is not in breach of the agreement or behind with the rent (see *Coatsworth* v *Johnson* (1886) 55 LJ QB 220). In the example given here Smith seems to have 'clean hands'.

Such an equitable lease would clearly bind Trollope, the question that needs to be considered however, is whether it would bind John, a third party to the contract. The answer should draw the examiner's attention to the fact that equitable interests are void as against a bona fide purchaser of the legal estate for value without notice. John appears to be a bona fide purchaser for value, but the facts tell us he has notice of Smith's rights. Does this mean that John is bound? The answer is that he may be! Where title to Wilton House was unregistered at the time of the agreement with Trollope, Smith's equitable interest would have had to be registered as an estate contract Class C(iv) under the Land Charges Act 1972, s. 2. John would only be bound if Smith has registered, as failure to register makes the equitable interest void even though John is aware of it (see *Hollington Bros Ltd* v *Rhodes* [1951] 2 TLR 691).

If title to Wilton House was registered at the time of the agreement then Smith would have an overriding interest under LRA 1925, s. 70(1)(g), which would be binding on John.

(c) If the agreement does not comply with s. 2 of the 1989 Act then you could argue that Smith may be able to establish proprietary estoppel (see first expression of the principle in the dissenting judgment in *Ramsden* v *Dyson* (1886) LR 1 HL 129) in order to give him an interest in the house. Smith would have to show that he acted upon a promise by Trollope that he would let Wilton House for 15 years to Smith in consideration of a rent of £1,000 per annum (see *Crabb* v *Arun District Council* [1976] Ch 179). Smith acted upon this promise as he took possession and paid the rent regularly. Consequently, Trollope could not go back on his promise. Case law should be quoted to support this argument, one interesting case being *J. T. Developments* v *Quinn* (1991) 62 P & CR 33, where the Court of Appeal held that proprietary estoppel could arise out of negotiations where there was no binding agreement for a lease.

The same issue as in (b) above still arises, namely if Smith was successful would the estoppel be binding on John as a third party?

An Essay Question

Another favourite exam question is on the lines of:

'An agreement for a lease is as good as a lease'. Discuss.

This then requires the student to show that he understands the fundamental differences between legal and equitable rights and can discuss in what ways an equitable lease might be defective, e.g., whether benefits and burdens pass on an assignment of an equitable lease.

EXCLUSIVE POSSESSION

In order to take effect as a lease the tenant must be given exclusive possession of the land, i.e., the right to exclude everyone, including the landlord, from the property. If there is anything less than exclusive possession then only a licence is created no matter what label the parties attach to it. Whether or not there is exclusive possession is a question of fact, the issue being whether the landlord retains overall control of the premises. For example, in *Appah* v *Parncliffe Investments Ltd* [1964] 1 WLR 1064 a woman who occupied a room in a residential hotel was held only to have a licence since the hotel owner kept a key to the room and entered to change the bed and empty the gas meter. The converse, which in the past much occupied both the courts and academics, is the issue whether the fact of exclusive possession automatically creates a tenancy. The test established in a long line of cases culminating in *Heslop* v *Burns* [1974] 1 WLR 1241 was one of intention to be inferred from all the circumstances. The issues raised were a popular area with examiners, and will probably remain so in view of the House of Lords decision in *Street* v *Mountford* [1985] AC 809 and the subsequent spate of cases arriving at the Court of Appeal. In that case, a very important one from a practical point of view, their lordships disapproved of a number of earlier cases and took the view that exclusive possession will lead to a presumption of tenancy which must be rebutted by the landlord. If you are now faced with this problem, the approach would seem to be to decide first whether there is exclusive possession. If there is exclusive possession then a tenancy will result unless reasons can be found why there should not be a tenancy, the parties' intention may then be relevant in a negative sense. The approach will *not* be to consider all the circumstances and from them decide whether the parties intended a licence or tenancy, nor will the name the parties give to their agreement be conclusive.

In *Street* v *Mountford* itself, the agreement was described as a licence. The effects of this important case have been discussed at length in various articles. R. Street [1985] Conv 328 comments that the decision 'turned the clock back more than a quarter of a century'. D.N. Clark [1986] Conv 39, however, welcomes the change to distinguishing a lease from a licence by a test of substance rather than form. He suggests, though, that the proper role of the issue of intent of the parties is not as simple as their lordships indicated. Indeed Rank (1988) 132 SJ 16, 550 is of the opinion that the *Street* case 'raised more problems than it solved'.

A good answer to a question in this area will be one which has considered these problems and recent decisions and made some attempt to either reconcile them with the House of Lords decision in *Street* or otherwise to comment.

There has been a great deal of litigation since *Street* v *Mountford* concerned with residential tenancies. Some recent decisions you may wish to refer to include the following:

(a) *Aslan* v *Murphy (Nos 1 and 2)* [1990] 1 WLR 766. Here the Court of Appeal held that even if an agreement between the occupier and the owner of the premises was not a sham, the court when deciding whether the occupier was a tenant or a lodger should consider the facts whether the terms of the agreement were part of the true rather than the apparent bargain made by the parties. On the facts the occupiers in that case had been granted exclusive possession and were therefore tenants. *Street* v *Mountford* was referred to in the judgment and the decision of the House of Lords in *Antoniades* v *Villiers* [1988] 3 WLR 1205 applied.

(b) *Antoniades* v *Villiers* and *A. G. Securities* v *Vaughan* are two cases heard as a joint appeal by the House of Lords and reported together. They are worth studying as they illustrate the difficulties the courts have with the lease/licence distinction.

In *Antoniades* it was held, reversing the Court of Appeal, that identical agreements, labelled as 'licences', executed at the same time by a man and woman, who were going to live together in a one bedroomed flat, but which stressed they were not to have exclusive possession, created a *joint tenancy*. Lord Bridge stated that the description of the agreements as licences was a sham to prevent the appellant enjoying the protection of the Rent Acts.

In contrast, in *Vaughan*, their Lordships decided that agreements again described as 'licences' and stating that there was no right to exclusive possession were found to be *genuine licences*. These agreements were entered into at different times by four individuals, who were initially strangers and provided that they should have separate rooms and when one left a new occupant was to be mutually agreed by the remaining licensees. To quote Lord Bridge:

> There is no artificiality — the arrangement seems to have been a sensible and realistic one to provide accommodation for a shifting population of individuals who were genuinely prepared to share a flat with others, introduced from time to time who would, at least initially be strangers to them.

Another useful judgment which discusses the above cases is that of Balcombe LJ in *Family Housing Association* v *Jones* [1990] 1 WLR 779 at p. 786.

The main thing to remember is that an examiner will expect answers to questions involving the lease/licence distinction not only to show an understanding of the reasoning behind the House of Lords decision in *Street* but to raise implications flowing from subsequent decisions.

(For a decision in the business field see *Ashburn Anstalt* v *Arnold* [1989] Ch 1 where there was exclusive possession and which brings to the forefront the notion of the gratuitous lease. The *Prudential* case does not alter the decision in *Ashburn Ansalt* on this point. See also *Skipton Building Society* v *Clayton, The Times,* 25 March 1993.)

Some courses, particularly professional ones, may require knowledge of different types of leases and issues such as surrender, merger or forfeiture. We do not intend to discuss these issues since many of the example questions on these topics tend to be of a 'bookwork' nature and do not require particular techniques.

IMPLIED OBLIGATIONS OF LANDLORD AND TENANT

The contents of leases vary according to the wishes of the parties, the type of property concerned and the length of the tenancy. For example, in a tenancy of a shop it would be common to require the tenant to insure against damage to plate glass windows. In a tenancy of a house obligations may relate to the use of the property and preservation of amenity.

Despite the wide variety of tenancy agreements certain covenants are commonly contained in leases and are known generally as the 'usual covenants', e.g., insurance covenants, repairing covenants and covenants against assignment. We will look at an examination question in this area as an example of the approach to be taken, but before dealing with that we will consider the covenants implied in tenancies since they form a popular basis for examination questions. Note that the statutory implied covenants have now been consolidated in the Landlord and Tenant Act 1985 and for clarity we will refer to both the old statutes and the equivalent sections of the 1985 Act.

Landlord's Implied Obligations

These are imposed by both common law and statute. Exam questions, however, usually merely refer to 'implied obligations' requiring the student to be aware of both types of obligation. At common law the landlord's obligations are to give quiet enjoyment and not to derogate from grant. In addition obligations concerning fitness for habitation are required by both common law and statute in the case of tenancies of dwelling-houses. We will deal with a problem covering these areas after looking at the basic requirements.

The covenant for quiet enjoyment, although commonly included in a lease, is nevertheless implied in every tenancy. It means that the landlord will not interfere with the tenant's physical enjoyment of the land. The question is essentially one of fact and applies to the landlord himself and those for whom he is responsible. One thing to remember is that there will normally be no breach of the covenant unless there is physical interference, e.g., causing physical discomfort by cutting off gas and electricity as in *Perera v Vandiyar* [1953] 1 WLR 672 (this may also amount to a criminal offence of harassment); but erecting an external staircase passing the tenant's bedroom and destroying his privacy is not a breach (*Browne v Flower* [1911] 1 Ch 219). Remember also that the covenant is not broken by the tortious act of a third party but is broken by the lawful act of a third party and a landlord is liable to the tenant in respect of any breach (see *Sanderson v Berwick-upon-Tweed Corporation* (1884) 13 QBD 547).

Non-derogation from grant means that the landlord, having granted the lease for a particular purpose, must not do any act which will prevent that purpose being realised. The obligation applies to the grantor and those claiming under him and the right of enforcement passes to the grantee's successors. The essence of breach of this implied covenant is that it makes the property substantially less fit for its purpose, not merely that it causes the tenant inconvenience or difficulty. For example, in *Newman v Real Estate Debenture Corporation Ltd* [1940] 1 All ER 131 a flat was let in a building which was intended to be let for residential purposes; it was held that the landlord committed a breach by letting a large part of the building for business purposes. In *O'Cedar Ltd v Slough Trading Co. Ltd* [1927] 2 KB 123 there was no breach when adjoining premises were let for purposes which increased the insurance premiums on the premises originally let.

Fitness for habitation applies only to a dwelling-house and obligations are implied at common law and by statute. It is a popular area for questions. The major problem for the student is to decide in what circumstances a particular obligation will be implied. We will therefore attempt to deal with the different situations and indicate the important points to remember.

At common law there is an implied condition in the letting of a *furnished* house that it is fit for human habitation when let. Provided the premises are fit when let, they need not remain so. Breach of the undertaking enables the tenant to repudiate and claim damages. An example is *Smith v Marrable* (1843) 11 M & W 5 where the house had previously been let to a tenant with tuberculosis.

The Landlord and Tenant Act 1985, s. 8 (previously Housing Act 1957, s. 6) applies only to houses let at a low rent, i.e., £80 p.a. or less in London and £52 p.a. or less elsewhere (if the letting was before 6 July 1957, the respective figures are £40 and £26). This section does *not* apply where the tenancy is for three years or more (Landlord and Tenant Act 1985, s. 8(5)). It is, however, applicable where the tenancy is periodic even though such a tenancy may last for more than three years. Where the Act applies it is wider than common law in that the property must be fit for habitation when let *and* must remain so. The Act cannot be excluded but the landlord is only liable for defects of which he has notice. In any event liability is restricted to situations where the defect can be remedied at reasonable cost, see *Buswell v Goodwin* [1971] 1 WLR 92. Breach is a question of whether the state of repair is such that 'by ordinary use damage may naturally be caused to the occupier, either in respect of personal injury to life or limb or injury to health' (per Lord Atkin in *Summers v Salford Corporation* [1943] AC 283). Guidance as to factors to be taken into account in deciding unfitness is given by Landlord and Tenant Act 1985, s. 10, and s. 604 of the Housing Act 1985 (as amended by Sch. 9 of the Local Government and Housing Act 1989) i.e., defects in respect of repair, stability, freedom from damp, internal arrangement, natural lighting, ventilation, water supply, drainage and sanitary conveniences, facilities for preparation and cooking of food and for the disposal of waste matter.

The Landlord and Tenant Act 1985, s. 11 (previously Housing Act 1961, ss. 32 and 33) applies *only* to short leases, i.e., for less than seven years. The section implies a covenant that:

(a)   the structure and exterior of the dwelling-house will be kept in repair, and

(b)   installations in the house for the supply of water, gas and electricity, for sanitation and heating will be kept in repair and proper working order.

Again the section cannot be excluded but can be modified by order of a county court if it is considered reasonable in the circumstances. The landlord is only liable for defects of which he has notice and the tenant must allow inspection of the premises upon receipt of 24 hours' notice. Where there is a breach the tenant cannot repudiate the tenancy but he can carry out the repairs himself after giving notice and set off the cost against future rent (see *Lee-Parker v Izzet* [1971] 1 WLR 1688). For a discussion of the extent to which the tenant's equitable right of set-off can be excluded by the terms of the lease see the Court of Appeal decision in *Connaught Restaurants Ltd v Indoor Leisure Ltd* [1994] 1 WLR 501.

Since the section implies two obligations on the landlord, you must be clear which you are dealing with. In relation to structure and exterior you may be required to discuss what constitutes the dwelling-house. For example, in *Brown* v *Liverpool Corporation* [1969] 3 All ER 1345 outside steps were part of the structure but in *Hopwood* v *Cannock Chase District Council* [1975] 1 WLR 373 a backyard path was not included. The distinction between the two cases appears to be that in the *Brown* case the steps were the only means of access to the house but in *Hopwood* there was another main entrance. The test therefore appears to be whether the area in disrepair was essential to reasonable use of the house. As regards water, gas etc. the obligation is twofold: to keep in repair and proper working order. Consequently it would seem sufficient that the installation works, even though it could be made to work more efficiently. For example, in *Wycombe Health Authority* v *Barnett* (1982) 264 EG 619 there was no duty to lag water pipes because they were in working order although perhaps not as efficient as they could be.

The Defective Premises Act 1972 imposes two obligations on the landlord which cannot be avoided. Under s. 4 the landlord is under a duty to take reasonable care to see that all persons who might reasonably be expected to be affected by defects are reasonably safe from injury. The section applies to all types of tenancies and rights of occupation arising by statute or contract. However, you must remember that the section only applies to defects the landlord knows of or ought to know of and where the landlord is under an obligation to maintain or repair *or* if he is entitled to enter the premises to maintain or repair. The duty does not go beyond the landlord's express or implied obligation. For example, if in a tenancy of a shop there is a landlord's covenant to keep in repair the sales floor, there would be no obligation under s. 4 to repair the living accommodation.

For an interesting discussion of the landlord's liability to repair see *Barrett* v *Lounova (1982) Ltd* [1989] 2 WLR 137 in which the Court of Appeal was of the opinion that an obligation for the landlord to carry out repairs could be implied if the circumstances justified it and it was necessary to give business efficacy to the lease. Kerr LJ was also of the opinion that the obligations under the Defective Premises Act 1972, s. 4, could be enforced by injunction in appropriate circumstances.

Under s. 1 of the 1972 Act there is a duty on anyone taking on work in connection with the provision or alteration of a dwelling to ensure the work is carried out in a proper and workmanlike manner and that the premises are fit for habitation. Breach of the duty gives the tenant the right to claim damages for damage or injury arising within one year of completion of the work. The section will principally arise where the landlord has authorised or carried out improvements or modifications to the property. In *Andrews* v *Schooling* [1991] 1 WLR 783 it was held by the Court of Appeal that s. 1 applies to a case of non-feasance as well as misfeasance. In that case renovation work had been carried out to a flat but no work had been done in the cellar other than painting the walls with the result that the flat remained damp. It was held the flat was unfit for human habitation where it was without some essential attribute on completion of the work, even though the work actually done had been properly carried out.

Tenant's Implied Obligations

There are two main obligations implied against the tenant: to pay rent and not to commit waste.

Payment of rent is invariably an express term of the lease but is implied in the absence of such express covenant. Rent is usually a money payment but payment in kind is allowed. It is essential that the rent is ascertained or ascertainable at the time the lease takes effect (see *Greater London Council* v *Connolly* [1970] 2 QB 100). Generally the obligation to pay rent remains even if the premises cannot be used, although this may now be subject to the contractual doctrine of frustration (see *National Carriers Ltd* v *Panalpina (Northern) Ltd* [1981] AC 675).

The more likely source for an exam question is the liablity for waste and this may particularly apply in professional courses. It is helpful to bear in mind the general elements of waste. The general aim of this covenant is to prevent a limited owner, such as a tenant, from damaging the premises so as to prejudice the interests of the reversioner, the landlord. The remedy is damages or an injunction. There are four types of waste:

(a)   Ameliorating, i.e., alterations which improve the land.

(b)   Permissive, i.e., failure to do that which ought to be done, e.g., non-repair of buildings.

(c)   Voluntary, i.e., doing that which ought not to be done to the detriment of the reversioner, e.g., cutting down trees.

(d)   Equitable, i.e., acts of wanton destruction, e.g., pulling down houses. Equitable and voluntary waste overlap and equitable waste is primarily important in settlements where the life tenant is not liable for voluntary waste.

In leases, liability for waste depends upon the type of tenancy. A tenant for years (i.e., a fixed term) is liable for voluntary and permissive waste in the absence of contrary agreement. Therefore the tenant must maintain the property in the condition in which he found it unless the lease contains a repairing covenant.

Under a yearly (i.e., a periodic) tenancy the premises must be kept in a tenant-like manner. The tenant is therefore liable for voluntary waste and he must take steps to prevent the premises falling into decay. In *Warren* v *Keen*

[1954] 1 QB 15 Denning LJ said that the tenant must take proper care of the property, he must clean the windows and chimney of a house but he need not carry out repairs which are caused by fair wear and tear or lapse of time.

A weekly tenant is not liable for permissive waste since there is an implied understanding that the house will be kept in a reasonable and habitable state by the landlord (see *Mint v Good* [1951] 1 KB 517). The tenant is however under a duty to behave in a tenant-like manner so that Denning LJ's dictum in *Warren v Keen* applies equally to weekly tenants.

A tenant at will is not liable for permissive waste but an act of voluntary waste automatically terminates his tenancy and he is liable in damages.

A tenant at sufferance is liable for voluntary waste.

ENFORCEMENT FOR BREACH OF IMPLIED COVENANTS

When answering a problem question involving a breach of an implied covenant by the landlord do not forget to refer to possible methods of enforcement open to a tenant as this is an important practical issue. If your course covers express covenants in leases then similarly you should be aware of the remedies for breach. You should refer to standard texts to become familiar with all the remedies available. However some points looked for by an examiner are noted below. This is not meant to be an exclusive list but is given as guidance.

Remedies Available at Common Law

Action for breach of contract
For breach of the implied covenants of quiet enjoyment and non-derogation from grant the usual remedies available for breach of contract are available, namely damages and/or injunction, the latter to restrain the landlord from persisting with the act or acts giving rise to the breach. The measure of damages awarded is the amount of damage suffered by the tenant. See *Kenny v Preen* [1963] 1 QB 499 where both remedies were granted, the landlord having threatened the tenant, with letters, shouting at her and banging on her door to get her to vacate the premises. Damages for injured feelings or mental distress are not recoverable (see Balcombe J (obiter) in *Branchett v Beaney, Coster & Swale BC* [1992] 3 All ER 910).

Action in tort
Breach of the covenant of quiet enjoyment may also give rise to an action in tort e.g., the landlord may cause a nuisance at law by causing unreasonable noise or may commit a trespass. In this situation a tenant may also frame an action in the relevant tort and exemplary damages may be awarded where the landlord's behaviour is regarded as outrageous. Such an award may bear

no relationship to the tenant's losses. See, for example, *Guppy's (Bridport) Ltd* v *Brookling* (1983) 14 HLR 1 where the landlords cut off all water supplies and sanitation and also *McMillan* v *Singh* (1984) 17 HLR 120.

Statutory intervention

Harassment and illegal eviction   A landlord's action amounting to a breach of the implied covenant for quiet enjoyment also amounts to harassment or unlawful eviction. Indeed if this is the case a criminal action may be instigated by the local authority under the Protection from Eviction Act 1977, s. 1(3), as amended by the Housing Act 1988, s. 29 which states that it is an offence for a landlord of a residential occupier or his agent to:

(a)   do acts likely to interfere with the peace or comfort of the residential occupier or members of his household, or
(b)   persistently to withdraw or withhold services reasonably required for the occupation of the premises as a residence,
and in either case he knows or has reasonable cause to believe that the conduct is likely to cause the residential occupier to give up occupation of the whole or part of the premises or to refrain from exercising any right or pursuing any remedy in respect of the whole or part of the premises.

If the tenant does in fact give up the premises then the landlord has committed the offence of unlawful eviction (see the Protection from Eviction Act 1977, s. 1(2)).

Remember the civil remedies discussed above are still preserved and a tenant may bring an action in tort or for breach of the covenant of quiet enjoyment.

In addition ss. 27 and 28 of the Housing Act 1988 introduced the right to claim damages in two situations, both of which result in the tenant giving up the premises:

(a)   where the landlord or any person acting on his behalf unlawfully deprives the occupier of his occupation of the whole or part of the premises (s. 27(1));
(b)   where the above persons are guilty of an attempt unlawfully to deprive the occupier of his occupation; or are guilty in effect of allowing harassment as a result of which the occupier gives up occupation of the premises (s. 27(2)).

Damages are based on s. 28 which, in brief, is the difference between the value of the premises (if sold on the open market), with a sitting tenant and with vacant possession. Clearly this is intended to be a deterrent to landlords who might otherwise pressure their tenants to leave. Note, however, that if a tenant is reinstated as a residential occupier before proceedings to enforce the liability are finally disposed of, then there is no statutory liability (s. 27(6)(a)). This is also the case where the court orders reinstatement. In these situations the tenant is left claiming as described above in contract or tort.

Statutory nuisance or unfitness   Most examiners will be looking to see if you are aware of remedies available to tenants provided by various statutes. How much detail you will need to go into will depend on your specific course and guidelines given by your tutor.

Two Acts in particular could be useful to a tenant;

(a)   The Environmental Protection Act 1990, s. 79(1)(a) which states that 'premises kept in a state which amount to a nuisance or are prejudicial to health' amount to a statutory nuisance within this section and are actionable by an individual (e.g., a tenant) in the magistrates' court. Alternatively, the tenant could complain to the local authority environmental health department who, if they are satisfied the premises amount to a statutory nuisance, may take formal action against the landlord requiring repairs, or other matters, to be carried out to remedy that nuisance. The local authority may take the case to the magistrates' court so that they may enter the property themselves and carry out the necessary work. The cost of the work is borne by the landlord and is registrable as a local land charge against the property. See, as an example of factors which can cause premises to be a statutory nuisance, *London Borough of Southwork* v *Ince* (1989) 21 HLR 504 (lack of sound insulation in council owned flats).

(b)   Similarly, if premises become 'unfit for human habitation' within the meaning of Part VI of the Housing Act 1985 (as amended by Housing Act 1988, Sch. 15) or where substantial repairs are necessary to bring it up to a reasonable standard, the local housing authority can serve a repair notice under s. 189 of the 1985 Act to compel the landlord to carry out repairs.

Only a brief outline of the possible forms of action are indicated above and students are advised to consult their land law textbook in relation to remedies and to widen their reading in this area.

SPECIMEN EXAMINATION QUESTION

Ernest is a student who is the tenant of one of several flats in a large house owned by Graball. In common with the other tenants Ernest signed a three-year lease which contained a covenant by the tenant to use the premises for residential purposes only. An adjoining flat is occupied by Moll, a prostitute, who disturbs Ernest by the rowdy behaviour of herself and her clients. Moll's behaviour is ignored by Graball since she pays twice as much rent as the other tenants. Graball has, himself, installed a new central-heating system, the boiler of which is located outside Ernest's flat. Ernest no longer has a hot-water supply and the heating system only works if kicked vigorously. Ernest has also discovered damp in the flat caused by leakage from the water system. He has now informed Graball that he does not intend to pay his rent until the defects are put right and something is done about Moll's behaviour.

Discuss.

Commentary

There is no difficulty here in identifying the parties: Graball is the landlord and Ernest the tenant. We are told that Ernest has signed a lease which is for a term certain. Assuming this is in a deed the formalities of LPA 1925, s. 52, are complied with and he has a legal lease. If only in writing, see s. 54.

Ernest has two complaints, One concerning Moll's behaviour and the other the state of his flat. It is therefore useful to divide the discussion into those two elements. With the exception of the tenant's covenant for residential use we are not told of any other express covenants so that Ernest will have to try to rely on implied covenants.

With regard to Moll's behaviour, Ernest must try to rely on implied covenants for quiet enjoyment or non-derogation from grant.

Can Ernest allege breach of the covenant for quiet enjoyment? There are two issues here: what amounts to breach and the landlord's responsibility for the acts of others. Generally breach only occurs where there is physical interference with enjoyment of the property. We are told that Ernest is disturbed by Moll's rowdy behaviour but, so far as we are aware, there is no physical interference with Ernest's use of the flat. Ernest could possibly argue that the noise is such as to amount to a tortious nuisance and hence that it interferes with use of the flat. If Ernest can show physical interference, which is doubtful, the interference is by Moll, not by Graball. The landlord is liable for his own acts but not for those of others, unless the breach arises by lawful use of the premises, e.g., in *Sampson* v *Hodson-Pressinger* [1981] 3 All ER 710 a landlord was liable for nuisance for noise caused by the lawful use of an inadequately insulated flat by another of his tenants. Here the interference, if any, is caused by Moll's unauthorised use of her flat since her lease permitted only residential use not 'business use'. It seems unlikely that Ernest could sue on the covenant for quiet enjoyment although he may, of course, have a cause of action against Moll in tort for nuisance.

The basis of non-derogation from grant is that the landlord cannot give with one hand and take away with the other. The premises here were let for residential purposes and all tenants in the building were required to covenant to that effect. Can Ernest claim Moll's use of her flat leads to derogation from grant? In *Newman* v *Real Estate Debenture Corporation Ltd* [1940] 1 All ER 131 letting parts of a building intended for residential use for commercial purposes was held to be a breach of the covenant. The situation here is different in that Graball has let the whole building for residential purposes but Moll is using her flat for the purposes of her own business. Graball has turned a blind eye to Moll's behaviour in return for double rent. Ernest could therefore try to argue that these two elements, taken together, amount to derogation from grant in that Ernest does not have the benefit of a quiet residential building in which to study (something that all students crave). If Ernest can establish breach, what remedy is available to him? He may well recover damages but that would not stop Moll's behaviour which is the remedy he really needs. Consequently it may be that Ernest will have a right but without an effective remedy. With regard to the state of Ernest's flat, he must try to rely on the implied covenants for fitness for habitation. We are not told whether the flat was let furnished so it is not clear whether the common law requirement would apply. Even if the letting was furnished, the facts do not indicate that the property was unfit when let so that Graball will not be in breach of the common law covenant. Again the facts do not disclose the rent payable so that we do not know whether the rent is low for the purposes of the Landlord and Tenant Act 1985, s. 8 (previously Housing Act 1957, s. 6). However, since the lease is for only three years it is unlikely that the rent would be as low as £80 or £52 p.a.

The next issue is whether Ernest can rely on the provision of the Landlord and Tenant Act 1985, s. 11 (previously Housing Act 1961, ss. 32 and 33). The lease is for less than seven years and the flat is a dwelling-house for the purposes of the Act so that there could be a breach of the implied covenant. We are told that Ernest no longer has a hot-water supply which would appear to be a clear breach of the covenant as the system is not in repair and working order. The heating system only works if kicked, so again it is not in proper working order. However, if the defect is caused by a faulty central-heating boiler the question could arise whether it is an installation *in* the dwelling-house. In *Campden Hill Towers Ltd* v *Gardner* [1977] 1 All ER 739 it was held that a house within the meaning of the Act means the particular part of the building demised, i.e., a flat, not the whole building containing the flats. On that basis Graball could argue that the boiler is not an installation within the dwelling-house. Note if the tenancy was entered into after January 1989 the Housing Act 1988 would deem the boiler to be part of the dwelling and thereby reverse the effect of the decision in *Gardner*. Ernest could presumably argue that the entire system is defective and not merely the boiler so that any necessary repairs in his flat should be carried out. Since Ernest has informed Graball about the defects the landlord cannot claim he has no notice and Ernest should be able to rely on the section. Ernest must be advised that he cannot withhold the rent but can set off the cost of any repairs he carries out against future rent (*Lee-Parker* v *Izzet* [1971] 1 WLR 1688).

Finally, if Ernest cannot establish any breach of implied covenants he could seek damages under the Defective Premises Act 1972, s. 1. We are told that Graball installed the central-heating system himself so that he owes an obligation to ensure the work was carried out in a proper and workmanlike manner and that the premises are fit for habitation. It seems clear from the facts that the system was not properly installed but is the flat unfit for habitation? This is a question of fact in every case and while the necessity to hit the system to make it work is not decisive, it might be possible to argue that a flat without hot water and adequate heating is unfit for habitation e.g., if as a result the flat is damp. This would only allow Ernest to claim damages for any injury or damage he has suffered as a result of the defective work. On the facts none appears to have been suffered by Ernest.

USUAL COVENANTS

As we have previously stated, a lease can contain any number of clauses and their meaning and effect is largely a question of construction: i.e., what did the parties intend when they entered into the lease? There are some covenants which are invariably contained in leases and which are known generally as the 'usual covenants'. Your particular course may or may not deal with them, very often it is a case of whether the lecture time available runs out before the lecturer has time to deal with them. To conclude this chapter we will look at a question on one of the usual covenants that is very popular with examiners — the covenant against assignment.

SPECIMEN EXAMINATION QUESTION

A lessee wishes to assign his interest in a lease of a shop. Advise him on his position if he has covenanted not to assign or underlet without his lessor's consent.

This is a question of a type which may well appear on a professional or non-law degree paper. It is essentially a bookwork question requiring the student to show his general knowledge of the topic rather than asking him to apply knowledge to a particular set of facts. In a law degree exam you would probably find a specific problem on assignment or a covenant against assignment would be one of a number of covenants to consider in the problem.

In approaching this particular question you should begin by showing the examiner you know what is meant by a covenant against assignment and then discuss the relevant authorities to show the considerations the tenant must bear in mind.

A covenant against assignment can either be a total prohibition or a qualified prohibition. Where there is a total prohibition the tenant cannot dispose of his interest at all. In a qualified covenant, as is the case here, the tenant can dispose of his interest only after obtaining his landlord's consent. The important point here is that the landlord's consent cannot be unreasonably withheld (Landlord and Tenant Act 1927, s. 19). The covenant may be specific or general, i.e., it may forbid assignment or, as is more usual, forbid 'assignment, subletting or parting with possession'. Again it would be useful to point out that covenants are construed strictly so that any disposition which does not fall within the strict wording is allowable. For example, in *Cook v Shoesmith* [1951] 1 KB 752 a covenant not to sublet was not broken by a sublease of part of the premises. Since the covenant here is against 'assignment or underletting' it may be useful to discuss what disposition the tenant may make. On a strict construction the tenant would be able to assign part of the premises but could he dispose of a lesser interest in the whole of the property, e.g., a licence? In *Marks v Warren* [1979] 1 All ER 29 it was held that a covenant against underletting or parting with possession was broken by an assignment since this required parting with possession, but Browne-Wilkinson J said that a restriction on alienation must be construed so as not to distort the ordinary meaning of words. It could be argued that the tenant could part with possession without breaking the covenant, since an assignment is a transfer of the residue of the tenant's term of years, which does not necessarily apply to parting with possession. However, we must here consider the possibilities of assignment, so you must discuss what considerations the tenant must take into account.

First, what is the position if the tenant assigns without first obtaining the landlord's consent? In that situation he is liable in damages and for forfeiture of the lease unless the court is prepared to grant relief. Note on this that in *Scala House & District Property Co. Ltd v Forbes* [1974] QB 575 the Court of Appeal held that a breach of a covenant against assignment is a once-and-for-all occurrence and is incapable of remedy. Relief under LPA 1925, s. 146, depends upon whether sufficient notice has been given. If the tenant applies for consent and this is refused he incurs no liability by assigning provided he can show the refusal was unreasonable. Note also the duty imposed on the landlord by the Landlord and Tenant Act 1988. This requires the Landlord to give consent or refuse it with stated grounds within a reasonable time of receiving the tenant's notice. If there is undue delay in replying the landlord becomes liable in damages for breach of statutory duty (s. 4).

The second point then to consider is the criteria which will be taken into account in deciding whether refusal was reasonable or not. The basic rule is that the landlord must have a substantial reason for his refusal, i.e., the prospective assignment must affect the value of his freehold reversion in some way. For example, in *Norfolk Capital Group Ltd v Kitway Ltd* [1976] 3 All

ER 787 refusal was reasonable because the prospective assignee could acquire the right to purchase the freehold reversion under the Leasehold Reform Act 1967, something which was not available to the existing tenant. Consent is unreasonably withheld if it is withheld for the landlord's own personal motives. For example, in *Anglia Building Society* v *Sheffield City Council* (1982) 266 EG 311 the landlord preferred a different type of use in order to maximise the rental value of other nearby property but was declared to have unreasonably withheld consent. The issue is always one of fact and the onus is on the tenant to show unreasonableness.

In considering refusal, one point to take into account is whether the landlord must rely on stated grounds for refusal or whether other factors can be taken into account. In *Bickel* v *Duke of Westminster* [1977] QB 241 Lord Denning MR was of the opinion that the court could take all the relevant considerations into account. The test therefore is *objective* not subjective. As Megarry put in (1963) 79 LQR 479 at page 482, 'in short what must be tested for unreasonableness is the withholding and not the landlord, the act and not the man'.

Finally, it must be remembered that consent cannot be refused on the ground of colour, race, nationality or ethnic or national origins (Race Relations Act 1976, ss. 1 to 3).

The final thing to remember in answering a question of this nature is that there are a vast number of cases on assignment, many of which depend on their own particular facts. You need not, therefore, give lots of examples; it is sufficient to state the principles, making it clear to the examiner that you appreciate the factors that the court will take into account. It may also be useful to refer to the Law Commission's report (Law Com. No. 141, 1985). Some of the proposals in that report were incorporated into the Landlord and Tenant Act 1988. The question refers to the tenancy of a shop so take care not to discuss irrelevancies, e.g., factors which can only relate to housing.

REVISION SUMMARY

Main Implied Obligations

LANDLORD	TENANT
Common law	
(a) To allow quiet enjoyment.	(a) To pay rent.
(b) Not to derogate from grant.	(b) To use premises in a
(c) To ensure premises are fit for human	tenant-like manner (if
habitation at start of tenancy (where tenancy	periodic).
is furnished).	(c) To allow landlord to
	enter and view if he is under
	a duty to repair.

Statute
(d) Landlord and Tenant Act 1985, s. 8: if a
house is let at a low rent and is let for less than
three years then the house must be fit for
human habitation at outset of tenancy and
must remain so.
(e) Landlord and Tenant Act 1985, s. 11: if a
house is let for less than seven years then the
landlord is under an obligation:
(i) to keep the structure and exterior in repair,
(ii) to keep in repair and proper working order
installations in the house.

SUGGESTED ADDITIONAL READING

The law of leases is generally dealt with only in outline in traditional land law
courses so that the coverage in standard land law texts would probably be
sufficient. Should more specialised reading be necessary, you could consult:

Evans and Smith, *Law of Landlord and Tenant*, 4th ed., 1993 (Butterworths).
J. Male, *Landlord and Tenant*, 3rd ed., 1990 (Pitman).
S. Bridge, *Residential Leases*, 1994 (Blackstone Press).

INDEX

TITLES IN THE SERIES